A Window in the Bosom

Twitenham. Feb. 11.
1737

Dr Sir

            I was in full hopes of
what I had long wished for, the pleasure of seeing
you, when I heard from Lady Codrington that
your ill health detain'd you, and now again
that you are still detain'd by a Return of yr
Asthma. I cannot say how much I am uneasy, till I know from your own hand the true
State of yr health; and my apprehension is
the greater, because Mrs Blount has since
writ me word you have taken Quicksilver
to no effect, which used to be yr sure Reme-
dy. I am now arrived to that part of Life, when
I cannot afford to bear the Hazard of a friend; &
every Attack wch Sickness makes on such an one
shakes me to the very Heart. Many times I
have wished, our fortune might have been to
have lived together; and tho' we cannot, I
can but just endure to be seperated from you.

Pope to Hugh Bethel 11 February 1737
Courtesy Beinecke Library

A

Window

in the Bosom

The Letters of Alexander Pope

BY

JAMES ANDERSON WINN

ARCHON BOOKS 1977

Library of Congress Cataloging in Publication Data

Winn, James Anderson, 1947-
   A Window in the Bosom

   Bibliography: p.
   Includes index.
      1. Pope, Alexander, 1688-1744—Correspondence.
   2. Poets, English—18th century—Correspondence. I.
   Title.
   PR3633.A43W5   821′.5 [B]   76-58361
   ISBN 0-208-01646-5

©James Anderson Winn 1977
First published 1977 as an Archon Book,
an imprint of The Shoe String Press Inc
Hamden, Connecticut 06514

Printed in the United States of America

To my Father,

who knew Greek

The old project of a Window in the bosom,
to render the Soul of Man visible, is what
every honest friend has manifold reason
to wish for.

Pope to Jervas

CONTENTS

PREFACE

ALEXANDER POPE's letters are the one part of his output largely ignored in the explosion of Pope studies since World War II. The publication, in 1956, of George Sherburn's splendid edition provided a complete and chronologically ordered text for the first time. In the twenty years since the publication of that edition, a few new letters have come to light,[1] and a few corrections to Sherburn's dating and annotation have been proposed, but no study of any length has sought to describe and analyze the letters themselves, perhaps because of the size and complexity of the task. Sherburn's compilation includes some 2,200 letters, about 1,500 by Pope, only 280 of which were published in Pope's lifetime. Anyone writing about this rich trove of material must necessarily confront both biographical and literary issues. The letters provide evidence which can help resolve questions of fact about Pope's career; they also serve to deepen our understanding of his complicated personality. C. W. Dilke, the first great student of the letters, was not exaggerating their importance when he asserted that no one should write Pope's biography without first editing his letters. But the letters are not merely raw historical material; they are literary documents as well, as Pope himself acknowledged by seeking to publish them. The imaginative and rhetorical processes Pope employed in writing his letters are often analogous to those he used in writing his poetry, so that the careful student of his letters becomes a better reader of his poems.

In the chapters which follow, I have sought to combine historical and analytical methods. Naturally, I have had to

select only a few of literally hundreds of possible topics, and I
can hardly claim that these have received exhaustive treatment.
Chapter 1 relates the complicated story of how those letters which
were published in Pope's lifetime came to be selected, edited,
printed, and sold. Here I have built on the painstaking factual
research which began with Dilke; my most important concern
in retelling the shory has been to speculate about the mixture
of motives which prompted Pope's actions. Chapter 2, in an
admittedly cursory way, seeks to sketch the history of the literary
letter in the West, indicating briefly what Pope learned from
his most important predecessors. Chapters 3, 4, and 5 discuss the
special characteristics of some specific correspondences, and here
the process of selection has been difficult. Those seeking detailed discussions of Pope's letters to Lyttelton, Orrery, Mallet,
Jervas, and the Richardsons, and many others will be disappointed. I have chosen the correspondents I *do* discuss both for
their intrinsic interest and to indicate the range and variety of
Pope's epistolary ourput. A summarizing epilogue presents some
concluding generalizations about Pope's presentations of himself in the letters.

My most important acknowledgment must be to the late
Professor Sherburn, whose twenty-two years of labor on his
edition produced such a usable text and solved firmly so many
problems which might otherwise have proved distracting. All
of my quotations follow his edition, *The Correspondence of
Alexander Pope* (5 vols., Oxford: Clarendon Press, 1956), except
for a few quotations from letters published since that edition.
In transcribing the texts, I have omitted the half brackets Sherburn employed to indicate passages excised when the letters came
to be printed. I have also omitted the full brackets he used to
indicate words or letters supplied in cases where a manuscript
is torn or damaged; this practice has made it possible for me to
introduce bracketed explanatory material into the quotations
from time to time. Except for a few duly noted instances, I have
accepted Sherburn's dates for the letters, the results of painstaking detective work on his part. In giving those dates, I have
followed his conventions: brackets around all or part of a date
indicate inferences; question marks indicate more serious doubt.

In quoting from Pope's poetry, I have followed the text of *The Twickenham Edition of the Poems of Alexander Pope* (10 vols., London: Methuen), quoting in each case from the latest editions: i.e., Volume I (1961), Volume II (1962), Volume III i (1950), Volume III ii (1961), Volume IV (1961), Volume V (1963), Volume VI (1964), Volumes VII-X (1967). I have used the abbreviation TE to denote this edition.

My first serious work on Pope came under the kind and stringent tutelage of Henry Knight Miller at Princeton. During my graduate studies at Yale, I benefited enormously from discussions of Pope with George DeForest Lord and the late William K. Wimsatt, Jr. My supervisor for the dissertation on which this book is based, Maynard Mack, whose immense erudition and precise judgment are too well known to need praise from me, has read the many versions of this study with painstaking care: his confidence in me has proved a most effective goad to labor. Others who read and commented on the manuscript at various stages of its development include Michael O'Loughlin, Ronald Paulson, Martin Price, and (at two different times) the late Professor Wimsatt.

My wife, Kathe Fox, has shielded me heroically from the thousand natural and unnatural shocks that a tyro scholar is heir to. Her unfailing sense of perspective has kept me from mistaking minor irritations for major crises.

> Oh! blest with Temper, whose unclouded ray
> Can make to morrow chearful as to day.

Schemes of Epistolary Fame

ON 22 MARCH 1705/6, the aging Restoration dramatist William Wycherley sat down to answer a witty letter (now lost) from a strange, young genius named Alexander Pope:

> My great Little Friend,—I have Receiv'd yours of the 17th Instant Yesterday, being the 21 and your Letter was the best, and most Wellcome thing I have Receiv'd since I came down, tho' I have receiv'd some Monny; But I must confess, you try my patience (as you say) in the beginning of your Letter; not by the many Lines in it, but the too many Compliments you make me for nothing; in which you prove yourselfe (tho' a sincere Friend) a man of too much fiction for I have not seen so much Poetry in Prose a great while, since your Letter is filled with so many fine words, and Acknowledgments of your Obligations to me (the only aseverations of yours I dare contradict) for I must tell you your Letter is like an Authors Epistle before his Book, written more to shew his wit to the World than his Sincerety, or gratitude to his Friend, whom he Libells with Praise, so that you have provoked my Modesty ev'n whilst you have Soothd my Vanity for I know not whether I am more Complimented than abused.
>
> (I, 14)

For the seventeen-year-old Pope, merely to correspond with a literary man of sixty-four, well established in the world of letters, must have been exciting. But to have Wycherley tell

him, even with a critical intent, that he wrote "Poetry in Prose"
and that his letter was "like an Authors Epistle before his Book"
must have been intoxicating. None of Pope's poems had yet seen
print; Tonson's first offer of publication was to come that same
spring. But surely his dreams already included whole books of
poetry, no doubt with the Author writing an Epistle as preface.
Perhaps it is not too fanciful to suggest that Pope's interest in
publishing his letters began in his teens, as a result of the sort
of praise they elicited from Wycherley and others.

Letters of various kinds were widely read in the London to
which Pope came in the first decade of the eighteenth century.
Schoolboys read letters by Cicero and Pliny. Tom Brown and
others indefatigably issued volumes of freely translated French
letters, so that even those who could not read French were
exposed to the tradition of Jean Louis Guez de Balzac and
Vincent Voiture. And everyone read the periodicals, which
were filled with letters. Many contributions to the *Tatler* and
Spectator were letters actually addressed to Addison and Steele
—edited, of course, as readers expected them to be.[1] But other
letters were simply essays by the main authors, masquerading
as fictitious correspondents. Whether real or counterfeit, most
of these letters took the form of essays on literary, social, or
philosophical subjects.

Not surprisingly, Pope was among the contributors of such
essay-style letters. Norman Ault, in *The Prose Works of Alexander Pope*, gives evidence for attributing to Pope all or part
of twelve *Spectators* and fourteen *Guardians*.[2] Usually Pope's
contributions take the form of letters, and in 1735 he reprinted
two *Spectators* and one *Guardian* as personal letters addressed
to Steele. That they really were letters to Steele is doubtful.
Steele introduced the earliest of them (in *Spectator* 406, for 16
June 1712) as a letter "from a Gentleman to a Friend, for whom
he has a very great Respect, and to whom he communicates the
Satisfaction he takes in Retirement,"[3] with no indication of how
he had received the text, and no implication that he was himself
the addressee. Ault concludes that the letter "was written to no
one in particular, but was simply a piece of literary composition
cast in the popular epistolary form expressly for publication
in *The Spectator*."[4] While entirely plausible, this conclusion

is not the only possible one. Pope could easily have written a version of this letter to Sir William Trumbull or another of his early correspondents[5] and subsequently polished it for publication. Whatever its history, the letter is a striking early statement of a theme to which Pope was often to return: the tension between urban involvement and rural retirement. Because its publication was anonymous, Pope could listen to the comments of the town without being known as the author, a technique he used repeatedly in his later career. He found such anonymity useful with some early poems as well: his *Messiah* appeared in *Spectator* 378 (13 May 1712), and his verses on a lady's fan (accompanied by an introductory note asking Mr. Spectator to "oblige a languishing Lover") appeared in No. 527 (4 November 1712).

Later that same month, however, Pope sent Steele some prose ruminations on the emperor Hadrian's dying speech, suggesting that the speech was more serious than readers had generally thought. After outlining his interpretation, Pope made a request: "If you think me right in my Notion of the last Words of *Adrian*, be pleased to insert this in the *Spectator*; if not, to suppress it."[6] Steele not only inserted it, but attributed it to Pope by name. No doubt, he meant no harm; Pope was, after all, becoming well known, and it would interest Steele's readers to know that the little poet was the author of the letter. Steele's introduction was quite complimentary:

> [Pope] enclosed for my Perusal an admirable Poem, which, I hope, will shortly see the Light. In the mean Time I cannot suppress any Thought of his, but insert his Sentiment about the dying Words of *Adrian*. I won't determine in the Case he mentions; but have thus much to say in favour of his Argument, That many of his own works which I have seen convince me that very pretty and very sublime Sentiments may be lodged in the same Bosom without Diminution to its Greatness.[7]

Pope quickly complained to his friend John Caryll:

> I only sent it as my private notion to Mr Steele, which yet I doubted of (as you see by the last lines of the letter itself)

not in the least dreaming that he would publish me as the
author of it by name.

([29 November 1712]; I, 157-8)

He probably also complained to Steele; at least he published a
letter in 1735 which, because it copies much of the authentic
Caryll letter on the subject, has been suspected as a fabrication.
It begins:

> I am sorry you publish'd that notion about *Adrian's Verses*
> as mine; had I imagined you wou'd use my name, I shou'd
> have express'd my sentiments with more modesty and
> diffidence.

(29 November 1712; I, 158-9)

While this particular text may be suspect, Pope probably did
express its crucial ideas to Steele:[8] he was not sorry to see the
"notion" published, but he had expected anonymity, and he
would have revised what he said had he known he would be
exposed as the author. Pope was to make similar statements
about later publications and later letters.

His next letter to a Steele periodical, the discussion of the
effects of illness in *Guardian* 132 (12 August 1713), was anonymous. Either Steele honored Pope's desire for concealment or
Pope submitted the text in a way that made tracing its author
impossible. Ault describes the headnote as "presumably by
Steele, but not impossibly by Pope himself."[9]

> Mr. IRONSIDE,
>   The following letter was really written by a young Gentle-
> man in a languishing illness, which both himself, and those
> who attended him, thought it impossible for him to outlive.
> If you think such an image of the state of a man's mind in
> that circumstance be worth publishing, it is at your service,
> and take it as follows.[10]

"An image of the state of a man's mind" is precisely what Pope
continually claimed his letters were. Both that phrase and the

insistence that the writer, described of course in the third person, "really" wrote the letter "in a languishing illness" suggest that Pope wrote the headnote. The anonymous prefaces he was to write for his published letters have much the same tone.

In fact, the entire story of these contributions to Steele's periodicals fits the pattern of Pope's later troubles with his letters: he instigates, but does not quite authorize, the publication of informal material; he complains after the printing has taken place, but his complaints do not seem entirely credible; finally, his response to the entire affair is to devise more complicated schemes for self-concealment. Later, this pattern was played out on a much larger scale, but even in the early years of Pope's career, the reasons for his complex attitudes toward the publication of his letters begin to emerge.

First, there were factors which made publishing his letters desirable. He recognized that some worthwhile ideas, useful phrases, and fugitive notions were tumbling out of him, even in his least formal letters. The thought that this material might be worth developing prompted him to ask for the return of his letters as early as 19 November 1712, when he wrote Caryll:

> I have an odd request to you that if you ever thought any of my epistles worth preserving, you will favour me with the whole cargoe, which shall be faithfully returned to you. I never kept any copies of such stuff as I write; but there are several thoughts which I throw out that way in the freedom of my soul, that may be of use to me in a design I am lately engaged in, which will require so constant a flux of thought and invention, that I can never supply it without some assistance and 'tis not impossible but so many notions, written at different times, may save me a good deal of trouble. Pray forgive this, and keep my secret which is of consequence.
>
> (I, 156)

The "design" might have been contributions for the *Guardian* or for the elegant entertainments Steele was planning for his "Censorium." But surely Pope already had plans of longer range.

He knew that there were witty moments in his letters; he had
every reason to believe that the recipients read them aloud or
showed them about, as he jokingly implied to the Duchess of
Hamilton:

> The two foregoing Periods, methinks, are so mystical,
> learned & perplext, that if you have any Statesmen or
> Divines about you, they can't chuse but be pleased with
> them.
>
> (October [1717]; I, 437)

In an earlier letter to Teresa Blount, he made a similar joke, but
a joke that shows what was on his mind, by concluding, after a
long underlined passage,

> When this letter is printed for the wit of it, pray take care
> that what is underlined be printed in a different character.
>
> (September [1714]; I, 258)

Twenty-one years later, in a revised, reorganized form, without
(alas) italics, the letter was indeed printed—by Pope himself!
    But his letters were not merely a grab-bag of reusable wit,
as Pope began to see quite early. He was fascinated by himself,
and saw his letters as raw material for self-examination. His
response when Caryll returned his early letters is typical:

> You have at length complied with the request I have often
> made to you; for you have shown me I must confess several
> of my faults in the light of those letters. Upon a review of
> them I find many things that would give me shame, if I
> were not more desirous to be thought honest than prudent;
> so many things freely thrown out, such lengths of unre-
> served friendship, thoughts just warm from the brain with-
> out any polishing or dress, the very *déshabille* of the under-
> standing. You have proved yourself more tender of another's
> embryos than the fondest mothers are of their own, for you
> have preserved every thing that I miscarried of. Since I know
> this I shall be in one respect more afraid of writing to you

than ever at this careless rate, because I see my evil works
may again rise in judgment upon me: yet in another respect
I shall be less afraid, since this has given me such a proof
of the extreme indulgence you afford to my thought. This,
dear sir, let me assure you, that the revisal of those letters
has been a kind of examination of conscience to me; so fairly
and faithfully have I set down in 'em from time to time the
true and undisguised state of my mind.

(5 December 1712; I, 160-1)

Despite the tone of self-depreciation, Pope betrays his conviction
that the embryonic quality of his letters makes them interesting.
They show "the true and undisguised state of [his] mind" more
clearly than his polished productions. As early as 1710, he had
told Wycherley, "I talk rather than write to you" (I, 84); in 1712,
he told Caryll, "my style, like my soul, appears in its natural
undress before my friend" (I, 155).

It is important to recognize that these statements represented,
for Pope's period, a new and surprising attitude toward letters.
Today, the foul papers and laundry lists of great men are routinely published; interest in "primary materials" is an expected
norm. But in the early eighteenth century, no one, certainly
no gentleman, would have declared his approval of the publication of unedited, first-draft letters. The attitude toward which
Pope was groping was new, and the eventual publication of his
letters was a powerful factor in changing the public attitude
toward published letters.

Pope's strongest statement on the subject comes in a letter to
the eccentric poet and projector Aaron Hill. In 1720, Hill had
praised Peter the Great in *The Northern Star*; consequently,
Peter's widow had sent Hill some private papers. Pope, sure
that Hill would follow normal practice and edit the letters,
urged him to publish them *verbatim*:

The Eye of Candour, like the Sun, makes all the Beauties
which it sees; it gives Colour and Brightness to the meanest
Objects purely by looking on them. I agree with you, that
there is a Pleasure in seeing the Nature and Temper of Men

in the plainest Undress; but few Men are of Consequence enough to deserve, or reward, that Curiosity. I shall indeed (and so will all Mankind) be highly pleased to see the Great Czar of *Muscovy* in this Light, drawn by himself, like an antient Master, in rough Strokes, without heightening, or shadowing: What a Satisfaction to behold that perfect Likeness, without Art, Affectation, or even the Gloss of Colouring, with a noble Neglect of all that Finishing and Smoothing, which any other Hand would have been obliged to bestow on so principal a Figure? I write this to a Man whose Judgment I am certain of, and therefore am as certain you will give the World this great Depositum, just as you have received it: There will be no Danger of your dressing this *Mars* too finely, whose Armour is not Gold, but Adamant, and whose Stile in all Probability is much more strong, than it is polish'd. I congratulate you, that this great Treasure is fallen into your Hands; and I congratulate all *Europe*, that it is to be delivered to them through the Hands of one, who will think it Sacrilege to touch upon, much less to alter, any great Lines of such an Original.

([September 1726?]; II, 405)

It is of course one thing to advocate candor in the publication of a dead man's papers, and another to use similar candor in publishing one's own. But Pope did grasp, and here stated clearly, the idea that a great man's informal writings might prove interesting. He knew that he was great, and he knew that his writings were interesting.

Equally powerful factors dissuaded Pope from publishing his letters. William Irving summarizes the social pressures neatly: "Few writers in those days would have had the effrontery to publish their own letters without excuse or polite subterfuge."[11] For Pope, such publication would not only have been effrontery; it might have been dangerous. He was vulnerable. He was a Roman Catholic in a country suspicious of Catholics as potential traitors and Jacobites. He was physically deformed, and he had enemies who were ready to exploit that deformity with the mindless but often-accepted

argument *mens curva in corpore curvo.* He was not a member
of the landed gentry; he held no university degree. After the
publication of his translation of the *Iliad,* he was notoriously
successful, which hardly endeared him to the starving hacks
of Grub Street. So Pope waited, calling in his letters from
time to time, occasionally searching his mind for ways to place
before the public those interesting embryonic thoughts, while
somehow protecting himself from exposure and attack.

When exposure came, it came from a predictable quarter. The
notorious printer Edmund Curll had been Pope's implacable
enemy since a hilarious skirmish in 1716, in which Pope took
vengeance on Curll for publishing some tasteless verses by
Mary Wortley Montagu (then his friend). He invited Curll
for a friendly glass of sack in a tavern, managed to slip an
emetic into Curll's drink, and published (anonymously) *A Full
and True Account of a Horrid and Barbarous Revenge by Poison
on the Body of Mr. Edmund Curll, Bookseller.*[12] Ten years
later, Curll had a splendid opportunity for revenge. A Mrs.
Elizabeth Thomas, who had been the mistress of Pope's early
friend Henry Cromwell, offered Curll autograph manuscripts
of twenty-five youthful letters from Pope to Cromwell. Curll
purchased the papers and issued them as the first part of his
Miscellanea (published in 1726; but dated 1727). A prefatory
letter to Cromwell from "the Editor" notes gleefully that Curll
has taken the necessary steps to secure the copyright, and con-
gratulates Cromwell on lying (in print) between "Sapho" and
"Corinna," whose supposed letters are included. An even more
gloating note to Pope begins the second volume. Curll is certain that Pope will take no legal action against Cromwell;
indeed, he expresses confidence that Pope will

> . . . *confirm* that *Friendship* which you have so strenu-
> ously and so frequently professed for him.
>   THEN, Sir, upon a happy *Consummation* of *all Things,*
> I doubt not but he will admit you to share his Felicity of
> *Lying in State* between them [i.e., Sapho and Corinna], not
> in *Linnen,* but *Paper* Sheets; for by that *Metaphor* no other
> Idea is conveyed than what is strictly consistent with the

purity of the *Platonick System*, all *Carnal Impurities* being
the Detestation of

> *Your humble servant,*
> *The* EDITOR

Terminis Trin: the final Day,
Succeeds the merry Month of *May*.

Even the doggerel date is cutting, as is the similar one Curll
affixes to the letter to Cromwell:

> As to fixt Time, the Tenth of June,
> When ev'ry *Tory's* Heart's in Tune.

Curll is imitating Pope's own youthful dating, in the very
letters being published:

> The twelfth or thirteenth Day of July,
> But which, I cannot tell you truly.

> The tenth of May; that is (in Meeter)
> Just fifty days before St. Peter.

Pope's response was complicated. The letters to Cromwell
were by no means his best: they were witty, but often in a forced
Restoration fashion; they were full of pedantry, for the young
Pope had been anxious to impress the much older Cromwell
with his literary knowledge; worst of all, they were often sala-
cious or impious. An astute reader could probably detect insincerity, as Elijah Fenton did. Fenton, who had worked hard
and had (he felt) been treated unfairly as a collaborator on Pope's
Odyssey, described the letters to his colleague Broome with ironic
mock-praise:

> I have read the collection of letters you mentioned, and
> was delighted with nothing more than that air of sincerity,
> those professions of esteem and respect, and that deference
> paid to his friend's judgment in poetry which I have some-

times seen expressed to others, and I doubt not with the same cordial affection. If they are read in that light they will be very entertaining and useful in the present age, but, in the next, Cicero, Pliny, and Voiture may regain their reputation.

(7 September 1726; II, 398)

Pope did feel called upon to complain about the publication, and predictably he used that complaint as a way of calling in more letters. To Caryll, he wrote again, asking him "to consult my fame, such as it is, and to help me to put out of Curl's power any trifling remains of mine" (5 December 1726; II, 419). To Hill, who had praised the letters, he expressed less concern about damage to his reputation; he actually claimed to be "very happy in the Envy and silly Attacks of such People, as have awakened the Generosity of so powerful a Defender" ([September 1726]; II, 404). And to Motte, a printer, he dropped what looks like a hint:

The advertisement of Curl is a silly piece of Impertinence, not worth notice, & it serves to tell every body what makes for my purpose & reputation, "That those Letters to Mr Cromwell were printed without My Consent or Knowledge."

(30 June [1727]; II, 438-9)

Ostensibly, Pope's "purpose," which he here alleged had been aided by Curll's advertisement, was simply to seem innocent of such vanity as publishing his own letters. But Pope's long-range purpose, perhaps already in his mind, was also aided by Curll's action: the public, knowing that Curll had published Pope's letters once without consent, was likely to expect a recurrence. Further evidence that Pope's distress over the publication of the Cromwell letters was limited to his embarrassment about the salacities and puerilities comes in the 1735 edition, which reprints edited versions of nineteen of the letters. Even Pope's "official" editions, the quarto and folio of 1737, include sixteen of the letters to Cromwell first issued in 1726.

On balance, Curll's publishing the Cromwell letters may very well have encouraged Pope in his subsequent plans to

publish. As we have seen, it was an excellent excuse for calling
in letters, and Pope wrote to a number of his friends at this time,
asking for them. His note to Bethel is particularly interesting:

> After the publishing of my Boyish Letters to Mr. Cromwell,
> you will not wonder if I should forswear writing a letter
> again while I live; since I do not correspond with a friend
> upon the terms of any other free subject of this kingdom.
> But to you I can never be silent, or reserved; and I am sure
> my opinion of your heart is such, that I could open mine
> to you in no manner which I could fear the whole world
> should know. I could publish my own heart too, I will
> venture to say, for any mischief or malice there's in it; but
> a little too much folly or weakness might (I fear) appear,
> to make such a spectacle either instructive or agreeable
> to others.
>
> I am reduced to beg of all my acquaintance to secure me
> from the like usage for the future, by returning me any
> letters of mine which they may have preserved; that I may
> not be hurt after my death by that which was the happiness
> of my life, their partiality and affection for me.
>
> (17 June 1728; II, 501)

Pope's *literary* reputation was not substantially injured by Curll's
publication; it may even have been enhanced. But the kind of
moral reputation he coveted with his soberer friends, such as
Caryll and Bethel, was bound to suffer, and it was necessary
for him to apologize for "folly or weakness." At the same time,
however, this very letter, ostensibly deploring publication,
seems to hint at Pope's desire to "publish my own heart." For
when he began to read through the old letters he was collecting,
he was soon convinced that they were interesting, as he reported
to Caryll:

> Some of my own letters have been returned to me, which I
> have put into order . . . ; and it makes all together an
> un-important, indeed, but yet an innocent, history of
> myself. . . . I thank God (above all) for finding so few

parts of life that I need be ashamed of, no correspondences or intimacies with any but good, deserving poeple, and no opinions that I need to blush for, or actions (as I hope) that need to make my friends blush for me.

(8 July [1729]; III, 38)

Discovering so little to blush for, Pope began to seek an occasion to publish some of these letters. Another Grub Street enmity soon provided what seemed a perfect situation.

Pope had published an edition of Shakespeare in 1725, with an interesting introduction but a text whose preparation, while comparatively painstaking for its time, was casual by modern standards.[13] Lewis Theobald, a more serious textual scholar, immediately attacked the edition in a pamphlet entitled *Shakespeare Restored*, which demonstrated the inadequacies of Pope's text; his rival edition was eventually issued in 1733. Another of Theobald's projects was the editing of some unpublished papers left at his death by Pope's old friend Wycherley. Wycherley's widow had married a Captain Shrimpton, who selected Theobald to edit the manuscripts, which duly appeared as *The Posthumous Works of William Wycherley Esq; In Prose and Verse. Faithfully publish'd from his Original Manuscripts, by Mr. Theobald. In Two Parts.* The preface, however, explained that only one part of the manuscripts was then being published, and promised that a second would follow "in a short time." Pope, who had revised many of Wycherley's late poems, and who had in his possession their correspondence relating to the poems, recognized at once that the *"Faithfully publish'd"* claim of the preface was false: Theobald had made many silent alterations. Still smarting from being exposed by Theobald, Pope saw an ideal chance to retaliate; he could attack Theobald on his own turf—as an irresponsible editor. Incidentally, he would adduce as proof his correspondence with Wycherley, edited to remove those follies and weaknesses he had mentioned to Bethel. Theobald had unwittingly provided an opportunity for the publication of letters which would show that Pope was valued, even as a boy, by the eminent Mr. Wycherley, and that he had revised Wycherley's work with a precocious skill far beyond the talents

of Theobald. The anonymity of the publication would protect
Pope from being suspected of vanity, and even if some readers
concluded (as well they might) that Pope was behind the volume,
the preface would emphasize the honorable purpose of the
publication: to clear Wycherley's reputation, which had been
harmed by Theobald's printing unfinished and undistinguished
pieces from the old poet's dotage.

To insure ostensible anonymity, Pope made use of his aristocratic connections. On about 15 September 1729, he wrote to
his good friend the Second Earl of Oxford, asking him to

> . . . suffer some Original papers & Letters, both of my own
> and some of my Friends, to lye in your Library at London.
> There seems already to be an occasion of it, from a publica-
> tion of certain Posthumous pieces of Mr Wycherley; very
> unfair & derogatory to His memory, as well as injurious to
> me; who had the sole supervisal of 'em committed to me,
> at his Earnest desire in his Life time: And Something will
> be necessary to be done, to Clear both his & my reputation,
> which the Letters under hand will abundantly do.
>
> (III, 54)

Three weeks later, he repeated the request, with a fuller explanation:

> My Lord,—I long since writ you a Letter, principally to
> enquire of your Lordships & Familys health: secondly to
> tell you of what I know you have the goodness to interest
> yourself in, my own; & thirdly to ask your leave to deposite
> certain Memorandums of me, & the best part of me, (my
> Friendships & Correspondence with my Betters) in your
> Library. I foresaw some dirty Trick in relation to my Friend
> Wycherley's papers which they were publishing; & nothing
> can at once do justice so well to Him & to Me, who was by
> him employd in them, as the divulging some parts of his
> & my Letters (with proper Guard & Caution to reserve what
> should not be published of private Letters pour raisons (as
> the French express it) d'honneteté. . . .

I would not appear myself as publisher of 'em, but any man else may, or even the Bookseller be suppos'd to have procurd Copies of 'em formerly, or now, it is equal. But certain it is, that no other way can Justice be rendered to the Memory of a Man, to whom I had the first obligations of Friendship, almost in my childhood.

(6 October 1729; III, 55-56)

Pope was of course more polite than honest in his assertion that the request for "leave to deposite certain Memorandums" stood third among his reasons for writing Oxford. He needed both the concealment and the stamp of aristocratic legitimacy that the depositing of the manuscripts would provide, and he was doubtless relieved by Oxford's cordial reply of 9 October allowing the use of the library.

Pope must have already done his selecting and editing, and probably had the fifty-one printed pages of his correspondence already set in type. Accordingly, on 4 November 1729 appeared *The Posthumous Works of William Wycherley . . . Vol II*, with a preface unquestionably by Pope. This carefully written preface informs the reader that Oxford "has been pleas'd, in the most Generous Manner, to comply with our Request, and to sacrifice a Private Curiosity to the Gratification of the Publick." It further promises that "the *Originals*, in the Author's own Hand-writing, may, upon Application, be view'd in the Harley-Library," and notes that some passages have been omitted.[14] Pope had warned Oxford on 16 October that he intended to do something like this:

My Lord,—I am extreamly obliged to you for your kind permission to Quote your Library, and to mention it in what manner I pleas'd: I consulted Mr Lewis upon the Turn of the Preface to those papers relating to Mr Wycherley and, have exceeded perhaps my Commission in one point, (tho we both judged it the Right way) for I have made the Publishers say, that Your *Lordship permitted them a Copy* of some of the papers from the Library, where the Originals remain as Testimonies of the Truth. It is indeed no more than a justice due to the Dead, and to the Living author; one of which (I have the happiness to know) You are Concerned for; and the other had too much Merit to have his Laurels blasted fourteen years after his death by an unlicend & presumptuous Mercenary.

(III, 58-9)

"I have made the Publishers say" constitutes as frank an admission as Pope ever made that the volume was his. To Swift, he was more indirect:

I speak of old Mr. Wycherley; some letters of whom (by the by) and of mine, the Booksellers have got and printed not without the concurrence of a noble friend of mine and yours, I don't much approve of it; tho' there is nothing for me to be asham'd of, because I will not be asham'd of any thing I do not do myself, or of any thing that is not immoral but merely dull . . .

(28 November 1729; III, 80)

As usual, Pope's phrasing is careful. He does not quite literally disclaim involvement in the project, and Swift may well have read this passage as a hinted acknowledgment of involvement, expressed in a way that the Post Office agents (who sometimes opened their letters) would not understand.

Whether Pope was hedging or hinting about the responsibility for the printing, he was correct about the contents: many of the letters to Wycherley are "merely dull," although he had edited out a good many trivial statements, as we know from the complete transcripts which still exist. After the slightly deceptive "To the Reader," Pope's volume reprints and annotates Theobald's Table of Contents, correctly labeling certain pieces as wholly or partially spurious. Then come the letters, then Pope's versions of the texts of Wycherley's maxims and poems. Vinton Dearing, in his detailed description of the one known copy of the volume, argues that "the text of Pope's volume of the *Posthumous Works* consists for the most part of documentation for his statements in the preface and the reprinted table of

contents.''[15]   Many of the footnotes are argumentative; one
notes that Wycherley's papers had "the misfortune to fall into
the Hands of a Mercenary," a repetition of the denigration of
Theobald Pope had made to Oxford.

But Pope's splendid revenge on Theobald seems to have mis-
fired. Only one copy of this book survives, and the later history
of the sheets containing the Wycherley correspondence makes it
clear that the book was withdrawn from publication. No contemporary document records the reason, but the best hypothesis
seems to be that Pope ran into copyright trouble.   Dearing,
following Sherburn's suggestion, speculates that Lintot, who
held the copyright for the "Epistle to Mr. Dryden," the "one
long, annotated example of Pope's revisions of Wycherley's
poems," threatened to sue Pope, and that Pope, "faced with the
necessity of cancelling it or of withdrawing the volume altogether, . . . not unnaturally chose the second alternative."[16]

This theory seems as good a guess at the reasons for the
suppressing of the edition as we are likely to have. Whatever
the reason, Pope was no doubt disappointed, not so much at his
failure to do Theobald more damage (he had, after all, enthroned
the hapless "Tibbald" as Prince of the Dunces in the 1728 *Dunciad*), but at his failure to advance what Swift accurately called
his "Schemes . . . of Epistolary fame" (26 February 1729/30;
III, 92).[17]   Furthermore, he was left with the sheets of what
was to have been his edition on his hands, and he was out of
pocket for the cost of printing.

While Pope seems to have formulated no active schemes for
publishing letters in the next several years, he did continue to
show interest in his letters, and in other people's.   On 3 April
1731; he sent Oxford some transcripts of his correspondence
with the exiled Jacobite bishop, Atterbury—letters about which
he was particularly concerned lest his enemies use his intimacy
with Atterbury to accuse him of treason.   And when Lady
Burlington had Pope look over some papers of her father and
grandfather, the first and second Marquesses of Halifax, he
proposed printing, among other items, a volume of their letters
(see III, 314).

Pope's next real move toward having his letters published

was an approach to his old enemy Curll. Not content with the
Cromwell letters, Curll had continued to show an interest in
potentially scandalous materials relating to Pope,[18] and had
repeatedly run advertisements soliciting such materials. Accordingly, on 27 March 1733, he received a mysterious note from
someone signing himself E. P. The note tells a story about
Pope's being whipped as a schoolboy for writing a lampoon
on his teacher. The last paragraph is curious:

> How much *past Correction* has wrought upon him, the
> World is Judge; and how much *present* Correction might,
> may be collected from this sample. I thought it a curious
> Fact, and therefore it is at your service, as one of the Orna-
> ments of this excellent Person's Life.
>
> (27 March 1733; III, 360)

We may imagine Curll's delight. The story was just the sort of
material he regularly introduced into his outrageous biographies
(Arbuthnot remarked that these "lives" were one of the new
horrors of death). The word "sample" suggested that E. P. had
more to offer, that Curll had actually opened a conduit to private
information about Pope. We may also imagine Pope having
some fun devising the tale and the letter (for they are surely his).
He must have enjoyed creating the ironic E. P., who implies that
neither past nor present correction will have any effect on Mr.
Pope, and who refers to the little story as "one of the Ornaments
of this excellent Person's Life." The excellent person himself
was aware of a further ironic twist in these words.[19]
     Curll took the bait, and announced his reception of the anec-
dote in an advertisement in the *Daily Journal*:

> *The SECOND Time of Asking*
> *(There is now Actually in the Press)*
>
> THE LIFE of Mr. POPE. Containing a faithful Account of him
> and his Writings. (Founded upon a Plan deliver'd by him-
> self to Mr. Jacob, with two Guineas, to insert it in his Lives
> of the Poets) Embellish'd with Dissertations, Digressions,

Notes, and all Kinds of poetical Machinery, in order to
render the Work compleat. Nothing shall be wanting but
his (universally desired) Death. Any Memoirs, &c. worthy of
his Deserts, if sent to Mr. Curll, will be faithfully inserted.

N. B. Pursuant to my former Advertisement in this Paper,
I received on Wednesday last, some Anecdotes relating to
*Mr. Pope's Behaviour, when he went to School to one Brom-
ley, a Popish Renegado. They are communicated by a
Gentleman, who declares, that he was Schoolfellow with
Mr. Pope, and the late D. of Norfolk at the same time, in
Devonshire-Street, Bloomsbury. The Fact is very remark-
able, as it is a Proof of that Natural Spleen which constitutes
Mr. Pope's Temperament, (as my Lord Bacon observes of
Deformed Persons) and from which he has never yet deviated.*

*As I intend to write this Life in a Chronological Method,
I desire those Gentlemen, who are willing to do Mr. Pope's
Character Justice, to be speedy in transmitting what
Memoirs they intend, that they may be placed in their
proper Order of Time; and shall be faithfully inserted in the
Words of the Writers.*

Burghley-Street in the Strand   E. CURLL
        March 30, 1733.[20]

After this letter and response, the ghostly and no doubt fictitious
E. P. vanished. To sell Curll the letters, Pope invented another
mysterious character, who had a longer and more successful
career.

The successor, an "old gentleman" named, or rather initialled,
P. T., ostensibly wrote in response to Curll's advertisement; like
E. P., he understood Curll's desire to write Pope's life, and he
provided Curll with some information on Pope's ancestry in a
letter dated 11 October 1733. Some of the information was false,
some of it was correct and detailed, and all of it was quite respect-
able. But P. T. made it clear that he wasted no love on Pope:

This is a true Account of Mr *Pope's* Family and Parentage.
Of his Manners I cannot give so good an one, yet as I would

not wrong any Man, both ought to be True; and if such be your Design, I may serve you in it, not entering into any Thing in any wise Libellous. You may please to direct an Answer in the *Daily Advertiser* this Day-sennight in these Terms—*E. C. hath received a Letter, and will comply with P. T.*

(III, 388)

Curll's appetite for more material on Pope, particularly for the derogatory description of Pope's "Manners" which P. T. seemed to be promising, was whetted, and he later claimed that he placed the dictated advertisement.[21] No such advertisement has ever been found, however, and P. T.'s next letter sounds as if none was placed:

Sir,—I troubled you with a Line sometime since, concerning your Design of the *Life* of Mr. *Pope*, to which I desir'd your Answer in the *Daily Advertiser* of *Thursday* the 10th[22] Instant *October*. I do not intend my self any other Profit in it, than that of doing Justice to, and on, that Person, upon whom, Sir, you have conferr'd some Care as well as Pains in the Course of your Life; and I intend him the like for his Conduct towards me. . . .

(15 November 1733; III, 395)

This beginning, although carefully ambiguous, seems to suggest that P. T. has been wronged by Pope and intends to retaliate through Curll, who has also been wronged. The letter continues with a concrete proposal:

A propos to his Life, there have lately fall'n into my Hands a large Collection of his *Letters*, from the former Part of his Days to the Year 1727. which being more considerable than any yet seen, and opening very many Scenes new to the World, will alone make a Perfect and the most authentick *Life* and *Memoirs* of him that could be. To shew you my Sincerity and determinate Resolution of assisting you herein, I will give you an Advertisement, which you may publish forthwith if you please, and on your so doing the Letters shall be sent you. They will make a Four or Five Sheet[23] Book, yet I expect no more than what will barely pay a Transcriber, that the Originals may be preserved in mine or your Hands to vouch the Truth of them. I am of Opinion these alone will contain his whole History (if you add to them what you formerly printed of those to *Henry Crom-Well*, Esq; . . .

(III, 395-6)

This very attractive offer seems to have made Curll suspicious. His subsequent behavior shows that he had not yet figured out that P. T. was Pope, but the circumstance of a "large Collection" falling into anyone's hands would have prompted caution. Further danger lay in an advertisement P. T. sent in the letter and insisted upon seeing published, which listed the correspondents whose letters were to be included and promised that Curll would be prepared to show the public original manuscripts to prove the authenticity of the book. Probably sensing at once the danger of making such claims without having seen any of the material, Curll held on to the letter, waiting for P. T. to make another move.[24]

Because of Curll's hesitation, the history comes to a halt here for a year and a half. This is a good point at which to review Pope's motives and methods. One plausible and simple hypothesis for this series of approaches in 1733 is that Pope merely wished to trick Curll into advertising; indeed, had Curll placed the proposed advertisement, some of Pope's friends would no doubt have urged him to head off the "piracy" by publishing an "authorized" edition. Curll would have looked foolish for promising originals when he had none, and might even have been successfully prosecuted. However, if Pope had already made his basic editorial decisions, he had indulged in some deceptions which might have bothered those of his correspondents who were still alive, especially John Caryll, letters to whom eventually appeared as if written to Addison, Steele, Congreve, and Trumbull. This redirection Caryll would surely have noticed and resented. Pope's other changes, omissions of irrelevant or embarrassing passages and occasional splicings together of parts of two letters as one, were so normal that they would not have offended any eighteenth-century reader (although they scandalized his nineteenth-century editors). But if Curll could be tricked into not merely advertising but actually publishing the letters, Pope's friends would of course attribute the redirections to Curll. Significantly, Caryll was safely dead (6 April 1736) by the time Pope's authorized, official edition of the letters appeared in 1737.[25]

Pope's motivation can never be called simple. In publishing the Wycherley edition, he had at least three purposes—vindication of Wycherley, editorial revenge on Theobald, propagation of his own correspondence as "documentation." Surely there were as many motives here—the old grudge against Curll, the social need to avoid what Dr. Johnson called the "imputation of vanity," the usefulness of stirring up journalistic mention of the letters *before* their publication (thus making them seem more controversial than they were and insuring a large sale), and the sheer joy of deception. This last motive is probably the hardest for twentieth-century readers to understand. Ours is an age of public nudity, both literal and figurative. The pages of our periodicals are filled with confessions of all kinds: aging homosexuals, surviving Nazi henchmen, and "happy hookers" "tell it like it was" and realize immense profits. But the eighteenth century was an age of splendid deceptions. Swift's major works, *A Tale of a Tub* and *Gulliver's Travels*, were published anonymously; Pope's *Dunciad* and *Essay on Man* acknowledged no author on their first title pages. Even the hacks of Grub Street knew that manuscripts "recently discovered" or "translated from the French" suggested mysterious sources and produced popularity. Similarly, the characteristic humor of the period relies on twists and deceptions; what reader of Swift's *A Modest Proposal* has not found himself fooled at some point by Swift's series of rhetorical disguises? Writers who were skillful at such games took particular pleasure in unravelling the deceptions of their friends, or even in suggesting new ones. Swift's note to Pope about the *Dunciad* is typical:

I would be glad to know whether the quarto edition is to come out anonymously, as published by the Commentator, with all his pomp of prefaces, &c. and among complaints of spurious editions?—I am thinking whether the Editor should not follow the old style of, This excellent author, &c. and refine in many places when you meant no refinement? and into the bargain take all the load of naming the dunces, their qualities, histories, and performances?

(16 July 1728; II, 505)

What Swift is here recommending is an act of fiction-making: Pope is to create an Editor who will comment upon the "excellent author." That both are Pope is part of the fun—the same kind of fun Swift had with his many *personae*, especially one Lemuel Gulliver, whose description of his travels was delivered to the printer by one Alexander Pope. In creating E. P., P. T., and (later) R. S., Pope was taking advantage of Curll's habitual shady dealings with the literary underworld, counterfeiting just those sorts of agents who might plausibly have stolen Mr. Pope's letters. The deceptions he and his initialled creations sold to Curll and the public are the most complicated, and the funniest, in a century of great deceptions. They are rendered more complicated by the fact that the only sources we have for understanding them are the accounts published afterwards by Pope and Curll, both of whom had reasons to lie and did. Pope's *A Narrative of the Method by Which the Private Letters of Mr. Pope have been Procur'd and Publish'd by Edmund Curll, Bookseller* contains his versions of nineteen numbered letters between Curll and the initialled agents, with a running narrative suggesting a largely incorrect (but more or less plausible) interpretation of those letters. When the *Narrative* appeared, Curll had already set type for his own account, a pamphlet called *The Initial Correspondence*, including many more letters. As a rebuttal to Pope, he reprinted the *Narrative* in full with contradictory footnotes, then added the *Initial Correspondence*, and published both as part of the front matter of *Mr. Pope's*

Literary Correspondence. Volume the Second. The consequent
division of Curll's history into two separately prepared accounts
confuses the order of the letters. All subsequent attempts to retell
the story have been based on these accounts, filled as they are
with accidental and deliberate errors. The appendix provides
one possible timetable of events, drawing on the accounts of
the two principals, and on later attempts to reconcile those
accounts. I should stress that *all* such versions of the story,
including mine, are necessarily speculative; no one will ever
know what happened beyond a few basic facts.

Those facts, in their simplest form, are as follows. In March
of 1735, Curll sent the letter and advertisement he had received
from P. T. in 1733 to Pope, and proposed a meeting to "close
all Differences." Pope quickly placed a public advertisement
as an answer, in which he claimed that any collection of letters
Curll might have must be a forgery; then, as P. T., he wrote
Curll accusing him of treachery in corresponding with Pope,
but still offering a collection of letters, now printed. After a
series of hesitations on both sides, a meeting between P. T. and
Curll was set up. James Worsdale, an actor hired by Pope,
arrived at this meeting and introduced himself as Mr. R. Smythe,
P. T.'s cousin. After many more letters, some of them now
written by R. S. rather than by P. T. himself, an agreement was
reached: as soon as Curll placed an advertisement listing the
correspondents (including several peers), he would receive the
sheets necessary to make up the book. On May 12, Curll finally
placed the dictated advertisement, and R. S. met him at a tavern,
accompanied by two porters with the long-awaited sheets. Curll
dispatched the porters and their load to his shop, where the books
were suddenly seized by officers of the Black Rod, acting on the
authority of the House of Lords. This seizure had been arranged
by Pope's friend Lord Ilay and was dependent on the fact that
the advertisement had implied that letters *from* peers would
be included (an illegal "breach of privilege"). Curll was called
to testify before a committee of the House of Lords; naturally,
this controversy stirred up considerable public interest in the
letters. There was much frantic correspondence between R. S.
and Curll; R. S. gave Curll instructions as to how to testify,
stressing the need to conceal P. T. from the Lords and Pope,

but Curll, more and more suspicious of R. S. and P. T., ignored those instructions and managed to recover his books when it became obvious that they contained no letters from peers. Actually, the books contained Pope's correspondence with Wycherley (the remainder sheets from the withdrawn *Posthumous Works*) and a number of other letters printed to match; there were many letters *to* members of the House of Lords, but none *from* them. P. T. and R. S. claimed that Curll had betrayed them and refused to deliver more sheets. Curll rushed into print with a reprint, and a number of booksellers issued editions of their own. The letters, not intrinsically a particularly interesting volume, became the literary event of the year.

In June, Pope published anonymously his plausible but false *Narrative* of what had happened in the previous month. Curll's fuller and much more accurate rebuttal, the *Initial Correspondence*, came out in July, but failed to convince the public. Finally, Pope issued an advertisement claiming that some of the letters published as his in May were not genuine and declaring himself "under a Necessity to publish such of the said Letters as are genuine, with the Addition of some others of a Nature less insignificant." His machinations had succeeded in making an "authorized" edition seem necessary.

Pope realized his major objectives. He fought Curll on his own ground and with his own weapons—deceit, forgery, and double-dealing—and achieved at least a draw, if not a victory. He disseminated his letters, and insured their popularity through the widely-publicized controversy. He saved the feelings of Caryll and other old friends by disclaiming the volume; at the same time, his editing saved the reputations of others. He indulged joyously in the complexity of the deception. To a degree, he satisfied his contradictory impulses toward self-exposure and concealment, impulses which are nowhere more clearly described, in all their contradiction, than in this passage of a letter to Orrery, written just one year after the first publication:

> I am tempted to say a great deal more to your Lordship, but so severe a fate, & such an Exposal of my private Thoughts as has befallen me in the publication of my freest

Letters, has given me a check that will last for life. So much Candour & Good nature as I know are in your mind, would draw out one's most naked Sentiments, without any Care about the cloathing them. And I am heartily sorry I can't expose myself to you alone. The same Excess of Humanity which sees all in the best light prompts to an Indulgence for whatever is well-meant; and that, joind to the great Partiality I find your Lordship has for me, would move you to keep my Trash, as our Friend Swift has done.

(10 May 1736; IV, 16)

The several levels of falsehood in this letter suggest the complexity of Pope's psychological state.   He claims that the publication of his "freest Letters" (hardly his freest, especially given the editing job) is a "severe . . . fate, . . . an Exposal of [his] private Thoughts."   But the "Exposal" was his own doing, for reasons he later acknowledges, in part, when he claims to be "heartily sorry I can't expose myself to you alone."   Still, the very fact that most of the sentiments expressed in the letter are clothed in polite falsehoods proves that Orrery was not really among those friends before whom Pope wished to stand figuratively naked.   In fact, what Pope is doing in claiming such a desire for intimacy is flattering Orrery so that he may use him as a tool in his campaign to recapture his letters to Swift.

Pope began that campaign because of the success of the 1735 volume—not merely its popular success as a sensation, but also the impression it made on such readers as Broome, who praised the morality of the letters:

I do not wonder at your caution in recovering your letters, after the late publication. Yet, after all, some few passages being retracted, where is the mighty grievance? With the good they certainly do you honour, and the worst that the ill-natured can say is what is no dishonour. You have, like our greatest beauties, shown there is such a thing as an excellence in trifling agreeably. It is a Laelius or a Scipio playing with pebbles, and, in my opinion, the humane companion, the dutiful and affectionate son, the compassionate and obliging friend, appear so strongly almost in every page, that I assure you I had rather be the owner of the writer's heart than of the head that has honoured England with Homer, his Essays, Moral Epistles, &c. These gain you honour with men, the other with heaven and angels.

(1 December 1735; III, 512)

Wealthy Ralph Allen of Bath, later the prototype for Fielding's Squire Allworthy, urged Pope to bring out an "authentic" edition, and offered to foot the bill. Pope's attempts to demur, such as this note to Fortescue, are extremely unconvincing:

Your too partial mention of the book of Letters, with all its faults and follies, which Curll printed and spared not, (nor yet will spare, for he has published a fourth sham volume yesterday,) makes one think it may not be amiss to send you, what I know you will be much more pleased with than I can be, a proposal for a correct edition of them; which at last I find must be *offered*, since people have misunderstood an advertisement I printed some time ago, merely to put some stop to that rascal's books, as a promise that I would publish such a book. It is therefore *offered* in this manner; but I shall be just as well *satisfied*, (if the public will,) without performing the offer.

(26 March 1736; IV, 7)

So the "official" edition was proposed, subscribed for, beautifully printed in quarto and folio, and published on 18 May 1737, providing Pope's wealthy friends who subscribed with highly edited, concise texts. A month later, J. Roberts published, as volumes v and vi of Pope's *Works*, an octavo edition, *"Wherein to those of the Author's own Edition, are added all that are genuine from former Impressions, with some never before printed."* This edition, which has considerably fewer omissions than the chaste folio, was never explicitly acknowledged by Pope, but it was clearly supervised by him and prepared before the folio, although published later.[26] For the next four years, Pope worked at recovering and publishing his correspondence

with Swift. His actions toward that goal, nearly as complex as
his machinations with Curll, but more difficult to understand
and defend, are discussed in chapter 5.

When Pope's chicanery was first uncovered by Dilke, his
Victorian editors, especially Elwin, were quick to describe his
actions as treachery, vanity, and fraud, perpetrated by a spiteful
and congenitally dishonest man. What they failed to see, and
what twentieth-century readers may be better equipped to
appreciate, was the complex artistry with which Pope's acts of
counterfeiting were carried out. How differently a letter promising to defend the obscure Caryll read when Pope hit upon the
expedient of labeling it as a letter to the famous Addison—and
how few alterations were necessary in the text itself! What a
convincing account the *Narrative* is, with the prose links suggesting such plausible ways to interpret the offered documents,
documents whose very ambiguities were carefully calculated by
Pope himself! What marvelously rounded characters P. T. and
R. S. became in the course of their careers! Hugh Kenner's recent
"historical comedy," *The Counterfeiters*, without explicitly
mentioning Pope's letters, contains some apposite commentary:

> The counterfeiter's real purpose is to efface himself, like the
> Flaubertian artist, so that we will draw the conclusion he
> wants us to draw about how his artifact came into existence.
> Thus it is difficult to discover any objection to a forged
> Vermeer, except that Vermeer did not paint it; to a forged
> banknote, except that the bank did not issue it; to the
> *Journal of the Plague Year*, except that it is not the journal
> it purports to be, but a fabrication; or to Crusoe's narrative,
> except that there was no Crusoe. Nor it is easy to decide
> whether a man who has made a banknote is a government
> employee, a counterfeiter, or a pop artist, unless we have
> evidence how how he meant his work to be regarded.[27]

Similarly, it is difficult to discover any objection to the 1735
letters, except that they are not what their title page and preface
claim; it is difficult to discover any serious objection to the

Narrative, except that it is prose fiction, not documentary. Pope's brilliance as a counterfeiter, evident as early as the contributions to the Steele periodicals but most brilliantly developed in the intrigues of 1735, was a talent he developed because of the realities of his vulnerability, which required self-concealment. However, in the case of the letters, he used his talents because of most un-Flaubertian needs: a man who seeks to publish his letters can hardly be seeking self-effacement. So the contradictory and powerful impulses toward self-exposure and imaginative disguise produced the actions which so infuriated the Victorians. I, for one, would allege that we know Pope better because of both impulses: if he had not wished to expose his private thoughts in some form, he would never have sought to publish his letters; if he had not enjoyed intrigue and the making of fictions, he would never have developed and maintained scenarios for their publication which now read like the plots of Gilbert and Sullivan operettas. Sometimes the impulses collided: perhaps the curious mistakes Pope made in the P. T. letters, the mistakes which eventually proved his complicity, resulted from a subconscious desire to have his cleverness eventually recognized and appreciated. But for the most part, Pope was a talented deceiver; when practicing deception against a sly and subtle adversary (and Curll was both sly and subtle), he plotted his moves like a bluffing poker player. If the results of his deceptions can be judged harshly by those for whom openness is synonymous with virtue, they can also be accorded more than grudging respect by those able to see skill in all forms of artifice—in a feigned letter or a hypocritical advertisement, as well as in a mock-heroic poem.

CHAPTER 2

Precedents and Predecessors

> You will do me a great favour, dearest friend, if you will
> help in collecting, as far as possible, the letters which I have
> written to various persons with more than usual care. . . .
> Scrape together what you can and from wherever you can,
> but do not send them except by the person I direct.[1]

THE MATTER AND MANNER of this paragraph suggest Pope, but the
letter was in fact written in 1505 by Erasmus, who was preparing
to publish a collection of his letters—a collection for which he
was later to disclaim responsibility in language which will also
be striking to readers of Pope:

> In the Epistles which have been published, there is
> nothing, I think, which will prejudice your reputation;
> but that publication was done by Peter Gillis, while I was
> paying my respects to my patrons in England. For my own
> part I had rather it had not taken place; but what cannot
> be altered must be endured.[2]

Like Pope, Erasmus recognized the worth of his letters and
arranged for their publication, but found it necessary to conceal
his involvement. The particular collection he sought to excuse
in the above letter was issued in 1517, and was unquestionably
the result of his own efforts, as other letters show.[3]

Like Pope, Erasmus was prolific: over 1,600 of his letters
survive, and there must have been more, for he speaks in 1523
of having written "such a mass of letters that two waggons

would hardly be equal to carrying the load."[14]   Like Pope, he lived to see a number of editions of his letters, some of which he authorized in part, using the same excuses Pope was to employ after him.   For example, in 1536, just a few months before his death, he penned a letter "to Friendly Readers" for use as a preface to a large edition of his letters then being printed. Like earlier prefaces, this one protested the triviality of the letters:

> The lucubrations which I publish myself, bring me discredit enough, without these people printing my nonsense, which I never wrote for the public.[5]

Describing as "nonsense" letters he had evidently worked hard to write and connived tirelessly to publish may have satisfied Erasmus's need to pretend to modesty about his lighter writings. Pope's similar needs, as argued in the preceding chapter, led him to make similarly disingenuous statements.

Yet there are more powerful reasons for considering Erasmus here: he occupies a central and consolidating position in the history of letter writing in the West. His letters, widely reprinted and translated, were looked on as models by letter writers in all parts of Europe. He was well versed in the letters of the three great Roman models: Cicero, Pliny, and Seneca. He recognized the rhetorical strategies of the classical letter, its relative looseness, its freedom from rules, but his knowledge of classical precedent did not make him a slavish imitator. He frequently diverged in practice and theory from the classical models, and it was, in part, his letters and his writing *about* letters that provided precedents for the epistolary achievements of Balzac, Voiture, and Pope.

About 1498, Erasmus wrote, for a student, a treatise *De ratione conscribendi epistolas.* A pirated version was printed in 1521, followed by an authorized edition in 1522. It is a thorough, tendentious, and witty performance, full of learning and practical good sense; it includes a full theory of letter writing, an exhaustive classification scheme for types of letters, and a host of skillfully chosen examples. Perhaps its most striking passage is

Erasmus's confident assertion that the letter is a unique *genre*, therefore deserving protection from the rules of the rhetoricians:

> You may look for order in letters, based on either nature or art, but less often on art. For if in making speeches, almost the whole arrangement is settled by pondering, not by rules, how much more should this be done in letters, which are read and not heard (and read by a learned man, not an oaf), and which, in the last analysis, not infrequently have no order at all; and if they actually do have order, they disguise it more than they display it. That is why those who chain up the freedom of the letter-form with required parts, and force letters into a kind of slavery that Quintilian never imposed on speeches, are concluding too exactly. In simple discussions, we shall follow that order that thinking will dictate to us, not petty rules. In miscellaneous letters, in which a heap of innumerable matters is jumbled together, either we shall spew forth anything that comes into the mouth, or we shall make up any old order (based on time, place, people, or things), which we can easily make clear with little transitional phrases.[6]

Pope's practice follows Erasmus's theory: even his most polished letters follow no set formula. In a letter to Molly Lepell, he describes himself as "a mortal enemy and despiser of what they call fine letters" ([1720]; II, 41). He frequently refers to his writing as negligent, hasty, or disconnected, even when he is actually writing carefully. He follows Erasmus's advice in writing letters which "disguise [their order] more than they display it." His accounts of his "rambles" use time and place as ordering devices, and his newsletters to Swift in Ireland use people, running through a litany of friends with a phrase or a sentence about each one. And the letters he selected for the 1735 volume satisfy most of the categories in Erasmus's classification scheme.[7]

The extent to which Pope's letters fulfill the requirements and categories of Erasmus suggests the continuity of an epistolary tradition rooted in classical antiquity. Erasmus was a pivotal part of that tradition because he was among the first group of scholars to be exposed to and influenced by the great classical letter writers. Cicero's letters were unearthed in the fourteenth century, by Petrarch; their impact on the way Erasmus and other *literati* of the Renaissance conceived of and composed letters cannot be exaggerated. Through Erasmus and others like him, an attitude toward letter writing based on Cicero (and Pliny and Seneca) became the norm. So when Pope's letters seem to follow the *dicta* of Erasmus, the resemblance for the most part should really be credited to common classical models.

Erasmus's treatise makes his dependence explicit. A chapter about any given type of letter is usually followed by an example or examples. Most of the examples come from Cicero's letters; Pliny, St. Jerome, and St. Augustine are cited less frequently. Sometimes there is a section of phrases and excerpts called, for example, *Laudatoriae Sylva,* or *Disputatoriae Sylva.* Such "forests" of citations, made to provide material for the fledgling letter writer, also cite Cicero above all others.

Cicero made this deep impression on Erasmus and virtually all later Western letter writers because his letters are not at all in the style we normally think of as "Ciceronian." Erasmus, after all, did publish a dialogue called *Ciceronianus,* in which there is considerable question about the worth of the rhetorical complexity of the Ciceronian oratorical style.[8] But Cicero's letters are something else: they are the ultimate source of the notions expressed by theorists of the letter ever since, that letters ought to be simple and natural. The letters *Ad Familiares* convey, in simple and unadorned prose, the picture of a man with normal sorrows and uncertainties, sharing his thoughts and emotions with his family and closest friends, without the characteristic periodic grandeur of his speeches.

Because the Latin of Cicero's letters is so simple, and because the letters were taken to be models, it is hardly surprising that children in seventeenth- and eighteenth-century England were given the letters as textbooks. One such book is a tiny pamphlet, brought out by Charles Hoole in 1660, called *A Century of Epistles English and Latine . . . By imitating of which, children may readily get a proper style for writing Letters.* The book includes letters by Cicero, Pliny, and Textor (i.e., Jean Tixier,

d. 1524), with English translations facing the Latin texts. The
selections begin with short letters and excerpts of the simplest
sort; one of the first formulas taught in Cicero's frequently-used
beginning: "Si valeas, bene est; ego valeo."[9]   Pope often argued
that the only needful content of a letter was contained in that
phrase:

> But the truth is, that all I ever think letters good for, is
> to convey to those who love one another the news of their
> welfare, and the knowledge that they continue in each
> other's memory.
>
> (5 August 1734; III, 425)

Whether or not Pope used Hoole as a textbook, he and his more
learned correspondents—especially Atterbury, Bolingbroke, and
Swift—were fond of quoting or alluding to Cicero's letters; on
at least one occasion Swift made up a Latin phrase and attributed
it to Cicero.[10]   And when a young man named George Selwyn
wrote for advice on a proposed translation, Pope was strongly
encouraging:

> I cannot enough approve of so laudable an Employment
> of your Youthful Studies, as the Translation of Tully's
> Epistles; I think it will be as Reputable, if you take Suf-
> ficient Time in the Work; and shall be very ready to *joyn*
> myself to the number of your Friends, whose Opinion you
> may take in the prosecution of it.
>
> (29 September [1738]; IV, 131)

What Pope got from Cicero is perhaps most readily demonstrated by sampling Cicero in one of the early English translations, *The Familiar Epistles of Marcus Tullius Cicero Englished
and Conferred with the French Italian and other Translations*
(1620). Here is Cicero on letter writing:

> You know, there are diuers sorts of letters in vse, but the
> chiefest is that by which the conueniencie was brought vs of
> writing, to giue notice vnto our friends, far off, about need-

ful matters, to vs, or them appertaining.   Letters of this
kinde I assure me, that you expect not from me.   For, of
your priuate occasions, you have them that giues You
notice, and those that brings you newes thereof: and in my
[affaires] there is no new thing happened.   There are yet
found two other kinds of letters, which much please me:
one familiar, and conceited: the other seuere, and weightie.[11]

There are numerous letters in which Pope similarly alleges that
he has no news to tell and proceeds, as Cicero does in the rest of
this letter, to discuss his emotional and intellectual responses
to events, rather than the events themselves.   But there are
important differences.   For Cicero, the events responded to, in
this letter and elsewhere, are public and political.   Pope, by
contrast, comes only in the last ten or fifteen years of his life to
anything resembling this concern with politics; more usually,
he responds to human events: his bodily illnesses and those of
others, a friend's success or failure in seeking a place, a fine lady's
slighting Martha Blount by not inviting her to a ball.   His
responses, like Cicero's, often take forms which could be called
familiar and conceited, or severe and weighty.   Like Cicero, he
also often rejects any purity of form and gives his reader a prose
which reflects more accurately the uncertainties and divisions
of his mind.   It is significant that in the letter quoted above
Cicero goes on to reject both of the "kinds of letters, which much
please me."   He continues, "of these, I know not, which is least to
my purpose."   He surely cannot joke with his friend about the
bad state of affairs in the Republic, nor is he sufficiently emo-
tionally composed to write a cogent philosophical analysis.
What he writes instead is a prose which seems close to the
process of thinking—improvisatory, unbalanced, additive.   That
a Cicero could write thus in his letters provided an all-important
precedent for Pope and others.

 The analogy runs deeper.   For Cicero, a final statement about
his response to public events usually took the form of a speech,
a fully rhetorical, balanced and organized, public expression.
For Pope, a final response to those people, ideas, and events
which most impressed him usually took poetic form; and Pope's

characteristic poetic form, the heroic couplet, is above all a
vehicle for tightly organized statement. But for both men, an
earlier stage, a lumpier sort of writing, is frequently found in
the letters. This less formal writing did not arise, for either man,
from false modesty. Cicero knew he was a skillful writer:

> And whereas you saie by waie of a iest, (for so I take it) that
> I possesse the treasures of the tongue, certainely I am not
> ignorant that of words I am not very barren, (for why should
> I dissemble) . . . [12]

And so did Pope:

> Will you never leave commending my poetry? In fair truth,
> sir, I like it but too well myself already.
>
> (28 May 1712; I, 144)

Both men claimed a special candor in their letters, a kind of
affectionate negligence. Cicero, asking Lucius Lucceius to
write his history, begins thus:

> I determine freely, to open my minde vnto you by letters,
> which doe not blush . . . [13]

Among hundreds of similar statements by Pope, compare this one
to Swift:

> Now as I love you better than most I have ever met with in
> the world, and esteem you too the more the longer I have
> compar'd you with the rest of the world; so inevitably I
> write to you more negligently, that is more openly, and with
> all but such as love another will call writing worse.
>
> (28 November 1729; III, 79)

The prose of the letters of Cicero and Pope is the result of a
conscious choice by men fully capable of more highly wrought,
artificial statement; because Cicero opted for the appearance of
simplicity, openness, and emotion in his letters, Pope found
those options more available. Of course, as both men always

realized, there is no such thing as a letter which perfectly mirrors the conscious and subconscious state of its writer's mind. Converting thoughts and feelings into sentences and paragraphs inevitably involves selection and definition. It was the *relative* lack of polish and order in the prose of Cicero's letters which impressed Erasmus and Pope, and which made that supposedly artless style a possible option.

Pope did not always exercise that option. He was capable of writing highly polished letters, and he often did. Here again, there were strong classical precedents. The two later Romans most often mentioned after Cicero as letter writers, Pliny the younger and Seneca, were much more concerned with artful style and order, much more obviously writing for publication. Pope's friend Bolingbroke, a great lover of Cicero's letters, argued for this distinction in a remarkable letter to Swift, asserting that Cicero's letters are special because *not* intended for publication:

> Pliny writ his letters for the Publick, so did Seneca, so did Balzac, Voiture &c. Tully did not, and therefore these give us more pleasure than any which have come down to us from Antiquity. when we read them, we pry into a Secret which was intended to be kept from us, that is a pleasure. We see Cato, and Brutus, and Pompey and others, such as they really were, and not such as the gaping Multitude of their own Age took them to be, or as Historians and Poets have represented them to ours, that is another pleasure. I remember to have seen a Procession at Aix la Chappelle, wherein an Image of Charlemagne is carried on the Shoulders of a Man, who is hid by the long Robe of the Imperial Saint; follow him into the Vestry, you see the Bearer Slip from under the Robe, and the Gigantick figure dwindles into an image of the ordinary Size, and is set among other lumber.
>
> ([9 April 1730]; III, 102-3)

Despite the force of the image Bolingbroke used, Swift was unconvinced; he suspected that Cicero had publication in mind even when protesting his negligence:

> I have observ'd that not only Voiture, but likewise Tully
> and Pliny writ their letters for the publick view, more than
> for the sake of their correspondents; and I am glad of it, on
> account of the Entertainment they have given me. Balsac
> did the same thing, but with more stiffness, and consequently
> less diverting.
>
> (21 October 1735; III, 505)

In fact, Swift was correct, perhaps because he remembered one
of Cicero's letters to Atticus:

> There is no collection of my letters, but Tiro has about
> seventy, and some can be got from you. These I ought to
> see and correct, and then they may be published.[14]

This is a crucial bit of evidence, for it argues that Cicero, like
Pope, was not only ready to write in a relatively candid, unre-
hearsed style, but sensed the worth and interest of what he had
written in that way, and was willing to see it published.

There is no question at all about the willingness of Pliny and
Seneca to see their work published; publication seems to have
been their primary object. For the most part, they divide between
them the two kinds of letters Cicero mentions in the letter quoted
above (p. 47); Pliny specializes in the familiar and conceited;
Seneca takes over the severe and weighty.

Pliny aims to entertain. His letters, at their best, fairly sparkle;
and the normal level is pleasant and diverting. He admits his
sense of what he is doing to Arrianus:

> Yet I do not wholly decline the Rhetorical expressions of our
> friend Marcus, so oft as I am admonished to digress a little
> from the purpose for seasonable delectability; for I desire to
> be witty [*acres*], not severe [*tristes*].[15]

Pliny's distinguishing talents are descriptive and narrative. His
most frequently collected letters, in the English translations of
Pope's age, are his two-part account of his uncle's death at the
time of the destruction of Pompeii, his description of his villa,
a rattling ghost yarn about a skeleton in chains, and a story

about a friendly dolphin who really carries a boy on his back. The slightly fantastic tale is Pliny's *forte*. Pope is never more like Pliny than in his letters about John Hewet and Sarah Drew, two rural lovers struck by lightening, especially the account he published as a letter from Gay to Mr. F_____ (9 August 1718; I, 482-3), which he must have written most of, and which lacks the love-letter elements of the accounts he sent to Martha Blount and Lady Mary Wortley Montagu.[16] Here is the description of the catastrophe:

> Perhaps in the intervals of their work they were now talking of the wedding cloaths, and John was suiting several sorts of poppys and field flowers to her complexion, to chuse her a knot for the wedding-day. While they were thus busied, (it was on the last of July between two or three in the afternoon) the clouds grew black, and such a storm of lightning and thunder ensued, that all the labourers made the best of their way to what shelter the trees and hedges afforded. Sarah was frightned, and fell down in a swoon on a heap of barley. John who never separated from her, sate down by her side, having raked together two or three heaps the better to secure her from the storm. Immediately there was heard so loud a crack, as if heaven had split asunder; every one was now solicitous for the safety of his neighbour, and called to one another throughout the field. No answer being return'd to those who called to our Lovers, they stept to the place where they lay; they perceived the barley all in a smoak, and then spy'd this faithful pair; John with one arm about Sarah's neck, and the other held over her, as to skreen her from the lightning. They were struck dead, and stiffen'd in this tender posture. Sarah's left eye-brow was sing'd, and there appear'd a black spot on her breast; her Lover was all over black, but not the least signs of life were found in either.

Compare this section from Pliny's account of his uncle's death:

> It was debated among 'em, whether they should stay within doors, or venture abroad in the open Air, for the Earthquake

was so violent, and the Houses reel'd and stagger'd so, that one wou'd have thought they had been torn up from their very Foundations. Now they were in the Fields, they had reason to fear the falling of Pumice-stones, tho' they were light and porous, which however of two Dangers were the least: with my Uncle, Reason overcame Reason, with the rest, one Fear overcame another, and they carried Pillows on their Heads to break the fall of any thing that might fall on 'em. In other places it was Day, but here it was as dark as possible Night itself could be, tho' it was somewhat lessned by the Flambeaux and other Lights. Then it was resolved to go to the Seashore, and see how the Sea stood affected, which still continued very Tempestuous. Here my Uncle, lying along upon a parcel of Cloaths, called once or twice for cold Water, and drank it off. After this the Flames, and a smell of Brimstone, which was used to precede the Flames, made the place too hot for 'em, so they waked my Uncle, who being supported by two Servants, got up; but in an Instant fell down again, being I supposed suffocated by the sulphureous Vapours: Three Days after this, his Body was found whole and intire, without the least hurt or mark upon it, and in the same Cloaths he last put on: in a Posture too, that made him rather look like one that was asleep than dead.[17]

The similarity of the events described is, of course, coincidental; my point is the similarity of style, the urbane, graceful, slightly detached tone of both letters. Clearly, Pliny was one of Pope's most important instructors in what William Irving aptly calls "the art of seeming artless."[18] One of his letters to Ferox shows his understanding of the effort necessary to write prose which reads effortlessly:

Your last Letter is a convincing Argument that you Study, and that you don't. You'll tell me I talk Riddles to you, and so I do, till I explain to you more distinctly what my Meaning is. In short, the Letter you sent me, shows you did not study for it, so easie and negligent it appears to be; and yet at the same time 'tis so polite, that 'tis impossible that

any should write it, who did not weigh every word; or else
you are certainly the happiest Man in the World, if you can
write Letters so Entertaining, without Care and Premedi-
tation.[19]

One could certainly make similar remarks about the smoothly
entertaining letters of Pliny himself—and about those of Pope
which seek and achieve the same polish. One could also remark
that such letters always seem directed to the world at large, which
is perhaps why those letters in which Pope seems most clearly
influenced by Pliny—the account of the rural lovers, the description of Stanton Harcourt, the letter on the hermaphrodite—are
all letters which he saw fit to send, with minor changes, to at
least two different correspondents.[20]

Seneca's letters seem even less directed to real individuals than
do Pliny's, and they smell distinctly of the lamp. Erasmus, with
his usual perception, classified them among "letters for which
the name of book seems more appropriate."[21] Seneca, of course,
did not admit to writing highly structured prose. On the contrary, he claimed "naturalness" in words much like those of
earlier and later letter writers:

> In the Matter of Composition, I would write as I speak;
> with Ease and Freedom; for it is more Friendly, as well as
> more Natural: And so much my Inclination, that if I could
> make my Mind visible to you, I would neither speak, nor
> write it. If I put my Thoughts in good Sense, the Matter of
> Ornament I shall leave to the *Orators*.[22]

The suggestion that letters are like talk is one often echoed by
Pope, and the phrase "make my Mind visible" suggests Pope's
"publish my own heart" (II, 501). The relegation of ornament
to the orators is a judgment Erasmus was later to make. But
Seneca did not practice what he preaches here; his letters are in
fact fully formal, although often disorganized. They are crammed
with *sententiae*, and Erasmus was certainly correct in calling them
books rather than letters, for there is little or no "naturalness"
in them, and plenty of ornament.

So it should not be surprising that Pope's letters contain just

one citation of Seneca, and that the citation comes in a letter to
Steele which appeared in the *Spectator*—just the kind of for-
malized philosophical performance that Seneca's own letters
usually are (see I, 146-7). Pope sounds most like Seneca when
he seeks to appear philosophical and sententious; a letter he
published as to Addison (14 December 1713; I, 201-3), having
fabricated it from an earlier version sent to Caryll (I, 185-6), is
one of his most "Senecan" performances:

> Good God! What an incongruous animal is Man? how
> unsettled in his best part, his Soul; and how changing and
> variable in his frame of Body? The constancy of the one
> shook by every Notion, the temperament of the other affected
> by every blast of wind! What is Man altogether, but one
> mighty Inconsistency! Sickness and Pain is the lot of one
> half of us; Doubt and Fear the portion of the other! What
> a bustle we make about passing our time, when all our space
> is but a point? What aims and ambitions are crowded into
> this little instant of our life, which (as *Shakespear* finely
> words it) is *Rounded with a Sleep*?

In constructing this letter, Pope clearly drew on two of Seneca's
most famous passages on the state of man:

> There is not so Disproportionate a Mixture in any Crea-
> ture, as that is in Man, of Soul and Body. There is Intemper-
> ance, join'd with Divinity; Folly, with Severity; Sloth,
> with Activity; and Uncleanness, with Purity.

> Either we are Puff'd up with Pride, Rack'd with Desires,
> Dissolv'd in Pleasures, or Blasted with Cares; and, which
> perfects our Unhappiness, we are never Alone, but in
> perpetual Conflict, and Controversie with our Lusts. We
> are startled at all Accidents. We Boggle at our own Shadows,
> and Fright one another. Lucretius says, *That we are as
> much afraid in the Light, as Children in the Dark; but,* I
> say, *That we are altogether in Darkness, without any Light
> at all; and we run on blindfold, without so much as Groping*

out our Way; which Rashness in the Dark, is the worst sort
of Madness. He that is in his Way, is in hope of coming to
his Journeys End; but Error is Endless.[23]

As usual, Pope's final version of his thoughts on this subject
took poetic form, in the opening of the second epistle of the
Essay on Man:

> Know then thyself, presume not God to scan;
> The proper study of Mankind is Man.
> Plac'd on this isthmus of a middle state,
> A being darkly wise and rudely great:
> With too much knowledge for the Sceptic side,
> With too much weakness for the Stoic's pride,
> He hangs between; in doubt to act, or rest,
> In doubt to deem himself a God, or Beast;
> In doubt his Mind or Body to prefer,
> Born but to die, and reas'ning but to err;
> Alike in ignorance, his reason such,
> Whether he thinks too little, or too much:
> Chaos of Thought and Passion, all confus'd;
> Still by himself abus'd, or disabus'd;
> Created half to rise, and half to fall;
> Great lord of all things, yet a prey to all;
> Sole judge of Truth, in endless Error hurl'd:
> The glory, jest, and riddle of the world!
>
> (II, 1-18)

Is it merely a coincidence that Pope's fine phrase "endless Error"
echoes Seneca's (and L'Estrange's) "Error is Endless"?

The most obvious Renaissance inheritor of Seneca's "heavy
sententiousness"[24] was Jean Louis Guez de Balzac, whose
elegant and courtly letters first appeared in France in 1624; in
1634 there appeared in London *The Letters of Mounsieur de
Balzac Translated into English, according to the last Edition,
by W*[illiam] *T*[irwhyt] *Esq*. Tirwhyt's preface praises Balzac
for reasons which were to become commonplace: he calls Balzac's
"stile right eloquent, and altogether unafected, his conceptions

high, and the whole Booke richly adorned with great varietie of learning, appearing almost in euery Page."[25]   Balzac himself admitted seeking such praise:

> Yea, had I pleased neuer so little to haue extended some of my *Letters*, they might have beene called bookes.   But besides, my designe, aiming rather to please, then importune, and that *I* tend to the highth of conceptions, and not at the abundance of words: When I treat with you, (my Lord) I suppose my selfe to be before a full assembly; and doe propose to my selfe neuer to write anything unto you, which Posterity ought not to read.[26]

The letters are frankly written for posterity, and written with careful aim at "highth of conceptions."   But they are also written in seventeenth-century France, and certain deviations from the classical models (especially Seneca) ought not to be surprising. Mistresses, for example, are now mentionable as part of the retired life:

> Whilst you imploy your houres in gayning hearts and Votes, and happily lay the foundation of some eminent enterprize; I here enjoy a reposednesse not unlike that of the dead, and which is neuer rouzed but by *Clorinda's* kisses.[27]

But for the last phrase, the sentiments might be those of Seneca; Clorinda's intrusion places us squarely in the world of French elegance; it was this part of Balzac to which Pope first responded:

> I made no question but the News of *Sappho's* staying behind me in the Towne wou'd surprize you.   But she is since come into the Country, and to surprize you more, I will inform you, that the first Person she nam'd when I waited on her, was one Mr. *Cromwell*.
>
> (25 April 1708; I, 47)

Pope's witty sallies to and about women often seem to derive from Balzac's part of the tradition.   One good example is his use of the language of servitude to describe affection. Here is Balzac:

> For my part, I ingeniously confesse, I do no longer liue vnder *Clorinda's* regency.[28]

Here is Pope, writing to Teresa Blount:

> My journey to Bath fell out in the three hundred seventy-sixth week of the reign of my sovereign Lady Martha [Teresa's sister]. At the present writing hereof, it is the three hundred eighty-ninth week of the reign of your most serene majesty, in whose service I was listed some weeks before I beheld her.
>
> (September [1714]; I, 258)[29]

Pope's social world, for all his attempts to make it seem so, was never as elegant as the circle of the Hotel de Rambouillet, in which Balzac and Voiture moved. But he did share with Balzac the problem of answering attacks by pedants. Balzac's response to those enemies who accused him of plagiarism and a host of other literary crimes is witty, dignified, and effective:

> It were enough that publike *Authority* should shelter me from the *tempest*, without exempting me from the *wind* and *dust*, and that it would guard my *Retrait* from *savage* beasts, without frighting away the *flies* also, and such importunate *Insects*. . . . It is well, that the heat of their braines, is *exhaled* out this way, and that their intemperance takes this course; and that to prevent their fury, men give some scope and liberty to their folly.[30]

In discussing his enemies, Pope used similar language:

> A State constantly divided into various Factions and Interests Occasions an eternal swarm of bad Writers.
>
> (9 April 1724; II, 227-28)

As the obtaining the love of valuable men is the happiest
end I know of this life, so the next felicity is to get rid of
fools and scoundrels; which I can't but own to you was one
part of my design in falling upon these Authors, whose
incapacity is not greater than their insincerity, and of whom
I have always found (if I may quote myself)
That each bad Author is as bad a Friend.
This Poem [the *Dunciad*] will rid me of those insects.
(23 March 1727/8; II, 481)

But I think a bright author should put an end to Slanders
only as the Sun does to Stinks; by shining out, exhale 'em
to nothing.
(14 December 1725; II, 349)

Yet Pope is much more antagonistic; he seems unable to stand as
aloof from his attackers as Balzac. And that difference is capable
of extension: Pope seems always more involved with his subject
matter than Balzac; Balzac's detachment, for all its elegance, was
not a lasting mode for Pope, who finally agreed with the judgment of hs early friend Sir William Trumbull:

I think a hasty scribble shews more what flows from the
heart, than a letter after *Balzac's* manner in studied phrases.
(6 March 1713/14; I, 212)

If Balzac is the inheritor of Seneca, his contemporary and
rival Vincent Voiture (1597-1648) is the inheritor of Pliny.
Voiture's letters are easily as artificial as Balzac's, but they
tend more toward sparkle and less toward sententiousness.
The Briscoe collection of 1700, in which Tom Brown translated
Pliny, begins with a selection of *Familiar and Courtly Letters*
by Voiture, translated by (among others) Dryden, Pope's enemy
John Dennis, and his two friends Thomas Cheek and Henry
Cromwell. The first long letter, translated by Dryden, is a perfect
example of Voiture's sprightly narrative style: Voiture tells the
Cardinal de la Valette about a magnificent party, a "Collation
to the Princess." There are splendid foods of all kinds, much

drinking (although the drinkers, Voiture admits, somehow forget to toast the Cardinal), music (including a sad Spanish song sung by Voiture), dancing, fireworks, and a wild coach ride back to Paris (during which the revellers encounter a group of seventeenth-century streakers).

Moving in such circles must have delighted Voiture, who was the son of a wine merchant, and who, like Pope, gained entrance to fashionable circles by his wit and his pen. Voiture's letters, with their scenes of courtly life and their elegant raillery, had a considerable vogue; indeed, they became more popular than Balzac's. They were first translated into English by John Davies in 1655, then selected and excerpted in numerous later collections, including Briscoe's. A complete *Works*, in two volumes, *Done from the Paris edition by Mr. Ozell*, which in fact reprints the translations by Dryden, Dennis, *et. al.*, was published in 1715 and reprinted several times. In this collection, the first item after the title page is a poem "To a Lady, with the Works of *Voiture*," by Mr. Pope.

The opening lines of Pope's poem give specific reasons for his admiration for Voiture:

> In these gay Thoughts the Loves and Graces shine,
> And all the Writer lives in ev'ry Line;
> His easie Art may happy Nature seem,
> Trifles themselves are Elegant in him.
> Sure to charm all was his peculiar Fate,
> Who without Flatt'ry pleas'd the Fair and Great;
> Still with Esteem no less convers'd than read;
> With Wit well-natur'd, and with Books well-bred;
> His Heart, his Mistress and his Friend did share;
> His Time, the Muse, the Witty, and the Fair.
>
> (TE VI, 62)

The aspects of Voiture's writing singled out for praise here are those aspects Pope sought to emulate: Voiture "lives in ev'ry Line," just as Pope wished to throw himself out on paper; Voiture's art seems natural; he makes unimportant trifles into elegant jokes; he charms without flattery. Pope's attempts to

do all these things, especially in his early letters, are often
directly related to his reading of Voiture.

He had read Voiture with some care. Even Curll noticed that
Pope's letter "to a Lady, with a *Book* of *Drawings*" (I, 4) was
based upon a letter of Voiture's to Madame Rambouillet.[31] And
his early correspondent Cromwell, having received a witty if
somewhat scabrous *rondeau*, found its source in Voiture.[32] But
Pope's general indebtedness is greater than even these easily-
documented borrowings indicate, for it was from Voiture that
he got some of his first operative assumptions about what a
letter should do.

First of all, a letter should compliment its recipient. Voiture,
thanking Madame Rambouillet for a mere thank-you note,
can claim that Alexander the Great "would have set more Value
upon this Honour, than he did on the *Persian* Diadem."[33] Even
though *he* has given her the gift for which the thank-you note
arrived, Voiture calls the lady's thanks "so rare a Favour" that
he feels himself on the "Pinacle of Glory." If such compliments
seemed overblown to Pope in later life, he was enthusiastic about
adopting the style as a young man. When Ralph Bridges thanked
him for the gift of of Tonson's miscellany volume of 1709 (which
contained the *Pastorals*), Pope replied, like Voiture, that the
thanks were more valuable than the gift:

> Sir,—I am very glad you receiv'd the Miscellany because it
> occasion'd the Favor of your obliging Letter to me, which
> deserves Thanks much more than so worthless a Present.[34]

The rules of such complimentary correspondence required self-
effacement, as Pope realized, and it must have cost him something
to pretend not to admire his own poems. Four years later, he
told Caryll, "It is the unfortunate consequence of a compliment,
that a man, for hearing a great deal more than his due said of
him by another, must afterwards say a great deal less than his
due of himself" (17 October 1713; I, 193). Perhaps the strain
of saying "a great deal less than his due of himself" was the
reason for Pope's later rejection of the extreme forms of the
complimentary mode, such as his criticism of Aaron Hill, in

1720: "I am . . . displeas'd, at your thinking it necessary to treat me so much in a Style of Compliment" (II, 36-37). Still, in order to understand Pope's early use of "a Style of Compliment" learned from the school of Voiture, and his later use of a chastened version of that style, modern readers must forget modern preoccupations with "sincerity." It probably never occurred to Voiture or to Madame Rambouillet to consider the literal sincerity of the extravagant comparisons in his letter; their very extravagance renders them comically charming. Voiture's compliments, and Pope's imitations of them, are designed to please by their witty artifice; inappropriate exaggeration is central to the mode. Neither Voiture nor his elegant hostess believed for a moment that he was actually so transported by her thank-you note as to stand on a "Pinacle of Glory," but both took pleasure in the phrase.

Pope understood these conventions perfectly. He told Cromwell, "As the fooling and toying with a mistress is a proof of fondness, not disrespect, so is raillery with a friend" (30 December 1710; I, 111). The exaggerated and brilliant compliments of Voiture struck him as a form of raillery; when he used such language, he usually meant it as a witty "proof of fondness," not as empty flattery.

The second assumption Pope got from Voiture was that a letter might be used to display learning; such display was what he had in mind in calling Voiture "with Books well-bred" in his poem. Here is Voiture presuming to rewrite Pliny:

> I fancy'd this Passage, *Nulli potest facillius esse loqui quam rerum naturae pingere*, &c. was out of *Pliny*, and I thought it very comical that you durst not name him any more to me. But even in your own Opinion, had not he better have said, *Nulli potest facilius esse loqui, quam rerum naturae facere?* . . . He thought he was mighty sublime with his *pingere*, and is quite the contrary.[35]

Pedantic? Certainly, but the young Pope had the same tune by heart, as his letters to Cromwell lamenting the indiscretions of Statius amply demonstrate.[36]

A more lasting influence was Voiture's incorporation of the

fanciful and romantic into his letters. In the letter about the
party mentioned earlier, Voiture calls the participants "god-
desses and demi-goddesses" and concludes with an appropriate
couplet from Boiardo. In his account of being tossed in a blanket,
he fancies himself attacked by cranes. He can even describe the
writing of letters as an act of magic:

> Even tho' I were utterly ignorant of your being a great
> Magician, and having the Art of commanding Spirits, the
> Power you have over my Affections, and the Charms I find
> in all you write to me, would be sufficient to inform me,
> that there is something supernatural in you. By the Help of
> your Characters, I beheld, upon a little Bit of Paper, both
> Temples and Goddesses; and you shew'd me all the Persons
> I love in your Letter, as in a Conjurer's Glass.[37]

Pope's imagination, the producer of the sylphs of the *Rape of
the Lock,* responded to and imitated this fanciful strain in Voiture. A passage in a letter to Lady Mary Wortley Montagu is
quite similar:

> The poetical manner in which you paint some of the
> Scenes about you, makes me despise my native country and
> sets me on fire to fall into the Dance about your Fountain
> in Belgrade-village. I fancy myself, in my romantic thoughts
> & distant admiration of you, not unlike the man in the
> Alchymist that has a passion for the Queen of the Faeries.
> I lye dreaming of you in Moonshiny Nights exactly in the
> posture of Endymion gaping for Cynthia in a Picture.
> ([Autumn 1717]; I, 439)

In both letters, a fanciful context makes possible such phrases
as Voiture's "the Power you have over my Affections" and Pope's
"my romantic thoughts & distant admiration of you." In both
cases, there is reason to suspect the writer of making admissions
in such a context that he would not or could not make in more
straightforward prose. A recent study argues that "the life
and letters of Voiture betray a 'malaise,' due to the tension pro-
voked by the flights of fantasy struggling against stark real-

ism."[38] Pope's letters to ladies, I shall be arguing, betray a similar struggle.

The idea of a special style for writing to ladies was a cultural norm when Pope began writing letters. Voiture cannot claim exclusive credit for creating such a style, but his letters to ladies are particularly skillful examples of the style; they were evidently useful examples for the young Pope. Voiture's letters betray an assumption, usually tacit, that *all* ladies, whatever their age or marital status, are to be approached as if they were objects for romance. In Voiture's case, if his boasting is to be believed, such an assumption may have had a measure of validity; he claimed that "he had made Love from the Scepter to the Sheep-Hook, and from the Coronet to the round-ear'd Cap."[39] For Pope, making such an assumption involved more imagination and less performance. In the letters of both men, the style based on the assumption uses raillery, compliment, and *double-entendre* to insinuate the writer's fundamentally sexual response to the woman being addressed. The writer usually portrays himself as languishing; again, exaggeration is fundamental. Both writers find a fine phrase too tempting to use just once; both send similar love letters to different ladies. Voiture even writes an all-purpose love letter "to his Unknown Mistress."[40]

Pope had coarser precedents for the racy elements in his letters to ladies. Tom Brown, indefatigable translator of Pliny, Voiture, and an obscure but smutty sixth-century Greek named Aristaenetus, was involved in producing innumerable letter collections, which included his own productions, some translations, and letters by such genuine rakes as John Wilmot, Earl of Rochester. It should not surprise us that various letters and sections of letters in these popular collections sound like Pope; such writers as Rochester knew Voiture and even Cicero, and they wrote in the style which was then the accepted pattern for epistolary discourse, elements of which Pope picked up—perhaps from them, perhaps from common sources. Here, for example, is Rochester to Henry Saville, on not writing news:

> You cannot shake off the Statesman intirely; for, I perceive, you have no opinion of a Letter, that is not almost a Gazette: Now, to me, who think the World as giddy as my

self, I care not which way it runs, and am fond of no News,
but the Prosperity of my Friends, and the Continuance of
their Kindness to me, which is the only Error I wish to
continue in 'em.[41]

Pope often makes similar assertions, such as this one to Mrs.
Knight:

> Madam,—I must keep my old custom of giving my friends
> now and then, once or twice a year, my testimony in writing
> that I love and esteem them, and that they have a place in
> my memory when I have been longest absent from them. I
> have never any thing else to say, and it is all that friendship
> and good will can, or ought to say: the rest is only matter
> of curiosity, which a newspaper can better gratify.
>
> (29 August 1735; III, 490)

Similarly, Pope's love letters, even those which insist on his
languishing state, are models of decorum compared to the love
letters Brown and other hacks were writing and collecting. It
will perhaps serve to place Pope's effusions in context to compare
a letter by Otway, also published by Brown:

> My Tyrant!
> I Endure too much Torment to be silent, and have endur'd it
> too long not to make the severest Complaint. I love You, I
> dote on You; *Desire* makes me mad, when I am near You;
> and *Despair*, when I am from You. Sure, of all Miseries,
> *Love* is to me the most intolerable: it haunts me in my *Sleep*,
> perplexes me when waking; every melancholy Thought
> makes my *Fears* more powerful; and every delightful one
> makes my *Wishes* more unruly. In all other uneasy *Chances*
> of a Man's Life, there is an immediate *Recourse* to some kind
> of *Succour* or another: In *Wants*, we apply ourselves to our
> *Friends*; in *Sickness*, to *Physicians*: But *Love*, the Sum the
> Total of all *Misfortunes*, must be endur'd with *Silence*.[42]

Next to this, even Pope's most carefully orchestrated ravings seem mild. Compare, for example, this distraught passage in a letter to Lady Mary Wortley Montagu of 3 February [1716/17]:

> I am now—I can't tell you what—I won't tell what, for it would grieve you—This letter is a piece of madness, that throws me after you in a distracted manner. I don't know which way to write, which way to send it, or if ever it will reach your hands. If it does, what can you inferr from it, but what I am half afraid, & half willing, you should know; how very much I was yours, how unfortunately well I knew you, and with what a miserable constancy I shall ever remember you?
>
> (I, 389)

Even Brown himself, all of whose collections seem calculated to entertain the most casual of readers in a superficial but effective way, may have had some influence on Pope, particularly in his ever-popular descriptions of the follies of the town. Here is a typical Brown production in this vein:

> I have been enquiring after the freshest Ghosts and Apparitions for you, Rapes of the newest date, dexterous Murders, and fantastical Marriages, Country Steeples demolished by Lightning, Whales stranded in the North, &c. a large Account of all which you may expect when they come in my way, but at present be pleased to take up with the following News.
>
> On *Tuesday* last, that walking piece of *English Mummy*, that *Sybil* incarnate, I mean my Lady *Court-all*, who has not had one Tooth in her Head, since King *Charles's* Restauration, and looks old enough to pass for Venerable *Bede's* Grandmother, was married—Cou'd you believe it?—To young *Lisanio*.[43]

One need only turn to Pope's letter to Mrs. _____ (presumably one of the Maids of Honor, although the letter smells as if its only intended recipient was the general public) to see similar writing:

I din'd with an old Beauty; she appear'd at the table like a
Death's head enamell'd. The Egyptians, you know, had
such things at their entertainments; but do you think they
painted and patch'd them? However the last of these objec-
tions was soon remov'd; for the lady had so violent an
appetite for a salmon, that she quickly eat all the patches
off her face. She divided the fish into three parts; not equal,
God knows; for she help'd Gay to the head, me to the
middle, and making the rest much the largest part took it
herself and cry'd very naive-ly, I'll be content with my own
tail.

                                                    ([1716]; I, 380)

This letter appeared in the 1737 octavo; Pope, like Brown, knew
the value of entertaining the public.

But Pope's contribution to the history of letter writing is not
merely a matter of his skill as an entertainer. To be sure, he was
careful to select for the 1735 volume letters which would appeal
to a wide variety of readers: for those interested in the serious and
philosophical, he printed the "Senecan" letter to Addison on the
state of man (quoted above, p. 54) and the letters on retirement
and illness which had already appeared in the *Spectator* and
Guardian (see I, 146-8); at the same time, he was not above satisfy-
ing the more prurient taste of Tom Brown's fans, as the letter
"To a Lady in the Name of her Brother," describing a visit to
see an hermaphrodite (I, 277-9), amply demonstrates. But these
letters are unusual, even in the 1735 volume, because they follow
their models closely, without displaying Pope's crucial break
with the tradition, a break which is clear in many of the letters
he chose to print in 1735. That feature, which must have struck
Pope's more perceptive readers as revolutionary, was his awareness of and interest in individuals, his insight into the personalities of his correspondents, the people he discussed, and himself.
After all, few letters of Cicero, Seneca, Pliny, Erasmus, Balzac,
or Voiture show such attention to human personality; indeed,
it seems to matter little who their addressees are. But even when
Pope uses these men as models, he moves beyond them toward

personal involvement with his correspondents. His letters, in short, are not merely literary.

Take for example the letter to Betty Marriot asking her to correspond with him:

> It is too much a rule in this town, that when a Lady has once done a man a favour, he is to be rude to her ever after. It becomes our Sex to take upon us twice as much as yours allows us: By this method I may write to you most impudently, because you once answer'd me modestly; and if you shou'd never do me that honour for the future, I am to think (like a true Coxcomb) that your silence gives consent. Perhaps you wonder why this is address'd to you rather than to Mrs. *M*—with whom I have the right of an old acquaintance, whereas you are a fine Lady, have bright eyes, &c. First Madam, I make choice of you rather than of your Mother, because you are younger than your Mother. Secondly, because I fancy you spell better, as having been at school later. Thirdly, because you have nothing to do but to write if you please, and possible it may keep you from employing your self worse: it may save some honest neighbouring Gentleman from three or four of your pestilent glances. Cast your eyes upon Paper, Madam, there you may look innocently: Men are seducing, books are dangerous, the amorous one's soften you, and the godly one's give you the spleen: If you look upon trees, they clasp in embraces; birds and beasts make love; the Sun is too warm for your blood, the Moon melts you into yielding and melancholy. Therefore I say once more, cast your eyes upon Paper, and read only such Letters as I write, which convey no darts, no flames, but proceed from Innocence of soul, and simplicity of heart.
>
> ([1714?]; I, 205-6)

Clearly, this letter belongs to the tradition of Voiture, but Pope adds his own characteristic humor to the elegant language of his model. His instinct for bathos shows in the suggestion that Betty is a more attractive correspondent than her mother because she

spells better. Ambiguous syntax, a comic technique frequent in
Pope's poetry, also features in this letter. Consider the possible
ways to read this sentence:

> Men are seducing, books are dangerous, the amorous one's
> soften you, and the godly one's give you the spleen.

Since both men and books can be amorous or godly, the non-
comittal use of "one's" and the minimal punctuation make any
number of readings possible. Even nature is full of suggestive
possibilities: trees, birds, beasts, the sun, and the moon can all
present amorous temptations. Pope's lively and sympathetic
imagination recognizes the possible effects of nature on an im-
pressionable teen-ager. To save herself from the alternatives of
sin or boredom, he advises Betty to "cast her eyes upon Paper"
and read his letters, "which convey no darts, no flames, but
proceed from Innocence of soul, and simplicity of heart."

Of course the letter is neither innocent nor simple. Its comic
surface does not hide Pope's real and important perception of the
difficulties young women of his time faced, just as his comic
treatment of Belinda in *The Rape of the Lock* does not conceal his
sympathy for her. The joke about the mistreatment of women
by men with which the letter opens is more than a humorous
gesture. Pope moves beyond Restoration wit: he exposes the
fact that such conventional phrases as "silence means consent"
are not merely funny, but cruel. He recognizes the restrictions
under which Betty must operate as she becomes a marriageable
young lady, and while playing the "Coxcomb" in his best witty
style, he indicates his awareness that Betty may well end up
married to a coxcomb. Several years before this letter, he had
written some lines to a woman about the plight of being confined
by custom:

> Too much *your Sex* is by their Forms confin'd,
> Severe to all, but most to Womankind;
> Custom, grown blind with Age, must be your Guide
> Your Pleasure is a Vice, but not your Pride;
> By nature yielding, stubborn but for Fame;

Made Slaves by Honour, and made Fools by Shame.
Marriage may all those petty Tyrants chace,
But sets up One, a greater, in their Place;
Well might you wish for Change, by those accurst,
But the last Tyrant ever proves the worst.

Significantly, these lines come from the *Epistle to a Young Lady,
with the Works of Voiture* (31-40). Like the letter to Betty
Marriot, the poem shows Pope's respect for and indebtedness
to Voiture; more significantly, both letter and poem show Pope's
ability to equal his model in writing comically about women,
while quietly surpassing him in understanding women.

A similar human concern informs the entertaining narratives
of the 1735 *Letters*, such as the account of Wycherley's deathbed
marriage to a young girl, in which Pope maintains a careful
balance between exploiting the comedy inherent in such a ludicrous act and understanding Wycherley's motives:

> The old Man then lay down, satisfy'd in the Conscience of
> having, by this one Act paid his just Debts, obliged a Woman
> who (he was told) had Merit, and shewn a heroic resentment
> of the ill usage of his next Heir.
>
> (21 January 1715/16; I, 329)

The same balance is evident in his story of a ride to Oxford with
the bookseller Lintot, who hoped to persuade him to do a little
translating to while away the time (I, 371-5). *Mutatis mutandis*,
Pliny could have told either of these stories, but he would not
have brought to them the imaginative insight into personality
that makes them, in Pope's hands, miniature exercises in character drawing. Pope helps us understand both Wycherley and
Lintot by a wealth of specific detail and an authorial attitude
which can laugh at both men without ridiculing them. Indeed,
it is a tribute to Pope's tact that when the account of their journey
was published, Lintot, far from being offended, wrote to Broome:
"There is one letter of Mr. Pope's to Lord Burlington, giving an
account of our journey together from Windsor Forest to Oxford,
—a merry one" (III, 489).

Even descriptive passages, always mere set-pieces for his pre-

decessors, become something more for Pope. Describing the
building of his villa at Twickenham, he writes to Robert Digby:

> Our River glitters beneath an unclouded Sun, at the same
> time that its Banks retain the Verdure of Showers: Our
> Gardens are offering their first Nosegays; our Trees, like
> new Acquaintance brought happily together, are stretching
> their Arms to meet each other, and growing nearer and
> nearer every Hour: The Birds are paying their thanksgiving
> Songs for the new Habitations I have made 'em: My Build-
> ing rises high enough to attract the eye and curiosity of
> the Passenger from the River, where, upon beholding a
> Mixture of Beauty and Ruin, he enquires what House is
> falling, or what Church is rising?
>
> (1 May 1720; II, 44)

This prose has the polish of Pliny; later in the same letter Pope
admits indulging in "Pomp of Style." But again he moves
beyond mere imitation. The striking feature of this description
is its persistently human scale of reference. Gardens, in this
world, exist to offer nosegays for people to smell. Trees embrace
"like new Acquaintance"—a striking reworking of an image in
the letter to Betty Marriot. Pope hears the songs of the birds as
"thanksgiving Songs for the new Habitations I have made 'em,"
and considers the impact of his new house on those who see it
from the Thames. He lifts the description beyond the realm of
the merely picturesque by considering the human importance of
each detail.

Not all the letters Pope chose to print, in 1735 and later, are as
striking as these examples. He had, after all, other motives for
selection besides excellence. He printed letters which would tend
to vindicate him, such as the Wycherley correspondence and the
fabrications to Addison. He selected letters that showed him
moving among the great, and this was one reason for the decision
to readdress letters to his obscure friend Caryll as if they had
been written to Addison or Congreve. But most of the letters
chosen have some definite intrinsic interest; they are worthy of
taking their place in the history of letter writing; in fact, they

extend and alter that history. With his knowledge of the tradition and his sense of the worth of his own contribution, Pope saw himself as belonging to the succession of great letter writers beginning with Cicero.

Precisely because Pope saw himself in this light, because he recognized (accurately) that he was writing for posterity, he felt compelled, like Cicero and every other figure mentioned in this chapter, to do some revising. Pope's nineteenth-century editors, discovering that he had revised his correspondence, judged him rather harshly—by standards not those of his own age. In fact, in those cases where we have both a printed text of a letter and an autograph or reliable transcript, close scrutiny fails to show Pope doing much more than editorial tightening. Very rarely is anything added to the letters; almost all changes are excisions, in which unnecessary phrases and repetitions are eliminated and uninteresting *trivia* suppressed. Even Pope's most deceptive revisions, such as the reworking of his letter to Caryll of 19 November 1712 (I, 154) to make it apply to Addison (see I, 183), involve a surprisingly small number of alterations. Here, as in his verse, Pope exhibits a talent for economy.

Unrevised texts are of interest for biographical scholars, for whom even the most trivial detail may prove useful, but for the general reader of the eighteenth or twentieth century, the texts Pope himself published will do very well. They include fewer than 300 of the 1,500 surviving letters Pope wrote in his lifetime, and while he had nothing like that number available from which to select in 1735, he may well have had as many as 500.[44] To be sure, the picture of Pope and his friends which emerges from a reading of only those letters which he chose to publish, in the form in which he published them, does not tally in all respects with the much fuller picture that emerges from reading the 2,200 letters to and from Pope in the Sherburn edition. But although Pope omitted many brilliant letters, although he indulged in some obvious deceptions in readdressing a few letters, although he often betrayed his desire to make himself a prominent place in the history of letter writing, the literary self-portraits he painted in his letters are of considerable value; if they do not show us Pope as he actually was with the fullness of the letters he did not publish, they do at least show us Pope as he wished to appear to the public—Pope as witty writer, sympathetic friend, serious thinker, sensitive observer, and (not least) educated practitioner of the epistolary form.

The horror the Victorians felt upon discovering that Pope had edited his letters was based upon a set of preconceptions about epistolary "naturalness' that Pope would never have understood. His famous predecessors had written carefully, even when protesting their negligence. They had selected letters for publication, edited texts, even connived to shift the responsibility for publication. In doing the same things, Pope, while he certainly was altering historical evidence, may well have thought he was giving posterity a more precise picture of himself. In one sense, he was right. Particularly where statements of belief are involved, those letters on which Pope labored the hardest are in some ways more dependable statements than those he wrote more hurriedly. A relatively "natural" or unselective letter actually has only a limited claim: it represents the writer's first response to a given situation, the first words that occur to him. Historically, such a letter has undeniable interest, and the historical consciousness that was to develop later in the century with Gibbon would place great value on such authenticity. But a letter which goes through several drafts, including a final revisal for publication, may make what Pope would have considered a larger claim: it represents the writer's best and most cogent thoughts on the subject discussed.

It was on such letters that Pope chose to rest his claim to be included among the great letter writers. If his awareness of the varying merits of Cicero, Pliny, Seneca, Erasmus, Balzac, Voiture, and even Tom Brown shows at times, it shows precisely because Pope, in prose as well as poetry, was always aware of his predecessors, knowledgeable about the characteristics and quality of the competition, able to use precedent skillfully, willing to break with precedent for a calculated effect. Pope's letters could no more have come into being without an epistolary tradition upon which to build than his poems could have been written without the classical and Continental poetic tradition. But in his letters as in his poetry, something powerfully new is created out of a dynamic relationship with the past.

CHAPTER 3

Compliments and Confessions

POPE'S USE, in his published letters, of assumptions, attitudes and styles based on those of the famous letter writers of the past is one of the ways he establishes, in those letters, a public version of himself—a *persona* related to, but distinct from, the *personae* he establishes in his poems. In the letters he did not publish, Pope seems conscious of his reader in a different way. The *personae* adopted in these letters are, if anything, more distinct, more precisely intended for the addressee; Pope wishes to make a particular impression on a particular reader. His tools, if sometimes less formal than those employed in the published letters, are by no means less literary—or less effective. Indeed, the skill with which he presents different versions of himself to his different correspondents is remarkable: he can be raffish and passionate when addressing ladies, careful and even submissive when addressing peers of the realm, and philosophical to the point of piety when addressing those friends whose admiration he treasured and needed. In creating such *personae*, Pope draws on traditional modes of address, but he inevitably modifies the tradition to serve his own purposes. In letters which at first seem highly conventional, there is often considerable self-revelation. Read closely, such letters show Pope (with varying degrees of self-consciousness) seizing upon real thoughts and traits and heightening them, while at the same time omitting or relegating to other letters equally real traits which were in conflict with those being used in a particular presentation of himself. I do not mean to suggest that Pope was a tireless conniver, deceitfully pretending to be a series of people he was not. What he was is quite clear in the letters: a man unusually aware of the various and often conflicting traits within him, with a talent amounting to genius for selecting and dramatizing those traits. In his best poems, the results of this dramatizing process are art of a high order; if not all the letters achieve the status of art, many deserve to be called skillful and effective examples of artifice.

Letters to his "Superiors"

In 1723, Pope sent Swift a letter describing and defending his mode of life, particularly his relations with famous men. The letter names an impressive series of aristocrats and credits Swift with having preceded Pope in their friendship. These Lords, bishops, and generals, Pope says, "may look upon me as one immediately entail'd upon them by You." Later, he boasts that

> The greatest Man in Power . . . shall hardly make me bow to him, unless I had a personal obligation to him & that I will take care not to have. The Top-pleasure of my Life is one I learnd from you both how to gain, & how to use the Freedomes of Friendship with Men such my Superiors. To have pleasd Great men according to Horace is a Praise; but not to have flatterd them & yet not to have displeased them is a greater.

(II, 184-5)[1]

No doubt the young Pope did learn "both how to gain, & how to use the Freedomes of Friendship" with the great from Swift, but Swift's prickly temper and prolonged absence from England meant that Pope soon surpassed his teacher. The two verbs in the phrase represent distinct and important skills: Pope's wide interests, entertaining wit, and penetrating insight into personality helped him gain the favor of great men; once he had gained their friendship, he knew how to use it.

He exhibited his talents in this area, like his poetic talents, at an early age. As a mere boy, he spent time with Sir William Trumbull, the retired Secretary of State, and the correspondence preserved between the two shows a close relationship. By 1714, he was confident enough to criticize what he calls Sir William's "style of compliment" (12 March 1713/14; I, 212-13), although in the same period he was sending to Sir William what seem quite fulsome compliments:

> One looks upon you as some Superior Being, that has been once among Men, and now sits above, at distance, not only to observe their actions, and weigh them with Truth and justice, but sometimes charitably to influence and direct them.[2]

Pope's claim to Swift that he never flatters the great cannot be taken seriously. Flattery, even in letters which loudly proclaim his aversion to flattery, is one of his basic means of making an impression on powerful men. An early example is his letter to Lord Lansdowne about dedicating *Windsor Forest* to him (10 January 1712/13; I, 172), in which he thanks Lansdowne "for having given my poem of Windsor Forest its greatest ornament, that of bearing your name in the front of it." The letter as a whole is more restrained than some effusive dedicatory epistles of its period, but it makes at least two more dubious claims. While Pope eagerly and sincerely submitted his work, throughout his life, to the criticism of those he respected, and while Lansdowne (George Granville) had been a part of Dryden's circle, Pope's request for "the free correction of these verses, which will have few beauties, but what may be made by your blots" can hardly be credited. Nor can the closing, in which Pope hopes "that many years hence the world might read, in conjunction with your name, that of, Your Lordship's, &c." Pope often later stated that it was *his* works which would preserve the names of those friends he mentioned in them. Perhaps at this early stage of his career, he was not yet fully confident of his future reputation, but even at twenty-four, he was hardly counting on Lansdowne's future fame to insure his own.

He had more immediate uses for such friends. Nine months later, Lansdowne dropped Pope a note, mentioning the pardon of a Jacobite named "Mr. Stafford, for whom you was pleas'd to concern yourself" (21 October 1713; I, 195). One assumes that

Lansdowne, at whose suggestion Pope had made *Windsor Forest* into a poem in praise of the Tory Peace of Utrecht, interceded with the Queen on Stafford's behalf.

By 1715, Lansdowne himself was out of favor and in the Tower. Like Oxford, Harcourt, Atterbury, Bolingbroke, and Edward Harley (later Second Earl of Oxford)—the friends Pope mentions in his letter to Swift—Lansdowne was out of power for the rest of his life. The "great" men with whom Pope corresponded were rarely men in real power. He had quarreled with Addison by the time Addison became Secretary of State, and while he attended dinners with and solicited favors from Robert Walpole, their relationship has been accurately called a "wary armed truce."[3] By the early 1730s that truce was broken, and Pope was engaged in open literary warfare with Walpole; a consequence of his more frankly political position was a new group of friends, also out of power, the "Patriot" Opposition typified by Lyttelton.

Still, even out of power, peers of the realm, bishops, and parliamentarians tended to be wealthy or at least comfortable, educated at least to the degree of "amateurism," and (Pope discovered) anxious to know the greatest living poet of their time. With a few such men—Atterbury, Bolingbroke, Oxford, Bathurst, Orrery—Pope built up relationships which were quite close, although he never forgot, even while affecting to disregard it, the "distance" between himself and his "superiors." A passage in his letter to Oxford on the death of his old nurse is typical:

> My Lord, forgive me: A more General & Common Style would better suit the distance between us: But Humanity renders men as equal, as Death does.
>
> (7 November 1725; II, 337)

Seven years later, he was still apologizing:

> I can't help this Style to my Betters, when they are such, as will make me Love as well as honour them; tho I have been much blamed by the Formalists of the Town for subscribing my Letter in print to Lord Burlington, with, *your Faithfull, affectionate Servant.*
>
> (22 January [1731/2]; III, 267)

There were two major consequences of Pope's consciousness of the distance to which he here alludes. One was stylistic: Pope's letters to his "betters," even when he concedes that their style may be improper, are always stylish. He usually wrote more carefully to these men than to correspondents with whom he felt on more equal terms. A second, often related consequence was Pope's seeking, in each of his relationships with the great, for ways to overcome the distance. He emphasized shared interests, opinions, or endeavors which might tend to place him on a par with his "betters," at least temporarily. He had understood the basic human appeal of this kind of approach for a long time, as one of his first letters to Wycherley indicates:

> In the first place, 'tis observable, that the Love we bear to our Friends is generally caused by our finding the same Dispositions in them, which we feel in our selves. This is but Self-love at the Bottom.
>
> (30 April 1705; I, 8)

With Oxford, Pope shared literary interests. The first Earl, Robert, had enjoyed relaxed tomfoolery with the Scriblerus Club, even while in office; Swift, Gay, Parnell, and Pope used to invite him to join them in ludicrous doggerel verses, to which he usually responded in kind. His son Edward, who became the second Earl in 1724, maintained a splendid library in which Pope worked, and was one of Pope's closest friends among the peers. We have over one hundred letters from Pope to Oxford, ranging in tone from simple notes of concern about the health of Oxford's wife and daughter to fully formal, carefully constructed letters in which Pope is altogether the professional writer. One good example of the latter kind is Pope's thank-you note for Oxford's gift of a gold cup and salver:

> My Lord,—Since till this very Day it was never known, that Poets receivd the same Prize as Horse Racers, or that Pegasus ever won the Golden plate ev'n in ancient times in any of the Olympian Pythian Isthmian or Nemean Games; I think It would be very natural & poetical to acknowledge your Lordships fine Present by a Quotation or Translation of the

Beginning of Pindar; And to confess, that it is a greater
Prize than ever that Poet carryd off for his Verses. But I must
differ from his opinion, that *Gold is only the best thing next
to Water.* I would correct the passage thus, that Gold is
the Best, & next Gold, Wine, not water. Both which your
Lordship has now given me the First opportunity I ever
had, to unite together.

I must have One Inscription upon it, which with me will
outweigh all Motto's whatever, That of your own Name,
and which will do me more Honour than Gold or pretious
stones. Would you expect it should be out of the Psalms?

Nomen tuum Dilectum super aurum & topazion.

I am calld in so much haste to dinner, & I go to it with so
much appetite, to drink with my friends your Health in your
own Bowl, (*Pleno me proluam auro*) That I can no more
write, than I could tell you if you were present (as I wish
you were) how much & with what grateful sense of many
favours superior to this I feel myself My Lord Your Ever
obliged faithfull Servant   A. Pope.

(26 December 1727; II, 465-6)

The allusions to Pindar, the Psalms, and Virgil are all undercut
by their jocular application, so that the letter's effect is far more
playful than pedantic. A more extreme example of the same kind
of humor is Pope's letter to Oxford about his new library at
Wimpole, with its execrable cross-language puns:

I wish a small Cellar of strong beer, were somewhere under
the Library, as a proper (brown) Study for the Country-
Gentlemen; while the Cantabrigians are imployd above;
unless any of the latter (for change and amusement) shall
chuse to Descend to the former, & De-*sipp*-ere in loco, as
Bentley's Horace has it. I hope my Lord you use Exercise
& *Bowl* daily, that Homer's saying may be fulfilled,

Διος δ'ετελειτο Βουλη

& that Lady Margaret rides, because Martial says

Ride si sapis, O puella, ride.

This advice is the best I can give, being perfectly Classical
& Cantabrigian. I must be forced to tell Lady Oxford in plain

English that I wish her all Health & pleasure, and that I
am while I live My Lord Your Lordships Most obliged faithful Servant A. Pun.

([June 1730?]; III, 115)[4]

Humor, even such ludicrous writing as this, worked for Pope
as an essential way of overcoming social distance. He had also
recognized this process early, as an early letter to Cromwell shows:

> I find I value no man so much, as he in whose sight I have
> been playing the fool. I cannot be *Sub-Persona* before a
> man I love; and not to laugh with honesty, when Nature
> prompts, or Folly (which is more a second Nature than any
> thing I know) is but a knavish hypocritical way of making
> a mask of one's own face.—To conclude, those that are my
> friends *I laugh with*, and those that are not *I laugh at*; so
> am merry in company and if ever I am wise, it is all by my
> self.

(30 December 1710; I, 112)

With Oxford, mock-pedantry was an easy form of humor, a way
Pope could bring about the laughter which he saw as bringing
men closer. His claim to Cromwell that laughter is a way of taking
off one's mask need not be taken too seriously; one may also
assume a comic mask in order to indicate one's love, and for Pope
at least, this was a frequent procedure.

In fact, like the licensed jester of legend, Pope often used a
witty context in order to make comments he might have been
unable to make seriously. To his friend Lord Bathurst, for
example, he sent a deft Biblical parody complaining of Bathurst's failure to write, and alluding to Bathurst's amorous
tendencies, to which he would allude again in *Sober Advice
from Horace*:[5]

> My Lord,—There was a Man in the Land of Twitnam, called
> Pope. He was a Servant of the Lord Bathurst of those days,
> a Patriarch of great Eminence, for getting children, at home
> & abroad. But his Care for his Family, and his Love for
> strange women, caused the said Lord to forget all his Friends

of the Male-Sex; insomuch that he knew not, nor once remembered, there was such a man in the Land of Twitnam as aforesaid. It were to be wisht, he would come & see; or if nothing else will move him, there are certain Handmaids belonging to the said Pope which are comely in their goings, yea which go comelily. If he will not vouchsafe to visit either his Servant, or his handmaids, let him (as the Patriarchs anciently did) send flocks of Sheep & Presents in his stead: For the grass of Marble Hill springeth, yea it springeth exceedingly & waits for the Lambs of the *Mountains*, (meaning Riskins) to crop the same

> Till then, all Mrs Howard's Swains
> Must feed—*no* flocks, upon—*no* plains.

([1725?]; II, 292)

If Bathurst received more than his share of such brilliant letters, he earned the right to Pope's best wit by being able to respond in kind. A letter in which he proposes to cart Pope off, house, gardens, and all, to a corner of his estate is one striking example, not only because of its humor, but because the basis of the humor, Pope's littleness, was not a subject about which he would have accepted joking from anyone but a close friend:

I'll cutt you off some little corner of my Park (500 or 1000 acres) which you shall do what you will with, & I'll immediately assign over to you 3 or 4 millions of plants out of my Nursery to amuse your self with. if you refuse coming I'll immediately send one of my wood-Carts & bring away your whole house & Gardens, & stick it in the midst of Oakly-wood where it will never be heard off any more, unless some of the Children find it out in Nutting-season & take possession of it thinking I have made it for them.

(19 September 1730; III, 134)

With Bolingbroke, there was much less humor, at least in the few letters that are preserved. Pope shared with the fallen leader a continuing concern for Swift and an interest in philosophy. Bolingbroke's letters to Pope seem very much under the spell

of Seneca, with whose fall from power Bolingbroke could identify; like Seneca, Bolingbroke writes as if posterity were glancing
over his shoulder: he is formal, highly rhetorical, and anxious
to defend himself. This serious pose, however, was not his
only epistolary mode; his letters to Swift and his earlier letters
to Prior at the time of the Treaty of Utrecht show considerable
wit. But for Pope, who was obviously impressed with him as a
thinker,[6] Bolingbroke played the philosopher, and Pope responded in kind; this moving passage on the difficulty of writing
well is typical:

> To write well, lastingly well, Immortally well, must not
> one leave Father and Mother and cleave unto the Muse?
> Must not one be prepared to endure the reproaches of Men,
> want and much Fasting, nay Martyrdom in its Cause. 'Tis
> such a Task as scarce leaves a Man time to be a good Neigh-
> bor, an useful friend, nay to plant a Tree, much less to save
> his Soul. Pray my Lord may not one ask this question, of
> so just, so grateful, and so deserving a thing, as the present
> Age?
>
> (9 April 1724; II, 227)

This dramatic rendering of the cost of writing represents the kind
of serious thinking Bolingbroke seems consistently to have drawn
from Pope. Of course, Pope's parodic wit shows in the allusion
to the scripture read in the marriage service, but the allusion has
a serious meaning: Pope, frustrated in courtship, took comfort
in claiming that he had wedded his Muse. What led him to share
this important metaphor with Bolingbroke was Bolingbroke's
similar sharing of some of *his* deepest concerns, the ethical
principles to which Pope's ultimate response was the *Essay on
Man*. Oxford or Bathurst would have received a more flippant
account of the writer's task, but for Bolingbroke, Pope chose
to dramatize a part of himself particularly congenial to a man
who prided himself on his thought.
    Even the deceit occasionally apparent in Pope's letters results
from such self-dramatization, for Pope's enthusiastic role-playing
sometimes led him to take positions which became practically

untenable.   His correspondence with Atterbury provides one
example. As Bishop of Rochester, Atterbury found time not only
for a correspondence with Pope (largely about books and ideas)
but for a surreptitious correspondence with the Pretender. Pope,
who was quietly friendly with a number of Jacobites, seems to
have been genuinely unaware of Atterbury's plotting.   Their
letters never mention politics; the typical concerns are literary,
and Atterbury never tires of giving Pope advice. He proposes
that Pope "review, and Polish" Milton's *Samson Agonistes* (II,
124), a suggestion Pope fortunately ignored. With considerably
better judgment, he recommends that Pope write satirical verse
(II, 104). Pope's replies are full of interesting literary ideas and
personal concern for Atterbury.

   In 1722, Atterbury's plot was discovered and he was sent to the
Tower. Since Pope knew nothing of Atterbury's guilt, he was
solicited as a witness in the trial before the House of Lords. His
testimony was designed to indicate that Atterbury spent his time
in reading and writing, not in political meetings. Pope loyally
but nervously went through with the testimony; he had reason
to fear implication, and he knew many of the lords. But his letters
to Atterbury in the tower trumpet boldly his determination to
remain loyal to his wronged friend. It was illegal to engage in
this correspondence, but one letter couches its defiance in resonant
Biblical terms, and seems to promise a future poetic celebration
of Atterbury:

> I fear there will be no way left me to tell you this great
> truth, that I remember you, that I love you, that I am grate-
> ful to you, that I intirely esteem and value you, but that one
> which I will find, even though it were death to correspond
> with you. A way which needs no open warrant to authorize
> it, or secret conveyance to secure it; which no Bills can pre-
> clude, nor any Kings prevent: a way which may reach to any
> part of the world where you may be, where the very whisper,
> or even the wish of a friend must not be heard, or even
> suspected. By this way I dare tell my esteem and affection
> for you to your enemies in the Gates, and you, and they, and
> their Sons shall hear it.
>
> ([23 April 1723]; II, 166-7)

On 16 May, however, the House of Lords found Atterbury guilty of treason and banished him. By 16 October Pope was writing to his friend Viscount Harcourt, soliciting aid in suppressing his letters, and even rumors of his letters to Atterbury:

> Speaking of Letters, puts me in mind of a Complaint I forgot when I last waited on you to trouble you with—(for your Lordship knows I have a sort of right by Precedent, to trouble you with all my Complaints; To other great men I am silent & patient, to you only a Grumbler) They have whisperd about the town a Story of a strange Letter writ by me to the Bishop during his Confinement: & I have met with one or two who have seen Copies of such a pretended Letter, which I never writ. I wonder at these things, & am in the dark to find for what end, or by what persons they can be propagated?
>
> (II, 206)

This is of course completely deceitful, but not quite a direct lie: Pope could claim that he denied here only writing the *copies*. Harcourt may even have been in on the secret, so that this careful note (innocuous enough if opened by the post office) constituted a signal to him to help keep Pope out of trouble. Whatever the case, Pope's duplicity is evident; he is covering his tracks. His sense that his friend had been wronged and deserted by many led him to make dramatic, foolish promises which he could not possibly keep, and certainly little would have been gained by his deciding to make a martyr of himself along with Atterbury. Pope did continue, by surreptitious means, to correspond with Atterbury in France until the Bishop's death, and he published edited versions of some of his letters in editions of the correspondence after 1737.

Apparently Pope's request to Harcourt was either successful or unnecessary, for he escaped any real damage. This was by no means the last or only time Pope asked his powerful friends to get him out of a scrape. Notable examples include the following: he persuaded Oxford, Bathurst, and Burlington to act as publishers of the *Dunciad*, protecting him from libel suits and concealing (temporarily) his authorship; he persuaded Oxford to allow Wycherley's papers to be deposited in the Harleian Library, and used this consent as a pretext to identify Oxford as the publisher of *The Posthumous Works of William Wycherley, Esq., Vol. II*; he got Lord Ilay to have the House of Lords seize Curll's "horse-load" of 1735 *Letters*; he used Orrery in his complex bargaining about the Swift correspondence. And these are only the most dramatic examples. Pope's powerful friends were constantly lending him coaches and chariots, putting him up for weeks at a time, voting for his candidates for various professorships and positions, and sending him items for his garden and grotto.

Not only did these powerful men constantly do favors for Pope, but they did so with little or no grumbling. Oxford, responding to the Wycherley request, writes, "I shall think my library very much Honoured by the deposite you propose" (III, 56); Orrery, in the midst of the negotiations with Swift, is even more eager: "In short my heart, my hand, my name is at your service, well knowing that they can never be more honourably employed . . . make use of me, and my name . . . in what manner you please" (IV, 294-5). To be sure, Pope was a charming and entertaining friend, and a famous man in his own right for most of his life; but those factors seem inadequate to account for the alacrity and eagerness with which his "superiors" so often served him.

To understand how Pope got this sort of response, it is necessary to examine his requests for favors, requests written with great psychological insight and skill. He was, after all, the poet who was so persuasive in portraying men controlled by various "ruling passions." He himself enjoyed doing good deeds and favors; Martha Blount reported to Spence that

> He did not know anything of the value of money, and his greatest delight was in doing good offices for friends. I used to know by his particular vivacity, and the pleasure that appeared in his looks, when he came to town on such errands or whilst he was employed in them, which was very often.[7]

Familiar himself with the gratifications of having done a favor, he was careful to appeal to the same sensibility in requesting favors. He knew the "ruling passions" of his friends well, and appealed to them. Here, for example, is his request that Oxford sign a statement about the *Dunciad*:

> My Lord,—I did not think so very soon to trouble you with a Letter: But so it is, that the Gentlemen of the Dunciad intend to be vexatious to the Bookseller & threaten to bring an action of I can't tell how many thousands against him. It is judgd by the Learned in Law, that if three or four of those Noblemen who honour me with their friendship would avow it so openly as to suffer their Names to be set to a Certificate of the nature of the inclosed, it would screen the poor man from their Insults. If your Lordship will let it be transcribd fair & allow yours to be subscribd with those of Lord Burlington, Lord Bathurst & one or 2 more, I need not say it will both oblige & honour me vastly. I beg a Line in answer, I cannot say how much I am Ever
>   My Lord your obligd affect: Servant A. Pope
>
> Whereas a Clamor hath been raisd by certain Persons, and Threats uttered, against the Publisher or Publishers of the Poem calld the *Dunciad* with notes Variorum &c. We whose names are underwritten do declare ourselves to have been the Publishers and Dispensers thereof, and that the same was deliverd out and vended by our Immediate direction.
>   ([18 April 1729]; III, 31-2)

There are many telling details. Oxford's doing Pope the favor becomes an open avowal of friendship; it protects a "poor man" (the bookseller, Gilliver, who stood to make a handsome profit); it will "oblige & honour" Pope himself; it is what Bathurst and Burlington are doing (the letter implies, as requests to those lords no doubt mentioned Oxford).

I am not seeking to impugn Pope's sincerity. On the contrary, I am suggesting that he knew himself and others well, and recognized in others, because he felt it himself, the almost uni-

versal human need to be thought generous. He appealed to great
men, not by toadying or obvious flattery, but by the more subtle
means of understanding their "ruling passions" and special
interests. To each of them, he presented a fitting side of himself:
if Bolingbroke fancied himself a philosopher, Pope could be
serious with him; if Oxford was proud of his library, Pope could
play scholarly games with him; if any great man relished his
power, Pope could provide him a chance to exercise it. Most
important of all, he never presumed to ignore their "greatness,"
even while effectively overcoming the distances that greatness
supposedly imposed.

Letters to Three Moralists—Caryll, Bethel, and Allen

Much of Pope's poetry is concerned with moral questions.
The ideal qualities praised in that poetry—moderation, generosity, tolerance, humility—appealed to Pope not only because
of his grounding in classical and Christian ethics, but because
they were qualities he saw and admired in some of his friends.
With three such men—John Caryll (1667-1736), Hugh Bethel
(d. 1748), and Ralph Allen (1694-1764)—he had extended correspondences.

John Caryll's home at Ladyholt was close to Binfield, where
Pope grew up, and Pope's first preserved letter to him (31 July
1710) reads as if they had already known each other for some
time. Caryll probably introduced Pope to Steele; certainly he
aided in the subscription for the *Iliad* and furnished the suggestion for the *Rape of the Lock*. Like the Blounts and the Engle-
fields, the Carylls were Roman Catholics; Pope's early letters to
Caryll from London usually include greetings to members of all
these families.

Living in London and immersed in the life of a man of letters,
Pope seems to have been concerned lest his works and reputation
offend the Catholic community in which he had grown up.
Apparently some took offense at a couplet in the *Essay on Criticism*, which Pope quickly defended to Caryll:

In your last you most charitably inform me of the mistaken

zeal of some people who seem to make it no less their business
to persuade men they are erroneous, than doctors do that we
are sick, only that thereby they may magnify their own cure
and triumph over an imaginary distemper. . . . The
very simile itself—
>   Thus wit, like Faith, by each man is applied
>   To one small sect, and all are damned beside.

if read twice may convince them that the censure of damning
here lies not on our Church unless they will call our Church
one small sect. And the cautious words *by each man,* mani-
festly show it a general reflection on all such (whoever they
are) who entertain such narrow and limited notions of the
mercy of the Almighty, which the reformed ministers of the
presbyterians are as guilty of as any people living.

(18 June 1711; I, 117-8)

He was to use his letters to Caryll repeatedly as vehicles for defending the orthodoxy of his poetry, perhaps because he sometimes needed to convince himself of that orthodoxy. The young
poet tasted attack as soon as he tasted success, and the attack
came from all sides, as he warned Caryll:

>   But let me tell you, you can hardly guess what a task you
>   undertake, when you profess your self my friend; there are
>   some *Tories* who will take you for a *Whig,* some *Whigs* who
>   will take you for a *Tory,* some *Protestants* who will esteem
>   you a rank *Papist,* and some *Papists* who will account you
>   a *Heretick.* . . .
>   I must expect an hundred attacks upon the publication
>   of my *Homer.* Whoever in our times would be a professor
>   of learning above his fellows, ought at the very first to
>   enter the world with the constancy and resolution of a primi-
>   tive Christian, and be prepared to suffer all sort of publick
>   Persecution.

(25 July 1714; I, 238-9)

The pose of resigned indifference to attack was a false one, of
course; the *Narrative of Dr. Robert Norris,* a violent attack on
Dennis, had been published in 1713, and Pope surely had a hand

in that pamphlet.[8] Pope knew that he was showing Caryll only
one side of himself, as he boasted to Martha Blount:

> Every one values Mr Pope, but every one for a different
> reason. One for his firm adherence to the Catholic Faith,
> another for his Neglect of Popish Superstition, one for his
> grave behavior, another for his Whymsicalness. Mr. Tyd-
> comb for his pretty Atheistical Jests, Mr. Caryl for his moral
> and christian Sentences, Mrs Teresa for his Reflections on
> Mrs Patty, and Mrs Patty for his Reflections on Mrs Teresa.
>   (post 24 November 1714; I, 269)

Still, "moral and christian sentences" were a part of Pope—
indeed, a more lasting part than "pretty Atheistical Jests." And
Caryll was no prude; Pope thought him capable of enjoying
his "Receipt to Make a Cuckold" (I, 267-8) and his rondeau
imitated from Voiture (I, 129). But in general, Pope communicated to Caryll his more serious responses to his life and work,
responses which he knew Caryll would take seriously. He
trusted Caryll enough to share with him even his deepest depres-
sions, such as this one while struggling with the *Iliad*:

> 'Tis really some advantage one receives from knowing
> the world that the more one sees of our fellow creatures, the
> more willing one grows to part with it and them. Which
> (to own an humble truth to you) is all I ever learned from
> experience that was to any purpose. If expectation is a jilt,
> experience is a downright whore, and stares us in the face
> with such confounded conviction, that it were better to be
> deceived as at first, unless we can heroically bear to leave
> this false prostituted thing the world, forever. I hope as a
> Christian, I can.
>   (11 October 1715; I, 317-18)

He also trusted Caryll in literary matters, soliciting his opinion
about samples of work in progress. Sometimes, most notably
when he sent Caryll the then-anonymous *Essay on Man*, he concealed his authorship in order to solicit an objective opinion.[9]

Pope's trust in Caryll and seriousness with him had several causes: their shared unpopular religion was one; Pope's admiration of Caryll's happy marriage was another; and after 1718, their ties became almost familial. Pope's father died on 23 October 1716; Caryll's eldest son, John II, followed him on 6 April 1718. After these deaths, it was as natural for Pope to seek fatherly advice from Caryll as it was for Caryll to be fondly concerned about Pope. Probably Caryll's greatest disappointment in the course of their relationship was that Pope did not marry Martha Blount, who was his goddaughter. He seems to have offered her with the dowry she did not have, but Pope set him straight:

> In the same manner I receive a secret contentment in knowing I have no tie to your God-daughter but a good opinion, which has grown into a friendship with experience that she deserved it. Upon my word, were it otherwise I would not conceal it from you, especially after the proofs you have given how generously you would act in her favour; and I farther hope, if it were more than I tell you that actuated me in that regard, that it would be only a spur to you, to animate, not a let to retard your design. But truth is truth. you will never see me change my condition any more than my religion, because I think them both best for me.
>
> (20 November 1729; III, 74-5)

Six years later, still hoping, Caryll misinterpreted the last line of the *Epistle on the Characters of Women* to mean that Pope intended marriage at last; again Pope corrected him (see III, 451). Caryll may have been led to keep hoping by the concern for Martha and her situation which Pope expressed to him in virtually every letter from 1730 on. He doubtless hoped Pope would rescue Martha from the domestic discord of the Blount household by marrying her, just as Pope hoped he, as Martha's godfather, might be able to bring about some change in her situation. At least twice before, the two men had been concerned about "unfortunate" ladies, but unable to do anything effective for them. In the early days of their friendship, they had much

correspondence about the ill treatment of a Mrs. Weston by her
husband; on this issue, Pope sided with Caryll and against his
own sister, Mrs. Rackett.[10] Later, both men were sending aid
to Caryll's cousin Mrs. Cope, who was in France and estranged
from her husband.[11] In neither case (nor, for that matter, in
Martha Blount's case) was either man capable of taking decisive
action: they sent concerned letters back and forth, but they never
confronted those responsible for the problems. Bold intervention
in the affairs of others was as foreign to Pope and Caryll as
concern was natural.

This shared trait, unwillingness to force confrontations and
give offense, goes part of the way toward explaining Pope's most
shameful action toward Caryll, the 1735 *Letters*, in which some
letters originally written to Caryll are printed as if to Addison,
Congreve, Sir William Trumbull, Robert Digby, and Steele;
several other letters to Caryll are headed "To the Honourable
J. C.," which no doubt led readers to infer that they were to
Pope's more famous friend James Craggs, especially since the
volume also includes several letters to Craggs. On 12 May 1735,
the first day on which Curll began to vend the letters, Pope
wrote to Caryll:

> But what makes me sick of writing is the shameless in-
> dustry of such fellows as Curle, and the idle ostentation,
> or weak partiality of many of my correspondents, who have
> shewn about my letters (which I never writ but in haste,
> and generally against the grain, in mere civility), for almost
> all letters, are impertinent farther than *si bene valeas, bene
> est, ego valeo* to such a degree that a volume of 200, or more
> are printed by that rascal: But he could never have injured
> me this way, had not my friends furnished him with the occa-
> sion by keeping such wretched papers as they ought to have
> burned.
>
> (III, 455)

This is certainly shameless equivocation, although with typical
skill Pope never flatly says that he has nothing to do with the
publication. Once he had yielded to his strong impulse to

publish the letters and had indulged his need to give them more variety and importance by redirecting a few, he was utterly unable to tell his old friend what he had done. Such a confession would have been offensive, as it would have involved admitting that he was less proud of his long friendship with the obscure Caryll than of his more fleeting relationship with, say, the famous Addison. To admit such vanity to a man whose humility he admired was not possible for Pope; it was easier to lead Caryll to believe that the mangling of the letters was the work of Curll—an eminently plausible theory. The most profound irony is that among the redirected letters are several dealing with ethics, in which the most painful and telling words are these:

> I ever must set the highest value upon men of truly great, that is honest Principles, with equal capacities. The best way I know of overcoming Calumny and Misconstruction, is by a vigorous perseverance in every thing we know to be right, and a total neglect of all that can ensue from it. 'Tis partly from this maxim that I depend upon your friendship, because I believe it will do justice to my intention in every thing; and give me leave to tell you, that (as the world goes) this is no small assurance I repose in you. I am Your, &c.

> (I, 198)

I quote from the version printed as to Addison and not dated in the 1735 *Letters*; in the actual letter sent to Caryll (12 June 1713; I, 177), Pope had underlined and made plural the word "intention," which deserves the emphasis. In the course of their friendship, Caryll did more than justice to Pope's intentions, believing, with the credulous fondness of a parent, that the admirable intentions he expressed in his letters were in fact his guiding principles. Principles they were, and Pope believed in them, but other motives frequently affected his behavior, even toward the man on whose conduct, in part, he based those principles.

Pope never explicitly declared to Caryll what the early words about intentions may have been hinting: that he recognized his failures to live up to his principles. To his friend Hugh

Bethel, however, he did admit that there were kinds of virtue he could not reach:

> I have now but too much melancholy leisure, and no other care but to finish my Essay on Man: There will be in it one line that may offend you, (I fear) and yet I will not alter or omit it, unless you come to town and prevent me before I print it, which will be in a fortnight in all probability. In plain truth, I will not deny my self the greatest pleasure I am capable of receiving, because another may have the modesty not to share it. It is all a poor poet can do, to bear testimony to the virtue he cannot reach; besides, that in this age, I have too few good examples not to lay hold on any I can find. You see what an interested man I am. Adieu.
>
> (9 August 1733; III, 381)

The line to which Pope alludes gives Bethel the epithet "blameless." How much Pope admired his simple virtues is apparent in an earlier letter:

> I have read much, but writ no more. I have small hopes of doing good, no vanity in writing, and little ambition to please a world not very candid or deserving. If I can preserve the good opinion of a few friends, it is all I can expect, considering how little good I can do even to them to merit it. Few people have your candour, or are so willing to think well of another from whom they receive no benefit, and gratify no vanity. But of all the soft sensations, the greatest pleasure is to give and receive mutual Trust. It is by Belief and firm Hope, that men are made happy in this life, as well as in the other. My confidence in your good opinion, and dependance upon that of one or two more, is the chief cordial drop I taste, amidst the Insipid, the Disagreeable, the Cloying, or the Dead-sweet, which are the common draughts of life. Some pleasures are too pert, as well as others too flat, to be relish'd long: and vivacity in some

cases is worse than dulness.   Therefore indeed for many years I have not chosen my companions for any of the qualities in fashion, but almost intirely for that which is the most out-of-fashion, sincerity.   Before I am aware of it, I am making your panegyrick, and perhaps my own too, for next to possessing the best of qualities is the esteeming and distinguishing those who possess it.   I truly love and value you, and so I stop short.

(17 June 1728; II, 501)

Here the virtue most emphasized, sincerity, is one which Pope, as we have seen, could not always claim.   In his letters to Bethel, Pope does "bear testimony to the virtue he cannot reach," not only by praising sincerity, but by practicing it.

The phrase about the "cordial drop" is also significant. Pope remembers the definition of love in Rochester's *Letter from Artemisa, in the town, to Cloe in the country*, as

> That Cordial-drop Heav'n in our cup has thrown
> To make the nauseous Draught of Life go down.

Pope was fond of the notion and the phrase, and used it twice in his later poetry: in the closing paragraph of *The Sixth Epistle of the First Book of Horace Imitated*, to Murray, and (significantly) in *The Second Satire of the Second Book of Horace Paraphrased*, which is dedicated to Hugh Bethel.   In that poem, the passage reads:

> Ill Health some just indulgence may engage,
> And more, the Sickness of long Life, Old-age:
> For fainting Age what cordial drop remains,
> If our intemp'rate Youth the Vessel drains?

(87-90; TE IV, 61).

Bethel's solid friendship did prove a "cordial drop" to Pope's ill health and old age, in part because Bethel was familiar with nauseous draughts.   He suffered from asthma, and was a lay expert on remedies, symptoms, and the varying merits of physicians. Pope consequently shared with him, as with no other friend, the details of his physical ailments, and of the treatments he underwent to ease them; these letters are by far our best source for information about Pope's diseases, and the medical case history of Pope in Nicolson and Rousseau's *"This Long Disease, My Life"* could never have been written without them. A letter Pope wrote in his last illness is typical in its details, and in the appalling picture it gives of eighteenth-century medical practice:

> Dr Burton is very watchful over me, he changd the warm Pills into a cooler regimen. I drink no wine, & take scarce any meat. Asses milk twice a day. My only Medcines are Millepedes & Garlick, & Horehound Tea. He is against crude Quicksilver till he is sure there is no fever, but prescribes Alkalizd Mercury in 5 pills a day: & proposes an Issue, which I fear may drain & waste me too much, it can't be imagined how weak I am, & how unable to move, or walk, or use any Exercise, but going in a Coach, for which the Weather is yet too cold.
>
> (19 March [1743/4]; IV, 508)

It was Bethel's simple and straightforward character that elicited from Pope these unique confidences about his body. In an undated fragment, Pope explained that he was most likely to be frank to such men; the claim rings true in this case:

> I am so aukward at writing letters, to such as expect me to write like a wit, that I take any course to avoid it. 'Tis to you only, and a few such plain honest men, I like to open myself with the same freedom, and as free from all disguises, not only of sentiment, but of style, as they themselves.
>
> (III, 519)

Perhaps more remarkable than Pope's frankness to Bethel about his ailments was his frankness about his frustrations with Martha Blount, with whom Bethel was friendly. A comment in a letter of 2 November 1736 is particularly telling:

I have so much, & so little, to say of Mrs Patty Blount that I wish you'd come, & join with me in forcing her to do herself right. I am tired with good Wishes for her, they are so ineffectual: her Virtues & her Weakness go hand in hand; I don't know which are greater: but every one who is her friend on account of the first must frett at the latter, since nothing can do her good for want of her own Coopera-tion. She is very sensible of any true Friendship, at the same time that she disappoints any true Friend. And her constant Memory & Regard of You in particular, is greater than I can express.

(IV, 39-40)

In all his letters to Caryll about Martha, Pope never approached this kind of emotional confession. In a later letter, frustrated by Martha's concern for her reputation (she would never even ride in the same coach with him), he hoped that Bethel might serve as a kind of chaperone:

Mrs Patty Blount is in Town, in the same unpleasant State as we have so long known and lamented her in: but always faithfully yours, & always remembring and regretting you. I'm sorry we are not allowed by Fate to be more constant Neighbours, & that Souls that think & feel alike must live in so disagreeing Spheres of Action, and Habit. We are equally Lovers of Quiet, but she has none at home, and I have none abroad. I hope in God you have in both. Had I Strength & health, I might travel sometimes & pass part of the Summers (which are my best days) in Yorkshire: Had she Resolution, we might both see her with more com-fort, in Winter in London. Nor would it be a Sin, or shame if we lived now & then all together at Twitnam.

(2 August 1740; IV, 255)

And when Bethel went to Naples in a futile attempt to improve his own failing health, Pope dreamed of coming to see him on a magic carpet:

> You can't imagine how often I wish myself with you,
> were there a Way of travelling without stirring, and one or
> two people I could waft along with me thro the Air, one
> of which you will guess.
>
> (1 January [1741/2]; IV, 378)

No doubt the friend whose identity Bethel was to guess was
Martha Blount, familiarly known to Pope and Bethel as Patty.

Pope's openness with Bethel on these two important but painful subjects, his body and his troubles with Patty, is indicative
of the unusual trust he reposed in him. Beyond the physical
pain Pope's body gave him, it was caricatured mercilessly, in
doggerel, prose, and cartoons, for much of his adult life. Similarly, the real pathos of his unfulfilled relationship with Patty
must have been considerably exacerbated by the malicious slander
which was spread about them from time to time (see below, pp.
120-23). Consequently, it is not surprising that Pope's references
to these aspects of his life are cursory and vague in many of
his letters; but something in Bethel inspired a special trust, and
the letters to him are invaluable for their frankness. Since so
little is known about Bethel, it is necessary to infer from Pope's
own testimony what it was that made him so particularly trustworthy. In that testimony, three qualities emerge as principally
responsible for this trust: Bethel was a plain man; he lived a
genuinely retired life; and his own discourse was characterized
by openness. As the relationships already examined in this
chapter reveal, Pope's qualities were different: he was complex;
the urge to retirement was only one part of his psychology,
balanced against a powerful need for involvement; and artifice
was so much a habit of thought, speech, and writing for him
that his communications with others were often ambiguous
or at least self-protective. It was his habit to assume a style
adapted to that of the person with whom he was dealing, a
partially imitative *persona*. In communicating with Bethel,
however, this habit resulted in his stripping away some of his
protective coverings, revealing some of the pain beneath the
gaiety. Of course, Pope could not succeed totally in his attempt
to be like Bethel, as a couplet of the poem he dedicated to his
old friend indicates:

His equal mind I copy what I can,
And as I love, would imitate the Man.

(131-2)

Pope also wished to imitate Ralph Allen, who was as plain
a man as Bethel, though much more prominent. From a boy-
hood so humble that his ancestors are now unknown,[12] Allen
rose to a position of wealth and power by devising an efficient
and lucrative system of cross-posts, so that no longer did every
letter mailed in England have to pass through London; he also
cornered the market on Bath stone. Despite his wealth, he
retained his humility and became famous for his many charities,
to individuals and institutions. Pope's couplet,

Let humble ALLEN, with an aukward Shame,
Do good by stealth, and blush to find it Fame.
(*Epilogue to the Satires, Dialogue* I, 135-6),

was a deserved tribute. Allen never sought credit for his benev-
olences, an attitude which made him impressive not only to Pope,
but to Fielding, who based the figure of Squire Allworthy on
him.

The story of Pope's friendship with Allen has been told in
great detail in Benjamin Boyce's recent biography, and needs
only to be summarized here. Allen approached Pope after the
publication of the 1735 *Letters*, with which he was very much
impressed, and was instrumental in the subscription for and
publication of the "official" version in 1737. The two men
shared interests in minerals (Allen sent stones for Pope's grotto
and gardens), in charitable causes (both did "good by stealth"
for Richard Savage and others in need), and in writing (although
here the relation was between a practicing professional and an
interested amateur).[13] Pope's admiration for Allen was genuine
and led to a regular correspondence and a number of visits; however, Pope was disingenuous with Allen on at least two issues:
he involved Allen in the delivery to Gerrard of the surreptitiously
printed volume of the Swift correspondence, but later told Allen
that the letters had been stolen by those around Swift (see IV,
273-4); and he got Allen to deliver at least one explosively politi-

cal letter to Lyttelton, while continually protesting his non-partisanship.[14] Allen, having a contract with the government, was at least officially sympathetic to Walpole, and Pope was by this time actively allied with those opposing the Prime Minister. Finally, there occurred at Allen's home in the summer of 1743 an unfortunate tiff between Martha Blount and Mrs. Allen.[15] This led to an estrangement which Pope worked hard at ending, writing and visiting Allen up to his death. But upon Pope's death, a provision in his will, giving Allen 150 pounds in repayment for various notes, gave renewed offense.

We have none of Allen's letters to Pope, but his letters to other correspondents, some of which Boyce quotes, show his simple and straightforward style. Pope's one attempt to imitate this style is fascinating:

> I will therefore only reply to your Six hearty Lines, in as plain a manner. I do really wish myself with you; I know not how to be so; I am afraid I cannot get so near you as within fourscore miles this Summer; My Infirmities increase ev'ry year: Tho my Spirit be prompt; my Flesh is weak. I have two great Tasks on my hands: I am trying to benefit myself, and to benefit Posterity; not by Works of my own God knows: I can but Skirmish, & maintain a flying Fight with Vice; its Forces augment, & will drive me off the Stage, before I shall see the Effects complete, either of Divine Providence or Vengeance: for sure we can be quite Saved only by the One, or punishd by the other: The Condition of Morality is so desperate, as to be above all Human Hands.
>   ([6 July 1738]; IV, 108-9)

For the first few clauses, Pope succeeds in keeping his grammar simple. But the attempt breaks down for reasons that reveal much about Pope's patterns of thought. As soon as he considers his attacks on vice, his habitual metaphor-making takes over: such words as "Skirmish" and "flying Fight" lead to the forceful image of the poet driven "off the Stage." And the antithetical rhetoric so common in Pope's couplets makes its appearance as well; the patterning which couples "Divine Providence" and "vengeance" and balances these nouns against the verbs "Saved" and "punishd" is unlike anything in Allen's letters.

Pope could not maintain an imitation of Allen's prose style, because his mind was more complex, more given to metaphor, but there is no reason to believe that he admired Allen's prose; he did admire Allen's morality, however, and admitted his inability to imitate it:

> Believe me as I believe you; I don't mean so good a man, but as sincerely inclined to be so, were I able, and Esteeming every good quality I cannot equal. Upon those Principles my friendship must last, & no Friendship can last upon other Principles, not even State-Friendships or Church Friendships.
>
> (17 April 1739; IV, 173)

As with Bethel, Pope emphasizes his inclination to follow Allen's moral example and his inability to achieve that ideal. Perhaps Pope's complexity, the very quality of mind that made him unable to write like Allen, also made him unable to act like Allen. Allen's humility was out of reach for Pope, who so needed fame that even cruel attacks on his person fascinated him; Allen's adherence to his simple ethical principles was also beyond Pope, who was willing to set aside principle for the sake of "pretty Atheistical jests" or "Schemes of Epistolary fame." So it is striking that in order to praise Allen, Pope resorted to clever Biblical and theological metaphors:

> If there were to be Another Deluge, I protest I don't know more than One Noah; and his Wife, (for he happens to have no children) whom I could expect God would save: I hope He will live forty years however, to preach in, before it comes.
>
> ([? 1 December 1742]; IV 429)

> Dear Sir,—
> For You are always truly so to me: and I know your Goodness so well, that I need not to be put in mind of it by your Benefactions . . . When We hear of Benefits, we ought

to be as Sensible of them as when we feel them: Yet this is
seldom the case; we Apply the Terms of Good, Benevolent,
Just, &c, meerly as relative to ourselves, and are in this as
unjust to Men, as Philosophers & Divines are to God, Whose
Ways & Workings they magnify or disapprove according to
the Effect they have on them selves only.

(19 April [1740]; IV, 234)

These passages are witty but not merely witty. In comparing
Allen to Noah, Pope implicitly includes himself among the
sinners who would drown in a second deluge; in comparing
Allen indirectly to God, he again includes himself (through
the plural pronoun) among those apt to be self-centered in
judging the "Benefactions" of God and man.

Pope, like Fielding, saw Allen as an exemplar of that ill-
defined but important eighteenth-century ideal, the Good Man.
In what may be his first poem, the "Ode on Solitude," he had
sought to define such a man; in the portrait of Axylus in the
Iliad, he had developed the definition further; and in the satires
of his last decade, it is the Good Man who serves as the standard
by which the frantic behavior of the characters who inhabit the
poems is measured and found wanting. In the wise and tender-
hearted Caryll, the understanding and trustworthy Bethel, and
the magnanimous and humble Allen, Pope saw parts of the
character of the Good Man, who was, above all else, a good
friend. That his own behavior toward these friends was not
always that of a Good Man was an irony which he did not always
recognize. But he did recognize, and could legitimately take
pride in, the fact that these three friendships were based upon
his sincere admiration for three good men. His *"intentions,"* to
recall the ill-fated letter to Caryll, were good ones, and his satisfactions in these friendships were real and important. A moving
passage in a letter to Allen may stand as a record of those satisfactions:

> The sentiments you express upon the Anniversary of your
> birthday shew you a Good Man, & therefore I have reason
> to be glad that you can account the Friendship I bear you

one of the Satisfactions of your life: Otherwise, it might be but a disgrace to be rank'd among the things you like, if you liked such things & Men, as many do like, & make their Enjoyments. I trust in God such a friendship will out-last all those that are built upon Vanity, Interest, or Sensuality, the common grounds upon which people build them. I am in haste, & need not add more; 'tis the most material, as well as most comfortable Reflection I can make, Adieu.

(26 July [1737]; IV, 83)

Letters to Ladies

When Pope first began to address ladies, Voiture was his principal model. The "courtly" style of Voiture, which was altered and somewhat degraded by such writers as Rochester, includes fulsome compliments, protestations of devotion, and sexual *double-entendres,* adding up to the implication that the writer is an incorrigibly wicked but irresistibly charming fellow. It is this pose which the young Pope adopts in his first published letter to a woman, entitled "To a Lady, with a *Book* of *Drawings*." As often noted, the letter is a close imitation of Voiture (see chapter II, p. 60, and note), but it departs from Voiture in its ending for a particularly heavy-handed series of *double-entendres*:

> The Painters are a very vain generation, and have a long time pretended to rival Nature; but to own the truth to you, she made such a finish'd piece about three and twenty years ago, (I beg your pardon Madam, I protest I meant but two and twenty) that 'tis in vain for them any longer to contend with her. I know You indeed made one something like it, betwixt five and six years Past: 'Twas a little girl, done with abundance of spirit and life: and wants nothing but time to be an admirable piece: But not to flatter your work, I don't think 'twill ever come up to what your Father made. However I wou'd not discourage you; 'tis certain you have a strange happiness, in making fine things of a sudden and at

a stroke, with incredible ease and pleasure. Madam, I am,
&c.

(I, 4)

This is rather like passages of dialogue in Restoration drama,
such as the "china closet" scene in Wycherley's *Country Wife*.
One doubts whether Pope actually sent this letter in just this
form, just as one doubts the suspiciously early date (1 March
1704/5) which he assigned to it in 1737. But there is no doubt
that he sent the *Rape of the Lock* to Martha Blount on 25 May
1712, with this accompanying note:

> Madam,—At last I do myself the honour to send you the
> Rape of the Locke; which has been so long coming out,
> that the Ladies Charmes might have been half decay'd,
> while the Poet was celebrating them, and the Printer
> publishing them. But yourself and your fair Sister must
> needs have been surfeited already with this Triffle; and
> therefore you have no hopes of Entertainment but from
> the rest of this Booke, wherein (they tell me) are some things
> that may be dangerous to be lookd upon; however I think
> You may venture, tho' you shou'd Blush for it, since
> Blushing becomes you the best of any Lady in England, and
> then the most dangerous thing to be lookd upon is Your-
> self—Indeed Madam, not to flatter you, our Virtue will be
> sooner overthrown by one Glance of yours, than by all the
> wicked Poets can write in an Age, as has been too dearly
> experienc'd by the wickedest of 'em all, that is to say, by
> Madam Your most obedient humble Servant,
> A: Pope:

(I, 143)

The innuendo here is certainly much milder, and the compliments
must have been charming to receive, but Pope's claim to be the
"wickedest" of poets, a claim hardly substantiated by the poem,
is an example of the *braggadocio* which was an essential part
of the "gallant" *persona* he adopted in such letters, and in his
more explicitly sexual letters to his male friends during the same
period (see, for example, I, 66-7).

It is a reasonable guess that this early and fasionable *persona* of the rake had a rather limited basis in fact. Pope may have tried to keep up with Cromwell, Cheek, Wycherley, and his other town friends in whoring, as we know he foolishly tried to hold his own in eating and drinking. Still, George Sherburn's assertion that "Pope, conscious of his physical inferiority, put up a brave front at being a rake" seems much the wisest explanation for Pope's frequent early suggestions that he knew well the ways of the prostitutes of Drury Lane.[16] No doubt there was more talk than action, but Pope's later urinary difficulties, for which he was operated upon in 1740, may actually have resulted from indiscretions in his youth. "Such urethral stricture as he experienced, medical authorities tell us, was probably the result of gonorrhea, contracted in youth."[17] Cheselden, Pope's surgeon, told Spence:

> I could give a more particular account of his [Pope's] health than perhaps any man. Cibber's slander of a carnosity [is] false. [He] had been gay, but left it on his acquaintance with Mrs. Blount.[18]

But all this is speculation, and it does seem likely that Pope's frequent illnesses and the constant frailty of his tiny frame rendered frequent expeditions to bawdy houses impossible. Cheselden's statement, presumably based on Pope's own remarks, seems reasonable too: Pope had good reason to abandon even the pretense of active raking upon meeting the lovely, eligible, and Roman Catholic Blount sisters.

Just when this meeting took place remains obscure,[19] but by 1711 he knew them well enough to feel the force of their considerable charms, and to report his feelings to Cromwell:

> . . . I am at this instant placd betwist Two such Ladies that in good faith 'tis all I'm able to do, to keep my self in my Skin. . . . Let me but have the Reputation of these in my keeping, & as for my own, let the Devil, or let Dennis, take it for ever! How gladly wou'd I give all I am worth, that is to say, my *Pastorals* for *one* of their *Maidenheads*, & my *Essay* for the other? I wou'd lay out all my *Poetry* in

Love; an *Original* for a *Lady*, & a *Translation* for a *Waiting
Maid*!

(I, 137-8)

The insinuation about maidenheads (suppressed, incidentally,
in Pope's published versions of the letter, but not in Curll's) is
endemic to the rakish style, but his suggestion that he would
barter his poetical works for the favors of the sisters implies that
he felt himself genuinely smitten. His description of his works as
"all I am worth" is not to be taken lightly, and despite the playful suggestion that a lady is worth an original, and a waiting maid
only worth a translation, one doubts that he would really have
traded a poem for any of the nameless (and perhaps imaginary)
"Saphos" about whom he joked with Cromwell and Wycherley.
    The Blounts were different. As respectable Catholic young
ladies who happened to be Pope's age and were blessed with
fine eyes, they must have struck Pope as ideal, and surely they
found him, at the very least, an interesting visitor. He was witty,
and sophisticated to a degree, and becoming rather famous.
But even his earliest letters to them show a tendency to keep his
wit under control, as he told them in 1713:

> You see Ladies, I can write Seriously when I am truly myself,
> tho' I only Railly when I am displasd with others. The most
> that any one shall get from me who would cause misunder-
> standings, is Contempt & Laughter; Those who Detest that
> evil way can have nothing less than an Entire Esteem such
> as will make me always Ladies, Your most obliged obedient
> humble Servant, A. Pope.

(I, 183)

Just two years later, in a letter to Martha alone, Pope rejects
wit even more pointedly:

> Madam,—I am not at all concern'd to think that this letter
> may be less entertaining than some I have sent: I know you
> are a friend that will think a kind letter as good as a diverting

one. He that gives you his mirth makes a much less present
than he that gives you his heart; and true friends wou'd
rather see such thoughts as they communicate only to
one another, than what they squander about to all the
world. . . . I wou'd cut off my own head, if it had nothing
better than wit in it; and tear out my own heart, if it had no
better dispositions than to love only myself, and laugh at all
my neighbors.

([February 1715?]; I, 280)

Pope's awareness that this kind of language was a break with
the gallant tradition shows in another letter of the same year, in
which he sends Martha a dense, serious opening paragraph
about temporality, city life, and death, and continues:

This is an odd way of writing to a lady, and I'm sensible
would throw me under a great deal of ridicule, were you to
show this letter among your acquaintance.

([1715]; I, 319)

It *is* an odd way of writing to a lady, and doubtless Pope was
correct in suggesting that his style might be ridiculed by Martha's
acquaintances. But there was a more serious kind of ridicule for
him to fear: laughter based on the ludicrous spectacle of a four-
foot, six-inch poet, however witty, courting the elegant and
stately Martha and Teresa. The Blounts lacked substantial
dowries, but they were young and pretty enough to be flattered
and flirted with by men much more attractive than Pope, who
had told Caryll as early as 1711 that he was "that little Alexander
the women laugh at" (I, 144). As George Sherburn astutely
points out, "he does not mean 'ladies,' "[20] but there was always
the possibility that the Blounts, who were "ladies," would laugh
at him as well. Pope's way of protecting himself from such
ridicule is delicate self-ridicule. He writes to Martha:

May you have all possible success both at your Devotions
this week, & your Masquerade the next: Whether you repent

or Sin, may you do all you wish; and when you think of me,
either laugh at me or pray for me, which you please.

([March 1716?]; I, 339)

And, with a wit that does not quite hide the pain, he tells Teresa;

> Madam,—I have so much Esteem for you, and so much of
> the other thing, that were I a handsome fellow I should do
> you a vast deal of good: but as it is, all I am good for is to
> write a civil letter, or to make a fine Speech. The truth is,
> that considering how often & how openly I have declared
> Love to you, I am astonished (and a little affronted) that
> you have not forbid my correspondence, & directly said,
> *See my face no more.* It is not enough, Madam, for your
> reputation, that you keep your hands pure, from the Stain
> of Such Ink as might be shed to gratify a male Correspon-
> dent; Alas! while your heart consents to encourage him in
> this lewd liberty of writing, you are not (indeed you are not)
> what you would so fain have me think you, a Prude! I am
> vain enough to conclude (like most young fellows) that a
> fine Lady's Silence is Consent, and so I write on.

(7 August [1716]; I, 349-50)

The psychological situation here is truly complex: Pope's only
real attraction, his way of competing with the Blounts' hand-
somer beaux, is his wit; but, as he confesses, he would like to
dispense with wit and confess his increasingly serious feelings
about them; however, the danger that they may laugh at a
declaration of love requires that that declaration be couched
in terms which are self-protective; and the mode of self-protection
which works best is—wit. So what amount to confessions of
love are disguised by such comical strategies as these comparisons of the ladies to foodstuffs:

> I love no meat but Ortolans [rich game birds], and no women
> but you. Though indeed that's no proper comparison but
> for fatt Dutchesses; For to love you, is as if one should wish
> to Eat Angels, or drink Cherubim-Broath.

(13 September 1717; I, 428)

For in very deed Ladies, I love you both, very sincerely and passionately, tho not so romantically (perhaps) as such as you may expect who have been us'd to receive more Complimental Letters and High flights from your own Sex, than ever I am like to reach to. In earnest, I know no Two Things I would change you for, this hot Weather, except Two good Melons.

([June 1717]; I, 409)

However, sometime after Pope's father's death on 23 October 1717, an occasion on which the Blounts were very kind to him, a severe misunderstanding occurred, or perhaps it was a series of misunderstandings. The letters from Pope to the sisters about this situation are among the most moving, and the most difficult to understand, that he ever wrote. In Sherburn's edition, they are conjecturally placed in late 1717 and early 1718 (see I, 455, 456, 458, 459, 460, 468). Not one has an absolutely certain date, and the order in which Sherburn chooses to place them is not the only order in which they might be read. The letters are openly, painfully emotional—like nothing which comes before in the correspondence. Gone are the rakish and self-protective effusions of wit. Pope writes in unmistakable pain, forced by that pain to acknowledge his real need for the Blounts, recognizing with excruciating clarity that his physical form makes impossible a satisfactory fulfillment of that need:

Dear Ladies,—I think myself obligd to desire, you would not put off any Diversion you may find in the prospect of seeing me on Saturday, which is very uncertain. I Take this occasion to tell you once for all, that I design no longer to be a constant Companion when I have ceas'd to be an agreable one. You only have had, as my friends, the priviledge of knowing my Unhappiness; and are therefore the only people whom my Company must necessarily make melancholy. I will not bring myself to you at all hours, like a Skeleton, to come across your diversions, and dash your pleasures: Nothing can be more shocking than to be perpetually meeting the Ghost of an old acquaintance, which is all you can ever see of me.

You must not imagine this to proceed from any Coldness, or the least decrease of Friendship to you. If You had any Love for me, I should be always glad to gratify you with an Object that you thought agreable. But as your regard is Friendship & Esteem; those are things that are as well, perhaps better, preservd Absent than Present. A Man that you love is a joy to your eyes at all times; a Man that you Esteem is a solemn kind of thing, like a Priest, only wanted at a certain hour to do his Office: 'Tis like Oyl in a Sallet, necessary, but of no manner of Taste. And you may depend upon it, I will wait upon you on every real occasion, at the first summons, as long as I live.

Let me open my whole heart to you: I have some times found myself inclined to be in love with you: and as I have reason to know from your Temper & Conduct how miserably I should be used in that circumstance, it is worth my while to avoid it: It is enough to be Disagreable, without adding Fool to it, by constant Slavery. I have heard indeed of Women that have had a kindness for Men of my Make; but it has been after Enjoyment, never before; and I know to my Cost you have had no Taste of that Talent in me, which most Ladies would not only Like better, but Understand better, than any other I have.

I love you so well that I tell you the truth, & that has made me write this Letter. I will see you less frequently this winter, as you'll less want company: When the Gay Part of the world is gone, I'll be ready to stop the Gap of a vacant hour whenever you please. Till then I'll converse with those who are more Indifferent to me, as You will with those who are more Entertaining. I wish you every pleasure God and Man can pour upon ye; and I faithfully promise you all the good I can do you, which is, the Service of a Friend, who will ever be Ladies, Entirely Yours.

(I, 455-6)

Even in this painful context, Pope mentions the disparities between his poetical talent, which the ladies presumably enjoy, and his sexual "talent," which he now realizes they will never taste. Earlier in the same year, in a slightly happier context, he had made a metaphor combining the two talents, telling the sisters that he "past . . . the day in those Woods where I have so often enjoyd—an Author & a Book; and begot such Sons upon the Muses, as I hope will live to see their father what he never was yet, an old and a good Man." This seems jovial enough, although certainly self-protective. The real pathos comes as the letter continues, with verses in which it is suddenly clear that, in poetry at least, Pope thinks of the Blounts as the Muses:

> I made a Hymn as I past thro' these Groves; it ended with a deep Sigh, which I will not tell you the meaning of.

> All hail! once pleasing, once inspiring Shade,
> 　　Scene of my youthful Loves, and happier hours!
> Where the kind Muses met me as I stray'd,
> 　　And gently pressd my hand, and said, Be Ours.

> Take all thou e're shalt have, a constant Muse:
> 　　At Court thou may'st be lik'd, but nothing gain;
> Stocks thou may'st buy & sell, but always lose;
> 　　And love the brightest eyes, but love in vain!
> 　　　　　　　　　　　(13 September 1717; I, 428-9)

Pope's realization that he was to love the Blounts in vain was no doubt building up for some time, but clearly the painful incidents recorded in the letters of late 1717 and early 1718 represent a climax of a sort. The immediate results included Pope's settling an annuity of forty pounds a year on Teresa (10 March 1717/18), with the condition that she not marry during the six years for which it was drawn up. These conditions have been called "curious" and "inexplicable," but as Pope explained to Teresa in a letter which seems to relate to the subject, she had "exprest [her] self desirous of increasing [her] present income" (I, 468). Pope's gift to her was certainly generous, and no doubt make it possible for her to keep up, in dress and style, with the court ladies whose friendship evidently meant so much to her. As to the provision about her marrying, it hardly seems unreasonable: if, as was far from impossible, some eligible man had decided to marry Teresa, it would have been embarrassing for him as well as for Pope for the annuity to be continued. In any case, the long-range result of the misunderstanding was a permanent break with Teresa; Pope last wrote to her in 1720, but Martha, by contrast, "remained to the end of his life, through slanders and imbroglios, the faithful center of Pope's affections."[21] About their devoted relationship, and about the letters in which Pope expressed his devotion to Martha, I shall have more to say.

When Pope was at work on *Eloisa to Abelard*, which would appear as one of the new poems in his collected works of 1717, he wrote to Martha Blount:

> I am here studying ten hours a day, but thinking of you in spight of all the learned. The Epistle of Eloise grows warm, and begins to have some Breathings of the Heart in it, which may make posterity think I was in love. I can scarce find in my heart to leave out the conclusion I once intended for it—
>
> ([March 1716?]; I, 338)

In the ending Pope printed, possibly that alluded to here, Eloisa suggests that some future poet may write of her romantic difficulties, concluding

> He best can paint 'em who shall feel 'em most.
>
> (366)

However, when the *Works* were in print, Pope sent them to Lady Mary Wortley Montagu, who was abroad, with this description, presumably alluding to the same passage:

> Among the rest, you have all I am worth, that is, my Workes: There are few things in them but what you have already seen, except the Epistle of Eloisa to Abelard; in which you will find one passage, that I can't tell whether to wish you should understand, or not?
>
> ([June 1717]; I, 407)[22]

In the same letter, he told Lady Mary, "I have left off all correspondence except with yourself" (I, 405-6); within a matter of
days he was sending his *Works* to the Blounts, with a sparkling
letter (see I, 409).

Indeed, during 1716-18, the climactic years of his relationship
with the Blounts, Pope was writing regular letters to Lady Mary.
He had met her in about 1715, and since they shared an interest
in and talent for poetry, a friendship sprang up. When Mr. Wortley Montagu went as ambassador to Turkey, taking his wife,
Pope began to write this remarkable series of letters, which Norman Ault has described as "both ardent and tinged with a playful
extravagance which suggests that his gallantry was not meant
to be taken too seriously."[23] Pope himself, however, often
suggests the opposite in the letters: he claims that his wit and
fancy are disguises for genuine and serious feelings. In a letter
of [October 1716], for example, he wittily carries forward a
recurring fantasy of these letters, a request that Lady Mary
purchase for him a fair Circassian slave (resembling herself,
of course) to be his concubine. Then he appears to break down,
of does he affect it?

> I can't go on in this style: I am not able to think of you
> without the utmost Seriousness, and if I did not take a
> particular care to disguise it, my Letters would be the most
> melancholy things in the world. I believe you see my Con-
> cern thro' all this Affectation of gayety, which is but like a
> Fitt of Laughing in the deepest Spleen or Vapours.
>
> (I, 364)

There is certainly a degree of self-dramatization here, but there
is no reason to doubt that Pope, at this time, found Lady Mary
genuinely attractive, and consequently indulged in a series of
fantasies relating to her. The Circassian slave was one; another,
alluded to in the same letter, was based on a legend about a queen
and a dwarf—a legend which had been told in an anonymous
quasi-Chaucerian poem in Tonson's 1709 *Miscellany*. Since
Pope contributed to this volume, he no doubt knew the story
from that source; it is interesting to speculate on his response
to lines like these:

> *Cynthio* was puzzel'd, and one may
> Give any one at least a Day
> To guess the Nymph that humbly su'd,
> And Swain so stubborn to be wo'd.
> Now who shou'd this *Adonis* be,
> But the King's ugly Dwarf! and she,
> In whose Embraces he was seen,
> The bright Astolpho's haughty Queen![24]

A third persistent fantasy concerns Pope's wish to follow Lady Mary, perhaps just as the Provencal poet Rudel had followed a Countess of Tripoli:

> The joy of following your Footsteps would as soon carry me to Mecca, as to Rome; and let me tell you as a friend, if you are really disposed to embrace the Mahometan religion, I'll fly on Pilgrimage with you thither, with as good a heart and as sound devotion, as ever Jeffrey Rudel the Provençall Poet, went after the fine Countess of Tripoly to Jerusalem. If you never heard of this Jeffery, I'll assure you he deserves your acquaintance: He lived in our Richard the first's time, put on a Pilgrims weed, took his voyage, and when he got ashore, was just upon the point of expiring, The Countess of Tripoly came to the Ship, took him by the hand: He lifted up his eyes, said, that having been blest with a sight of her, he was satisfied; and so departed this life. What did the Countess of Tripoly upon this? She made him a Splendid funeral, built him a Tomb of Porphyry, put his Epitaph upon it in Arabic verse, had his Sonnets curiously copied out and illumind with letters of gold, was taken with Melancholy, and turnd Nun. All this Madam you may depend upon for a truth and I send it you in the very words of my Author.
>
> (I, 440-1)

Of course, all of these fantasies were impossible, as both Pope and Lady Mary knew. He was far too frail to travel to France, let alone Turkey; she was not about to purchase him a concubine (nor does one imagine Pope's mother allowing even a pretty Circassian at Twickenham); and within a few years, far from copying out Pope's writings in gold, she was actively satirizing him. But these and other fantasies function in these letters as the "courtly" witticisms function in many of the Blount letters: aside from making entertaining reading, they allow Pope to dramatize his feelings toward Lady Mary, but in a form far enough from being explicit that his own feelings are protected. Consequently, Pope's occasional admissions that the fantasies are "the meer disguise of a discontented heart" (I, 83), though even those admissions themselves are couched in suspiciously dramatic language, are admissions of an important truth: the maker of the *persona* recognizes both his tools and his reasons.

Pope was reminded every day of the physical deformity that made him different from others. The fantasies in which he could imagine that difference as overlooked or altered or reversed deserve special attention. Certainly the tale of the queen in love with the dwarf is one of these. Pope was probably thinking of that tale when he wrote to the Blounts, in the letter quoted in full on pp. 107-8, "I have heard indeed of Women that have had a kindness for Men of my Make." A more complicated fantasy about nakedness occurs repeatedly in letters to both Lady Mary and the Blounts. Its first development comes in a particularly dense paragraph to Lady Mary:

> I think I love you as well as King Herod could Herodias, (tho I never had so much as one Dance with you) and would as freely give you my heart in a Dish, as he did another's head. But since Jupiter will not have it so, I must be content to show my taste in Life as I do my taste in Painting, by loving to have as little Drapery as possible. Not that I think every body naked, altogether so fine a sight as yourself and a few more would be: but because 'tis good to use people to what they must be acquainted with; and there will certainly come some Day of Judgment to uncover every Soul of us. We shall then see how the Prudes of this world owed all their fine Figure only to their being a little straiter-lac'd, and that they were naturally as arrant Squabs as those

that went more loose, nay as those that never girded their loyns at all.

(18 August [1716]; I, 353)

This series of metaphors is connected as brilliantly as we expect such metaphors to be connected in Pope's poems, but it is the last one which is most important. Even Pope's choice of words is telling: when he suggests that "Prudes" will be exposed on the Day of Judgment as "arrant Squabs," he is using one of the cruel epithets John Dennis had hurled at him in his attack on the *Essay on Criticism*—an attack which was only the first of many pamphlets shamelessly exploiting Pope's deformities. Dennis had called Pope "a young, squab, short Gentleman . . . and the very bow of the God of Love."[25]   Ruefully viewing his own twisted body, constantly reminded of its flaws by Dennis and others, aware that there was no queen ready to disrobe for him, Pope devised his expressive fantasy of the Last Judgment, in which people whose earthly bodies had been normal, but whose souls were twisted, would be exposed.   Laughed at by women for whom his appearance was his most important quality, he took understandable refuge in his poet's pride, as he explained to the Blounts in a darker version of the same image:

How can a poor Translator and Harehunter hope for a Minute's memory? Yet He comforts himself to reflect that He shall be rememberd when people have forgot what colours you wore, and when those at whom you dress, shall be Dust! This is the Pride of a Poet, let me see if you dare owne what is the Pride of a Woman, perhaps one article of it may be, to despise those who think themselves of some value, and to show your friends you can live without thinking of 'em at all. Do, keep your own secrets, that such fellows as I may laugh at ye in the valley of Jehosaphat, where Cunning will be the foolishest thing in nature, & those white Bums which I dye to see, will be shown to all the world.

(8 October [1718]; I, 515)

That there is a certain violence in this fantasy cannot be denied, but it also cannot be denied that Teresa Blount cared mightily about dress and appearance. It was that care which caused her cruelty to Pope, who had recognized it as early as the autumn of 1716, when he wrote to Martha, who was at home in the country while Teresa went to the birth-night party for the Prince of Wales:

> Let your faithless Sister triumph in her ill-gotten Trea-
> sures; let her put on New Gowns to be the Gaze of Fools,
> and Pageant of a Birth-night! While you with all your
> innocence enjoy a Shadey Grove without any leaves on, &
> dwell with a virtuous Aunt in a Country Paradise.
>
> (I, 375)

The phrase "without any leaves on" may be read as a bit of pastoral whimsy, since a leafless grove is hardly shady, but the overtones of "innocence" and "Paradise" make another reading possible. The phrase may modify "you," making of Martha an unclothed and unfallen Eve, in contrast to her fashionable but worldly sister. If this suggestion is really operative, it is worth considering how sharp the contrast is between the mythical landscape of Eden, its inhabitants innocently nude because they are unconscious of having anything to hide, and the mythical landscape of Pope's fantasy of the Last Judgment, with the "arrant squabs" stripped of their hypocritical coverings. Years later, in a letter to John Knight, Pope explicitly compared Martha to Eve:

> Her love for the place she banished herself from [Knight's
> estate] resembles Eve's passion for Paradise, in Milton,
> when she had got herself turned out of it. However, like
> Eve, who raves upon tying up the rose-trees, and cultivat-
> ing the arbours in the midst of her grief, this Lady too talks
> much of seeing the lawn enlarged, and the flocks feeding
> in sight of the parterre, and of administering grass to the
> lambs, and crowning them with flowers, etc.
>
> (8 November 1729; III, 68)

The qualities in Martha that made Pope think of her in these terms included her innocence, virtuousness, and receptiveness to his own "romantic" imagination. It was to her that he sent

long descriptions of picturesque villas, landscapes, and ruins.[26]
It was to her that he sent an elegiac account of the deaths of the
rural lovers struck by lightning, with his epitaph for them and
a personal application at the end of the story:

> After all that we call Unfortunate in this Accident, I cannot
> but owne, I think next to living so happy as these people
> might have done, was dying as they did. And did any one
> love me so well as Sarah did John, I would much rather dye
> thus with her, than live after her. I could not but tell you
> this true and tender ˙Story, and should be pleasd to have
> you as much mov'd by it as I am. I wish you had some
> Pity, for my sake; and I assure you I shall have for the
> future more Fear, for yours; since I see by this melancholy
> example, that Innocence & virtue are no security from what
> you are so afraid of.
>
> (6-9 August 1718; I, 481)

What Pope takes to be the innocence of the simple folk in his
little pastoral tragedy reminds him of Martha's innocence. To
the more wordly Teresa, he sent quite a different note, affecting
rakish unconcern:

> Madam. Since you prefer three hundred pounds to two
> true Lovers, I presume to send you the following Epitaph
> upon them, which seems to be written by one of your Taste.
>   Here lye two poor Lovers, who had the mishap
>   Tho very chaste people, to die of a Clap.
> I hope Miss Patty will not so much as smile at this: if she
> does, she may know, she has less pity than I.
>
> (I, 349)[27]

And to Lady Mary, he sent a letter whose story is similar but
whose personal appeal is more muted than that sent to Martha:

> Upon the whole, I can't think these people unhappy:
> The greatest happiness, next to living as they would have
> done, was to dye as they did. The greatest honour people
> of this low degree could have was to be remembered on a

little monument; unless you will give them another, that
of being honoured with a Tear from the finest eyes in the
world. I know you have Tenderness; you must have it: It
is the very Emanation of Good Sense & virtue: The finest
minds like the finest metals, dissolve the easiest.

But when you are reflecting upon Objects of pity, pray do
not forget one, who had no sooner found out an Object of
the highest Esteem, than he was seperated from it: And who
is so very unhappy as not to be susceptible of Consolation
from others, by being so miserably in the right as to think
other women what they really are. Such an one can't but
be desperately fond of any creature that is quite different
from these.

(1 September [1718]; I, 496)

Far from shedding a tear, for the lovers or for Pope, Lady Mary
responded in her best burlesque vein:

Here lies John Hughes and Sarah Drew;
Perhaps you'll say, What's that to you?
Believe me, friend, much may be said
On that poor couple that are dead.
On Sunday next they should have married;
But see how oddly things are carried!
On Thursday last it rain'd and lighten'd,
These tender lovers sadly frighten'd,
Shelter'd beneath the cocking hay
In hope to pass the time away.
But the BOLD THUNDER found them out
(Commission'd for that end no doubt)
And seizing on their trembling breath,
Consign'd them to the shades of death.
Who knows if 'twas not kindly done?
For had they seen the next year's sun,
A beaten wife and cuckold swain
Had jointly curs'd the marriage chain;
Now they are happy in their doom,
FOR POPE HAS WROTE UPON THEIR TOMB.

(I, 523)[28]

To be sure, her poem is devastating, and perhaps Pope's tenderness toward John and Sarah was a trifle affected, but it must have been Lady Mary's habitual refusal to exhibit sympathy, here perfectly exemplified, which led to her ultimate break with Pope. Certainly her letters to him from abroad—well-written, newsy travelogues—ignore consistently Pope's obvious and repeated pleas for some form of emotional attention. There are many versions of their final quarrel. Lady Mary may have been disappointed about the loan of a harpsichord (see Pope's apology to her, 15 September 1721; II, 82-3). Or there may have been some difficulty about a proposed satire, as Pope apparently told Arbuthnot, though Lady Mary, who was the source for this story, vigorously denied it. Or there may have been some basis in fact for the story kept alive by rumor and innuendo throughout Pope's life: that he made a serious declaration of love to Lady Mary, upon which she laughed in his face. I doubt this last theory, for Pope seems to have had ample reason to expect just this response. But the story, whatever its veracity, has a measure of symbolic truth. What happens, in the course of Pope's letters to Lady Mary, is precisely what supposedly happened on this mythical occasion: he exposes his feelings to her, and she callously laughs at him.[29]

That he missed her cannot be doubted. When he had finished Twickenham, he recorded his sense of her absence in moving lines which he sent to Gay:

> Ah friend, 'tis true—this truth you lovers know—
> In vain my structures rise, my gardens grow,
> In vain fair Thames reflects the double scenes
> Of hanging mountains, and of sloping greens:
> Joy lives not here; to happier seats it flies,
> And only dwells where WORTLEY casts her eyes.
> What are the gay parterre, the chequer'd shade,
> The morning bower, the eve'ning colonade,
> But soft recesses of uneasy minds,
> To sigh unheard in, to the passing winds?
> So the struck deer in some sequester'd part
> Lies down to die, the arrow at his heart;

There, stretch'd unseen in coverts hid from day,
Bleeds drop by drop, and pants his life away.

(TE VI, 225-6)[30]

But Pope was not a wounded deer; he was tougher than this
poetical projection, and he developed ways of coping. By 1722,
he was reusing a version of the last eight lines in a letter to the
poetess Judith Cowper (II, 142). His letters to her (we have
twelve, all written in 1722 and 1723) are interesting as chastened
descendants of his earlier witty and fantastic styles. There is
plenty of sparkle and some fantasy, but never is there any believ-
able suggestion that Pope contemplates serious emotional involvement with the lady. He wishes to be her friend, he suggests
that they have a kinship as poets, but he does not go farther:

I challenge a kind of Relation to you on the *Soul*'s side,
which I take to be better than either on a Father's or Mothers;
and if you Overlook an ugly *Body* (that stands much in the
way of any Friendship, when it is between different Sexes)
I shall hope to find you a True & constant Kinswoman in
Apollo. Not that I woud place all my Pretensions upon
That Poetical foot, much less confine 'em to it; I am far more
desirous to be admitted as yours on the more meritorious
title of Friendship. I have ever believd this as a sacred
maxime, that the most Ingenious Natures were the most
Sincere, & the most Knowing & Sensible Minds made the
Best Friends. Of all those that I have thought it the felicity
of my life to know, I have ever found the most distinguished
in Capacity, the most distinguished in Morality: and those
the most to be depended on, whom one esteemd so much as
to desire they shoud be so. I beg you to make me no more
complements. I coud make you a great many, but I know
you neither need 'em, nor can Like 'em: Be so good as to
think I don't.

(18 October [1722]; II, 138-9)

By this time in his life (he was thirty-four), Pope had settled
into his villa at Twickenham, and had decided to remain single.

He had realized that his only sons would be begotten upon the poetical muses. He was even able to praise his single state in a letter to Broome denying a rumor that he planned to marry:

> Your report of my quitting, or being in the least inclined to quit, the easy, single state I now enjoy, is altogether groundless; as idle, as the news which people invent, merely because they are idle.
>
> (18 September 1722; II, 134)

However, rumors persisted, and some were nasty, suggesting that Pope and Martha Blount were secretly married, or that she was his mistress. These rumors are not dead today. In the chronology at the beginning of the recent Penguin critical anthology on Pope, F. W. Bateson, without comment or proof, makes this entry:

> 1727 . . . Martha Blount becomes Pope's mistress about this period.[31]

There remains no reliable evidence to support this allegation. Pope's denial to Caryll, written in 1725, is worth quoting at length:

> A very confident asseveration has been made, which has spread over the town, that your god-daughter Miss Patty and I lived 2 or 3 years since in a manner that was reported to you as giving scandal to many: that upon your writing to me upon it I consulted with her, and sent you an excusive alleviating answer; but did after that, privately and of myself write to you a full confession; how much I myself disapproved the way of life, and owning the prejudice done her, charging it on herself, and declaring that I wished to break off what I acted against my conscience, &c.; and that she, being at the same time spoken to by a lady of your acquaintance, at your instigation, did absolutely deny to alter any part of her conduct, were it ever so disreputable or exceptionable. Upon this villanous lying tale, it is further added by the same hand, that I brought her acquainted with a noble

lord, and into an intimacy with some others, merely to get quit of her myself, being moved in consciousness by what you and I had conferred together, and playing this base part to get off.

You will bless youself at so vile a wickedness, who very well (I dare say) remember the truth of what then past, and the satisfaction you expressed I gave you (and Mrs Caryll also expressed the same thing to her kinswoman) upon that head. God knows upon what motives any one should malign a sincere and virtuous friendship! I wish those very people had never led her into any thing more liable to objection, or more dangerous to a good mind, that I hope my conversation or kindness are.

(II, 353-4)[32]

Everything about this letter rings true. Pope, to be sure, could and did "equivocate genteely" about his authorship of indecent verses and other trivial matters, but there are many reasons to believe him on this serious subject. His mother was alive and remained in his home until her death in 1733. She was a woman of principle, leaving the table once when Voltaire told an indecent story, and would certainly not have allowed in her house even the *appearance* of a liaison. Patty Blount often visited Mrs. Pope, and was appreciated, as a letter from Pope on one of his rambles records:

Wherever I wander, one reflection strikes me: I wish you were as free as I; or at least had a tye as tender, and as reasonable as mine, to a relation that well deserved your constant thought, and to whom you wou'd always be pull'd back (in such a manner as I am) by the heart-string. I have never been well since I set out; but don't tell my Mother so; it will trouble her too much: And as probably the same reason may prevent her sending a true account of her health to me, I must desire you to acquaint me.

([15 June 1724]; II, 236)

And when Teresa became involved with a married man in 1729, Pope's concern that Martha's reputation and tranquility would be damaged by her continuing to live with her mother and sister in London seems fully genuine. At the same time, his lack of power over her is indicated by the fact that she did continue to live there. His letters to Caryll on the subject are frank and concerned;[33] it is impossible for me to believe that he would have taken such positions while carrying on an affair himself.

Patty remained his "virtuous friend." His feelings for her—tender, protective, critical, appreciative—are recorded in the letters he wrote to her during the last twenty years of his life: letters as bare of artifice as any Pope wrote. One written from Stowe in 1739 gives perhaps the fullest description of these mature feelings:

> Dear Madam,—I think you will not complain that I don't write often enough, but as to long Letters, it is hard to say much, when one has nothing to tell you but what you should believe of course, and upon long experience. All is Repetition of only One Great Truth, which is lessened when it really is so, by too frequent Professions. And then the other things are of Places & Persons that little or not at all affect you, or interest you: You have often rebuked me for talking too much of myself & my own Motions, & it is surely more triffling & absurd to write them, than to talk them; considering too that the Clerks of the Postoffice read these Letters. . . . So I go on, to tell you that I am extremely well, as well as ever I expect to be in every thing, or desire to be, except my Constitution could be mended, or You made happier. Yet I think we have both of us the Ingredients about us to make us happy; Your natural Moderation is greater than mine, yet I have no sort of Ambition nor Vanity that costs me an Uneasy moment. Your Temper is much more chearful; and That Temper, joined with Innocence, & a Consciousness of not the least Inclination to hurt, or Disposition to envy another, is a lasting Security of that Calm of Mind which nothing can take from you, nor Sickness nor Age itself. But the *Skill* of your *Conduct* would be, to avoid & fly as far as possible from all Occasions of ruffling it, or such Vexations, which tho they can't destroy it, can

& will cloud it, & render you the *more liable* to be uneasy,
for being *more tender*, & *less inclind* to make or see others
uneasy.

(IV, 187)

There is much to notice here. Pope's devotion expresses itself
principally in his concern for Martha's situation with her family.
He perceives that her desire to avoid confrontations and unpleas-
antness prevents her from asserting herself; at the same time, he
recognizes that agreeableness and even submissiveness are among
her charming qualities. While he chides her gently, here and in
other letters, a tone of acceptance runs through the late letters.
She will never change (his phrase for her is *semper eadem*), but
he accepts her with her temperamental weaknesses, just as she,
perhaps more than any other friend, came to accept his physical
weaknesses.

But there are moments of pathos in these late letters. At the
end of the letter quoted above, Pope wishes Martha would come
to a neighboring country-house, and realizes that she will not,
and concludes:

But this, I know, is a Dream: and almost Every thing I wish,
in relation to You, is so always! Adieu. I hope you take
Spaw waters tho you mention it not. God keep you, & let
me hear from you.

Another moving moment comes in Pope's reply to Bathurst's
jocular proposal to cart Pope's entire villa off to a corner of his
estate (see above, p. 80). Responding in kind to Bathurst's wit,
Pope proposed that Patty be brought along, to look after the
children:

Mrs Patty has always a Partiality for you, notwithstanding
your eternal neglect, of which she thinks there cannot be a
greater proof than your never proposing to put her among
the other things in the Cart. She can't be so humble as not
to imagine, Her Person might be as much an Ornament to
your Wood, as a Leaden Statue. She says she could look

after the children that you resolve to give My House to; and
for my part I assure your Lordship, I should think myself
not so much disgracd by the Company you assign me, but
be proud to pass my time with the only honest & unprej-
udic't Part of the Nation; Those children, my Lord who
may come to assert, what their Fathers have given up.

(1 October [1730]; III, 137)

Pope's participation in Bathurst's fantasy and the political implication of the last sentence fail to hide his real pain at having
no children, a pain he was to acknowledge only in an aside to
Fortescue:

In particular I wish the Honour, the Spirit, and the In-
dependency of this free Nation may continue when I am
dust and ashes, & tho' no Child of mine (but a Poem or two)
is to live after me.

(27 March [1739]; IV, 169)

Pope speaks the truth here. His poems were his only children,
and the energy and care with which he engendered them may be
among the many results of his lack of success in love. Other
results of Pope's being thwarted in his early attempts to find a
wife include his need for understanding, trustworthy friends
(male and female) and his ability to look with a somewhat jaun-
diced eye at the sexual foibles of others, an attitude which
emerges in *Sober Advice from Horace*, and in the *Epistle on the
Characters of Women*, dedicated, although with typical modesty
she would not allow the use of her name, to Martha Blount.

CHAPTER 4

The Life of Writing: Grub Street and St. James's

"THE LIFE OF A WIT," Pope wrote in the preface to the 1717 *Collected Works*, "is a warfare upon earth," and while the word "wit" had a number of distinct meanings in the eighteenth century, he used it here to mean a wit who writes. Unprotected by anything like modern copyright laws, forced to publish through a relatively small group of legitimate booksellers, in constant danger from pirate printers, working without significant secretarial assistance, and almost always underpaid, the eighteenth-century writer had considerable difficulty getting his work before the public.[1] Once he did so, he faced a critical establishment ready to damn him, either for slavish allegiance to rules and models or for shocking disregard of them. Even if a work was judged pleasing on aesthetic grounds, there were always political dangers: the practice of reading subversive allegory into innocent works, which Pope satirized in *The Key to the Lock*, was real.[2]

In this difficult world Pope functioned brilliantly. He was acutely aware of the actions and motives of his allies and antagonists in the inky battles of Grub Street. He understood his booksellers' need for profit, and managed to satisfy that need while supporting himself as well.[3] His indefatigable reading of pamphlets and periodicals kept him aware of the productions of the Dunces, and he knew how to use lesser writers for his own purposes.[4] He was, above all else, a thorough professional, and he had a special respect for those few other writers he took to be similarly professional—most notably his colleagues from the Scriblerus Club.

In his shrewd dealings with his booksellers, Pope showed a
complete understanding of their world, a world inhabited by pirate printers and hungry lesser writers, eager for any task and
generally exploited by the powerful booksellers, the Tonsons and
Lintots.[5] But when he sought to comment on that world, he
tried to seem above its petty concerns; one humorous example
is his somewhat fictionalized account of a ride to Oxford with
Bernard Lintot, who (according to Pope) hoped to persuade
the poet to do a little impromptu translating:

> As Mt. *Lintott* was talking, I observ'd he sate uneasy on
> his saddle, for which I express'd some sollicitude: Nothing
> says he, I can bear it well enough; but since we have the day
> before us, methinks it would be very pleasant for you to rest
> a-while under the Woods.   When we were alighted, "See
> here, what a mighty pretty *Horace* I have in my pocket?
> what if you amus'd your self in turning an Ode, till we
> mount again?   Lord! if you pleas'd, what a clever *Miscellany*
> might you make at leisure hours."   Perhaps I may, said I,
> if we ride on; the motion is an aid to my fancy; a round trott
> very much awakens my spirits.   Then jog on apace, and I'll
> think as hard as I can.
>
> Silence ensu'd for a full hour; after which Mr. *Lintott* lug'd
> the reins, stopt short, and broke out, "Well, Sir, how far
> have you gone?"   I answer'd seven miles.   "Z____ds, Sir,
> said *Lintott*, I thought you had done seven stanza's. *Olds-
> worth* in a ramble round *Wimbleton-hill*, would translate
> a whole Ode in half this time.   I'll say that for *Oldsworth*,
> (tho' I lost by his *Timothy*'s) he translates an Ode of *Horace*
> the *quickest* of any man in *England*.   I remember Dr. King
> would write verses in a tavern three hours after he couldn't
> speak: and there's Sir *Richard* in that rumbling old Chariot
> of his, between *Fleet-ditch* and *St. Giles*'s pound shall make
> you half a *Job*."
>
>   ([November 1716]; I, 373)

Pope portrays Lintot, here and throughout the letter, as the
thoroughgoing business man, for whom literature is in essence
a product.   The wretched authors Lintot praises are singled out

for the speed with which they can produce printable translations under any conditions. By refusing to fall in with Lintot's little scheme, Pope seeks to separate himself from such men; *he* does not write whatever Lintot suggests, nor does he produce to order on horseback. The humor is good-natured enough, but the distinction is one Pope often insisted on: while he certainly was concerned to make a fair return on his works, he did not like to be thought of as writing principally for money. Whatever the true state of affairs, Pope clung to the old version of the gentleman author, writing for the sake of truth and his own friends. Years would pass before Dr. Johnson, who did think of himself proudly as a professional writer, would tell Boswell, "No man but a blockhead ever wrote, except for money."[6]

Pope's pretensions to a kind of "gentleman author" status were reinforced by his awareness of a world other than the world of Grub Street: two years before he wrote the description of the ride with Lintot, he had enjoyed the company of such part-time writers as the learned Dr. Parnell, the powerful politician Dr. Swift, and the Queen's own physician Dr. Arbuthnot. With these men and others, Pope formed the Scriblerus Club. Their discussions of literature and joint projects, laughed over in Arbuthnot's chambers in St. James's palace, were no doubt far removed from the notion of literature as a means of survival which prevailed in Grub Street.

In his letters to the lesser writers with whom he engaged in joint ventures or controversy, Pope betrays his understanding of their world. But at the same time, his evidently superior (even snobbish) attitude toward them reflects not only his sense of his own greater talent, but his identification with the Scriblerus group, whom he treated as literary peers. The letters to both groups shed invaluable light on Pope's notions about his profession.

Letters to Allies and Adversaries

Lytton Strachey was only the most eloquent of many readers of Pope who have seen him as a monkey pouring boiling lead down on his enemies from the comparative safety of a window.

Like most partial views of Pope, this one has a measure of validity: Pope was unable to ignore the cruel and constant attacks
made on him by lesser ,writers; his counterattacks, usually in
poetic form, were always forceful and sometimes vicious; but
his desire to seem above the Grub Street battles led him to
disown or explain away his own missiles in those battles. Pope's
letters to his adversaries reveal other equally valid aspects of
his attitude toward the Dunces. They show his willingness to
forgive men who had made scurrilous and unprovoked attacks
on him, his eager responses to overtures of reconciliation, and
his genuine appreciation of those who withheld attacks they
might have made.

Again, the coexistence within Pope's mind of conflicting
impulses is confusing. How can the same person have acted
alternately as the all-forgiving Good Man, eager for reconciliation, and the angry satirist, skewering his victims? The
famous story Pope's friend Jonathan Richardson told Dr. Johnson goes part of the way toward explaining the combination:

> One of Cibber's pamphlets came into the hands of Pope,
> who said, "These things are my diversion." They sat by
> him while he perused it, and saw his features writhen with
> anguish.[7]

Johnson clearly believed that the anguish was Pope's real
response, that "insensibility to censure and criticism" was
always a pretense, that "he wished to despise his critics, and
therefore hoped that he did despise them."[8]

The last phrase contains a valuable hint, for Pope did wish
to maintain an amiable aloofness toward Grub Street, and as
some letters show, occasionally achieved it. But his usual
response to attack was not indifference but simultaneous fascination and pain. About 1734, he asked the younger Jacob Tonson
to do an unusual bit of binding for him:

> Sir,—I desire you'l take these five Setts of the Odyssey, &
> do what you can with 'em.
> I desire also you'l cause the Pacquet I send, to be bound

together, as many in a Volume as are tyed together. Let the Octavo be made to match in colour & Size this which is already bound, & Letter it Libels, On Pope &c. Vol. 2d

Pray Bind the duodecimos also in another vol. the same colours, Letterd Curl & Company.

And Bind the Gulliveriana, & letter it (Same Colour) thus, Libels on Swift & Pope.

In this you will oblige Sir Your Very faithful Servant A. Pope.

I don't know but soon we may have some better business together.

Pray send me Philip's Freethinkers, and the first or second Vol. of Blackmores Essays, in which is his piece of Heroic poetry.

One of these pamphlets is imperfect at the end, of which I desire you'l procure an entire one.

(III, 399)

Pope's desire to have perfect copies of all the attacks on him and his care in having them bound are strong evidence of the fascination these largely ephemeral productions had for him. Being attacked and caricatured was then, as it is now, evidence of fame, and Pope was justly proud of his fame. At the same time, the kind of abuse these writings contained was certain to be painful; Pope can hardly have enjoyed reading them. But to ignore them completely was impossible. The best he could manage was the pretense of aloofness. Swift and others urged him repeatedly to ignore those who "scribbled" against him, and he himself saw such an attitude as ideal. That he could not consistently achieve it is hardly surprising.

The simple fact of Pope's success was probably the basic reason why such struggling hacks as Gildon and Budgell attacked him. He never wrote to such men; their inclusion in the *Dunciad* was a sufficient response. (Possibly, he may have also been responsible for attacks on them in the *Grub-Street Journal*.)[9] Probably it was with such men in mind that he wrote to Swift, five years before the *Dunciad*:

I have carefully avoided all intercourse with Poets &
Scriblers, unless where by great Chance I find a modest
one. By these means I have had no quarrels with any personally, & none have been Enemies, but who were also
strangers to me. And as there is no great need of Eclaircis-
sements with such, Whatever they writ or said I never
retaliated; not only never seeming to know, but often really
never knowing any thing of the matter.

([August 1723]; II, 185-6)

Of course, even at this relatively early stage of his career, this
claim was false. Pope had retaliated in print against Dennis
as early as 1713 (see above chapter 3, p. 87 and note), and he
seems to have been consistently well-informed about attacks on
himself. But the attitude toward "Poets & Scriblers" described
here represents something Pope *wished* he could achieve. His
partial successes in maintaining equanimity toward his enemies
were based on this ideal, and on a principle he often enunciated:
that attacks on his poetry and on his person were very different
things. When Dennis published his *Reflections Critical and
Satyrical, upon a late Rhapsody, call'd An Essay upon Criticism*,
which included some acute comments on the poem and an un-
conscionable personal attack (quoted in part above, chapter
3, p. 114), Pope wrote to Caryll:

I send you Mr. Dennis's Remarks on the *Essay*, which
equally abound in just criticisms and fine railleries. . . .
To give this man his due, he has objected to one or two
lines with reason, and I will alter them in case of another
edition: I will make my enemy do me a kindness where he
meant an injury, and so serve instead of a friend.

(25 June 1711; I, 121)[10]

Late in life, in the prose maxims he published along with the
Swift correspondence, Pope made a rule of this attitude:

Get your Enemies to read your works, in order to mend

them, for your friend is so much your second-self, that he
will judge too like you.

And he did change the lines Dennis criticized, just as he did not
let his rage at Theobald's *Shakespeare Restored* stop him from
adopting some of Theobald's emendations in later editions of
his own Shakespeare.

Dennis and Theobald are prime examples of enemies to whom
Pope eventually showed kindness. As early as 1719, perhaps
with a touch of superiority toward a largely vanquished foe,
but not without compassion, Pope wrote of Dennis, in a letter
to Broome:

> If my gains by Homer were sufficient, I would gladly
> found an hospital, like that of Chelsea, for such of my
> tribe as are disabled in the muses' service, or whose years
> require a dismissal from the unnatural task of rhyming
> themselves, and others, to death. Poor Gildon should have
> his itch and—cured together, and old Dennis not want good
> looking after, and better accomodation than poets usually
> meet with in Moorfields.
>
> (II, 3)

Two years later, there actually was a cease-fire. Pope subscribed
for Dennis's *Original Letters*, and Dennis edited the letters to
leave out their quarrel. The exchange of letters is illuminating:

> Sir,—As you have subscrib'd for two of my Books, I have
> order'd them to be left for you at Mr. *Congreve*'s Lodgings:
> As most of those Letters were writ during the Time that
> I was so unhappy as to be in a State of War with you, I was
> forced to maim and mangle at least ten of them, that no
> Footsteps might remain of that Quarrel. I particularly
> left out about half the Letter which was writ upon pub-
> lishing the Paper call'd the *Guardian*. I am, Sir, Your
> most obedient, Humble Servant, John Dennis.
>
> (29 April 1721; II, 75)

Sir,—I call'd to receive the Two Books of your Letters from

Mr. *Congreve*, and have left with him the little Money I am in your Debt. I look upon myself to be much more so, for the Omissions you have been pleas'd to make in those Letters in my Favour, and sincerely join with you in the Desire, that not the least Traces may remain of that Difference between us which indeed I am sorry for. You may therefore believe me, without either Ceremony or Falseness, Sir, Your most Obedient, Humble Servant. A. Pope

(3 May 1721; II, 75-6)

Of course, shots were fired again over the *Dunciad*, at which time these letters were quoted by both sides to prove bad faith. Early issues of the *Grub-Street Journal* were frequently critical of Dennis.[11] But in 1731, when Dennis was old and blind and in desperate need, Pope was actively trying to get subscribers for a proposed edition of Dennis's *Works*.[12] When that subscription failed, and when Dennis suggested that Pope's aid was evidence of fear, Pope quietly helped the old man financially, through his friend, the young playwright David Mallet, to whom he wrote on March 18 [1732/3]:

I have not forgot J. Dennis; if you find occasion, pray Extend my Debt to you by giving him a little more.

(III, 357-8)

In December of the same year, just a few months before Dennis died, a benefit night was organized for him, to which Pope contributed an anonymous and often misinterpreted prologue.[13]

If Theobald, the first Prince of Dunces, neither deserved nor got this sort of generosity, Pope at least maintained a sense of fair play toward him. Mallet's *Of Verbal Criticism*, which contained an attack of Theobald, was delayed in publication because Pope wished to give even "piddling Tibbald" a fair chance for profit from a play then on the boards. His request that Mallet postpone publication cames in the same letter:

It comes into my mind to desire you to postpone publishing your Poem (in which Tibbald is touched upon with so much justice, as your subject required) till after he has had a

Benefit-Night for a Play of his call'd *Secret Love* or some such name; It may perhaps, else, be some prejudice to him.

These kindnesses are hardly the acts of Strachey's spiteful monkey. They are the acts of a man who, despite all his own comfortable success, remained conscious of the struggle for existence in the rough-and-tumble world of literary London, sympathetic to a degree with men of far less talent, who were bothersome to him whether they attacked him or sought his favor. Despite the bother, civility remained important to Pope: the man who could attack without giving quarter in a published poem or a deft advertisement rarely confronted his enemies for face-to-face quarrels—or wrote them angry letters. Samuel Johnson's great defiant letter to Chesterfield has no parallel in Pope's letters.[14] On the contrary, Pope so needed to appear civil in one-to-one intercourse, including letters, that his attempts to deny having satirized people with whom he had personal dealings led him into hopelessly tangled lies and deceptions.

Pope's relations with Aaron Hill are the classic case. Hill has been called, with some justice, "the most persistent and colossal bore of the century,"[15] but his sheer energy was remarkable. He wrote reams of bad verse, including an epic poem; numerous tragedies, with essays on how they should be acted; and, if his letters to Pope are at all typical, interminable correspondence. He knew and worked with Handel, devised projects including a scheme to extract oil from beech trees, and fathered children whom he named Urania, Astraea, Minerva, and Julius Caesar. He was handsome and wealthy, and he had provided Pope's friend John Gay with employment as his secretary from 1708 to 1711.[16] Hill's remarkable self-confidence, even audacity, included a sensitivity to real or imagined attack greater even than Pope's. So when Bernard Lintot (hardly the most dependable of men) told Hill that Pope had questioned the propriety of Hill's *The Northern Star*, a panegyric of Peter the Great, Hill flew into a rage. In a "Preface to Mr. Pope," printed in the first edition of the poem (Pope had apparently seen the manuscript), Hill vigorously defended himself and needlessly maligned Pope. Admirably and not atypically, Pope remained silent. Two years later, Hill apparently repented, sending Pope his new effort,

The Creation, with an apology which makes up in effusiveness for what it lacks in grammar:

> If you needed an Inducement to the strengthening your Forgiveness, you might gather it from these two Considerations; *First*, The Crime was almost a Sin against Conviction; for though not happy enough to know you personally, your *Mind* had been my intimate Acquaintance, and regarded with a kind of partial Tenderness, that made it a little less than Miracle, that I attempted to offend you. . . .
>
> ([1720]; II, 35)

Pope responded, accepting both the poem and the apology, although his remark about the poem is cleverly ambiguous. Hill may have read it as a compliment, but Pope hardly meant it as one:

> I will say nothing of the Poem you favour me with, for fear of being in the wrong; but I am sure, the Person who is capable of writing it, can need no Man to judge it.
>
> (2 March [1719/20]; II, 37)

What Pope really thought of Hill's writing is probably more clearly indicated by the inclusion of a certain "A. H." among the Flying Fish in the *Peri Bathos* of 1728. As Dorothy Brewster suggests, "possibly he was so impressed with the absurdity of some passages in Hill's works that the critic in him could not refrain from putting Hill where he belonged."[17]   Hill retaliated with satires on both Pope and Swift, only to find what he took to be himself participating in the diving contest of *Dunciad* II:

> H——— try'd the next, but hardly snatch'd from sight,
> Instant buoys up, and rises into light;
> He bears no token of the sabler streams,
> And mounts far off, among the swans of Thames.
>
> (II, 283-86)

This flurry took place all in one spring: the *Bathos* came out in March, Hill's attacks in April, the first *Dunciad* in May. So far as we know, Hill remained silent. When the lines were repeated in the 1729 *Dunciad*, "H____" became "**," but a footnote made the identification with Hill unmistakable—at least to him:

> This is an instance of the Tenderness of our author. The person here intended writ an angry preface against him, grounded on a Mistake, which he afterwards honourably acknowledg'd in another printed preface. Since when, he fell under a second mistake, and abus'd both him and his Friend.
>
> He is a writer of Genius and Spirit, tho' in his youth he was guilty of some pieces bordering upon bombast. Our Poet here gives him a Panegyric instead of a Satire, being edify'd beyond measure, at this only instance he ever met with in his life, of one who was much a Poet, confessing himself in an Error: And has supprest his name, as thinking him capable of a second repentance.
>
> (TE V, 136)

Hill's response took two forms. He published an anonymous poem entitled *The Progress of Wit: A Caveat*, criticizing Pope for wasting his talent in attacking the Dunces, and he wrote Pope a friendly letter, enclosing one of his daughter Urania's poems, with a complaining postscript:

> If, after this, I should inform you, that I have a gentle complaint to make to, and against you, concerning a paragraph in the notes of a late edition of the *Dunciad*, I fear, you would think your crime too little to deserve the punishment of so long a letter, as you are doomed to, on that subject, from, Sir. Your most humble, and Most obedient Servant, A. Hill.
>
> (18 January 1730/1; III, 164-5)

Pope's response was needlessly self-defensive:

Sir,—I am oblig'd to you for your Compliment, and can
truly say, I never gave you just Cause of Complaint. You
once mistook on a Bookseller's idle Report, and publickly
express'd your Mistake; yet you mistook a second time,
that two initial Letters, only, were meant of you, tho' every
Letter in the Alphabet was put in the same manner: And,
in Truth (except some few), those Letters were set at Random
to occasion what they did occasion, the Suspicion of bad
and jealous Writers, of which Number I could never reckon
Mr. *Hill.* and most of whose Names I did not know.

. . . As to the Notes [to the *Dunciad*], I am weary of telling
a great Truth, which is, that I am not Author of 'em; tho'
I love Truth so well, as fairly to tell you, Sir, I think even
that Note a Commendation, and should think myself not ill
us'd *to have the same Words said of me.*

. . . I do faithfully assure you, I never was angry at any
Criticism, made on my Poetry, by whomsoever: If I could
do Mr. *Dennis* any humane Office, I would, tho' I were sure
he would abuse me personally Tomorrow; therefore it is no
great Merit in me, to find, at my Heart, I am your Servant.
I am very sorry you ever was of another Opinion. . . . I vow
to God, I never thought any great Matters of my poetical
Capacity; I only thought it a little better, comparatively,
than that of some very mean Writers, who are too proud.
—But, I do know *certainly*, my moral Life is *superior* to
that of most of the *Wits* of these Days. This is a silly Letter,
but it will shew you my Mind honestly, and, I hope, convince you, I can be, and am, Sir, Your very affectionate and
humble Servant, A. Pope.

                              (26 January 1730/1; III, 165-6)

As Pope admits in the last paragraph, this is indeed a silly letter.
His claims that he did not mean Hill in the *Bathos* and that he did
not write the notes to the *Dunciad* are almost certainly false. His
further claim that he "never was angry at any Criticism, made
on my Poetry" is at least a little too self-congratulatory, more
a statement of his ideals than of his practice. His "vow" that
he "never thought any great Matters of my poetical capacity" is

similarly imaginary. Unable to admit in the direct intercourse of a letter that he has in fact criticized Hill, he resorts to a description of his actions and feelings which tallies with his notion of how he *ought* to respond to attacks, but which is in fact so far from the truth that even Hill was not fooled. Hill's longer reply has been praised with some justice by Johnson and later scholars; it exposes the deceptive reasoning of Pope's letter, threatens politely to publish another attack, and proffers forgiveness in its final paragraph:

> Upon the Whole, Sir, I find, I am so sincerely your *Friend*, that it is not, in your own Power, to make me your Enemy: Else, that unnecessary Air, of Neglect, and Superiority, which is so remarkable in the Turn of your Letter, would have nettled me to the Quick; and I must triumph, in my Turn, at the Strength of my own Heart, who can, after it, still find, and profess myself, most affectionately and sincerely, Your humble Servant, A. Hill.
>
> (28 January 1730/1; III, 169)

Pope's reply, self-confessedly a weak one, feebly continues some of the protestations of innocence, but opens with a paragraph whose tone is nearly confessional:

> Since I am fully satisfy'd we are each of us sincerely and affectionately Servants to the other, I desire we may be no further misled by the Warmth of writing on this Subject. If you think I have shewn too much *Weakness*, or if I think you have shewn too much *Warmth*, let us forgive one another's Temper. I told you I thought my Letter a silly one; but the more I thought so, the more in sending it I shew'd my Trust in your good Disposition toward me. I am sorry you took it to have an Air of *Neglect*, or *Superiority*: Because I know in my Heart, I had not the least Thought of being any way superior to Mr. *Hill*; and, far from the last Design to shew Neglect to a Gentleman who was shewing me Civility, I meant in Return to shew him a better Thing, Sincerity; which I'm sorry should be so ill express'd as to seem Rude-

ness. I meant but to complain as frankly as you, that all
Complaints on both Sides might be out, and at a Period for
ever: I meant by this to have laid a surer Foundation for
your Opinion of me for the future, that it might no more
be shaken by Mistakes or Whispers.

(5 February 1730/1; III, 169-70)

This was good enough for Hill, and there were no more misunderstandings. Pope, however, conscious of having been
detected in his disingenuousness, was condemned to put up
with Hill's letters for the rest of his life. These letters included
requests that Pope read Hill's atrocious tragedies, and Pope
actually did read *Athelwold* and *Caesar*—more than once! Hill's
self-confidence was remarkable. He wrote letters to Walpole
filled with gratuitous advice about politics. He instructed David
Garrick in the art of acting—privately in letters and publicly in
his theatrical periodical *The Prompter*. As Professor Lounsbury wryly puts it,

No one escaped his mania for giving advice. No station in
life, no position in the public service, no eminence in any
profession led him to hesitate about bestowing upon the
occupant or possessor the result of his reflections upon
matters to which they might reasonably be assumed to have
themselves devoted years.[18]

Pope did not escape. In 1738, Hill sent him tedious instructions
for possible improvements in the *Essay on Criticism:*

When such a writer as *you*, for example, took a resolution
of describing the swiftness of *Camilla*, under the most agile
hyperbole of lightness; even to her treading upon *cornstalks*,
without *bowing* them; nobody can doubt, but your meaning,
in such a description, must have been, that she *skimm'd* the
scarce-touch'd plain, she *flew over*;—yet, when, on the contrary, your expression says, that she *scours* it—that unwary
mis-use of one word, checks the speed of your airy idea, and

presents to the fancy, a quite opposite image of *pressure,*
attrition, and *adherence.*

(IV, 96-7)

Pope's polite reply seems a little weary:

> As to the Subject-matter of the Letter, I found what I have
> often done in receiving Letters from those I most esteemed,
> and most wished to be esteemed by; a great Pleasure in
> reading it, and a great Inability to answer it. I can only say,
> you oblige me, in seeming so well to know me again; as
> one extremely willing that the free Exercise of Criticism
> should extend over my own Writings, as well as those of
> others.

(9 June 1738; IV, 102)

The history of their relations and Pope's real need to *seem* polite
necessitated such forbearance, but I cannot help believing that
it was with Hill in mind that Pope wrote, in the *Epistle to Dr.*
Arbuthnot:

> A Fool quite angry is quite innocent;
> Alas! 'tis ten times worse when they *repent*.

(107-8)

However, reading and commenting on his tragedies was as
close as Pope came to a professional relationship with Hill. With
William Broome and Elijah Fenton, men considerably less arro-
gant than Hill, but no more talented, Pope collaborated on his
translation of the *Odyssey*. His first request to Broome for aid
in preparing the notes for the *Iliad* sets the tone of their correspondence:

> If you have leisure, and can engage, without failing me,
> to read over in order the commentaries of Eustathius, on
> the four first Iliads, and to place a mark upon all the notes
> which are purely critical, omitting the grammatical and

geographical and allegorical ones, you will oblige me
particularly by informing me. I should be glad you had
the time to translate them afterwards, and I should think
myself under an obligation to pay a lawful tribute for the
time you spent in it.

([November 1714]; I, 266)

The sequence of the first three phrases is telling. "If you have
leisure" sounds like the beginning of a casual request, and
Broome, comfortably settled in his parish at Sturston, certainly
had leisure. " . . . and can engage," with its strong verb,
suggests that Pope is seeking a firm commitment. And " . . .
without failing me" is almost a threat. The results, from Pope's
point of view, were satisfactory: Broome waded through Eusta-
thius and excerpted material Pope found useful in the notes to
the *Iliad*, and despite Pope's offer of payment, Broome did this
work for nothing. He had married well and needed no money.

In the *Odyssey* project, Broome did all the notes and translated
eight books; Fenton, humorously castigated by both Pope and
Broome for his laziness, produced four books of translation.
Again, profit was not a motive for Broome, but this time he did
hope to share in the fame. But the initial plan to conceal the
collaboration altogether was compromised by Broome's telling
too many people of his involvement; the decisions made about
what would be told the public were dishonest; the truth, when
finally told, proved somewhat embarrassing to all concerned.
And Pope's "complimentary" inclusion of Broome in the *Dunciad*, coming just after he had quoted some unfortunate lines
of Broome's in the *Bathos*, set off a chain of events similar to
what occurred with Hill. There were letters of accusation and
denial, and an eventual reconciliation.[19]

But Pope's letters to Broome and Fenton during the actual
period of collaboration are altogether different, and show Pope's
skill as a taskmaster. In the early days of the collaboration, for
example, when the three men were still choosing books, Fenton
planned a visit to Broome, which Pope announced in this clever
note:

Our friend Fenton tells me you speak of the old Greek, as one is apt to do of a companion one has had too much of. The best company tires a man sometimes, if one is to travel long with it. But you that have gone already to Hell with him, and to Circe's island, and Scylla, and Charybdis, methinks may pass a peaceable dull day or two in his house, eating and drinking by his fireside with his wife and children. And yet, it seems, the second book is a weariness of spirit to you. Well, be of good cheer, I will do the third, and save you the trouble of hearing old Nestor's long stories. Let us, like good christians, bear one another's burthens, that we may persevere to the end. Fenton intends to see you with a book in his hands, as a sample that he deserves his meat and drink at yours, and is not a mere vagabond, such as you find strolled about in Homer's days, and told everybody Jupiter was their particular friend. You will, I doubt not, receive him as cordially as good Eumaeus himself could have done, and teach your very dogs good manners on his arrival at the vicarage. Mrs. Broome will meet him, if you have any respect for Homerical rites, with a bason and ewer, to wash his head and feet; and if you slew a tithe pig by the force of your own arm, and broiled it with your own hands, you will do no more than becomes you, either as an hospitable friend or a sober priest. I do not absolutely require, that if you give him a calves' head, you should tip the horns with gold, in the manner of Laerceus, but you must be void of all humanity if you do not provide one of your maids for his bedfellow.

(April [1722]; II, 110-111)

Pope's in-jokes and implication of *camaraderie* soften but do not alter the fact that his purpose in this letter is to urge Broome to get on with Book II. At a later stage in the project, Pope's orders become somewhat more brusque:

The indolence of our friend obliges me to write at his request, though I have no time, and he a great deal. It is just to tell you, first from myself, that I have received the eighth book, though I think it a great providence that I did so, for it came half-opened by the penny post. I beg you for the future to give better directions, or send by surer hands. The consequences would be very bad, if any accident should happen.

(24 April 1724; II, 231)

Finally, when Broome had completed his labors on the notes, Pope responded with some tenderness and a surprising metaphor:

Your last, very last, packet happily arrived two days ago. I wish you joy, and myself; we have been married now these three years, and dragged on our common load with daily and mutual labour and constancy, lightening each other's toil, and friends to the last. We want only now a glorious epiphonema, and crown to our work. Why should we not go together in triumph, and demand the bacon flitch at Dunmow, or some such signal reward? Or shall I, like a good husband, write your epitaph, and celebrate your great obedience, compliance, and wife-like virtues; while you, in your turn, make a kind will at the conclusion of your career, and express all the kindness you can to your beloved yoke-fellow? Something must be done at the close of this work by us both, as a monument equally of friendship and of justice to each other.

(20 January [1725/6]; II, 363)

The flitch of bacon to which Pope alludes here was a prize awarded to any couple who could prove they had not quarrelled for a year and a day; perhaps at this point, Pope and Broome could have claimed it, but within the next year they quarrelled bitterly. The "monument . . . of friendship and justice" Pope proposed making became a statement signed by Broome at the end of the folio *Odyssey*, falsely alleging that he had done but three books, and Fenton but two. There followed a period of suspicion and anger, aggravated by the *Dunciad* and the *Bathos*; by May of 1728, Broome was writing to Fenton:

You ask me if I correspond with Mr. Pope. I do not. He
has used me ill, he is ungrateful. He has now raised a spirit
against him which he will not easily conjure down. He
now keeps his muse as wizards are said to keep tame devils,
only to send them abroad to plague their neighbours. I
often resemble him to an hedgehog; he wraps himself up
in his down, lies snug and warm, and sets his bristles out
against all mankind. Sure he is fond of being hated. I
wonder he is not thrashed: but his littleness is his protection; no man shoots a wren.

(II, 489)

A number of later critics have concurred with Broome's angry
suggestion here, concluding that Pope was indeed "fond of
being hated." A larger statement about Pope's actions when
engaged in controversy, however, all require taking more into
account. When Pope was attacked or imagined that he was, his
responses were complex: he was fascinated, to be sure, by attacks
on himself, and that fascination led to his collection of libels
and his complete and detailed familiarity with the abuse the
Dunces heaped upon him; he resented the attacks, naturally
enough, and his resentment sometimes led to retaliation—overt
(as in the *Dunciad*, although even there the device of initials
was self-protective), partially disownable (as in the notes to the
Dunciad or the examples in the *Bathos*, both of which Pope
habitually attributed to others), or entirely covert (as may have
been the case with the *Grub-Street Journal*); finally, after immediate resentments were over, he was often sorry for his retalia-
tions, and sought to deny responsibility for them.

His behavior with Broome fits this pattern. In an attempt at
reconciliation in 1730, he claimed not to have known that Broome
was quoted and criticized in the *Bathos*:

Indeed, when I saw that passage in the book, I never suspected it to be yours, but imagined I had remembered it in
Cowley, mistaking the one for the other.

(III, 107)

And when Broome's admirable refusal to cooperate with Curll

in denigrating Pope led to a full reconciliation, Pope rectified his errors of the past, admitting quietly in the preface to the *Works* of 1735 that he had done only twelve books of the *Odyssey*, and omitting the reference to Broome in the 1736 *Dunciad*. He reported both services to Broome:

> I had also a mind not to write to you till I could perform my promise of altering the line in the Dunciad. I have prevailed with much ado to cancel an impression of a thousand leaves to insert that alteration, which I have seen done, and I will in a week send you the small edition of my works, where you will find it done, by your carrier, when I find the direction whither to direct the books, which I have mislaid. In the meantime, I enclose the leaf. You will observe I have omitted the note as well as the verse, and again told them I translated but half the Odyssey.
>
> (12 January[1735/36]; IV, 2-3)

In a letter of the same spring, Pope makes a revealing general statement about their reconciliation:

> I truly wish you health and long life, and shall upon all occasions be glad to show you my disposition is friendly to all mankind, and sorry at any time, whether through mistakes or too tender resentments, or too warm passions —which are often nearer akin than undiscerning people imagine—to have wounded another.
>
> (25 March 1736; IV, 5)

This statement is at least as much a part of the truth about Pope as the popular view of the poet as a spiteful and resentful monkey (or hedgehog, as Broome put it). In a way, the word "another" is the crucial one, for when Pope recognized that he had attacked another person, another poet, another vulnerable human being, he was sooner or later genuinely sorry. When attacking the Dunces, Pope seems to have thought of them not as people, but as phenomena or symptoms, forces responsible for the breakdown of what he accurately took to be important values. The fumbling incompetence of their writing enraged him; it was an assault on language, on the kind of lucidity which he saw as an essential quality of civilization. Their continual involvement in party controversies he saw as an abandonment of more fundamental human values. Their usual lack of learning threatened to undermine the assumptions about classical and Christian heritage and world-view which he was anxious to preserve. But when he thought of the Dunces as people, he responded differently: when Dennis was not merely the name printed on the title page of a vituperative pamphlet, but an old, blind man, struggling to stay alive; when "Tibbald" was not merely the prince of textual piddlers but a man who needed the profits of a play to eat; when Broome stood revealed as a man with some natural pride in even his meager talents as a versifier, Pope could no longer remain on the offensive. That his forgiveness almost never took the form of an honest admission that he had attacked and a straightforward apology is regrettable but understandable. It is important to see in Pope's denials of responsibility not merely his inability to admit that he had struck out against these men, but his wish that he had not, that he had conformed to his ideal of equanimity. Pope seems never to have learned that he could not blot out the facts of his past actions as easily as he could blot our lines he wished to reject from his poetry.

Letters to the Scriblerians

On frequent Saturdays in the spring of 1714, in Dr. Arbuthnot's chambers in Queen Anne's palace, Pope joined Arbuthnot, Swift, Parnell, and Gay for the meetings of the Scriblerus Club. After an early plan to publish a burlesque journal to be called *An Account of the Works of the Unlearned*, the Club had settled on the project of writing the memoirs of one Martinus Scriblerus, "a man of capacity enough; that had dipped into every art and science, but injudiciously in each."[20] The actual productions of the Club durings its active life were meager, but Swift's *Gulliver's Travels* (1726), Pope's *Peri Bathos* (1728), and of course the *Memoirs of Martinus Scriblerus* (1741) were among projects begun or inspired during the Club's short life. The death of the Queen on 1 August 1714, which removed Arbuthnot from his comfortable position as her physician and ended Swift's political career, also effectively finished the Scriblerus Club. Parnell died in 1718, but with Arbuthnot, Gay, and Swift, Pope maintained active correspondence of a special kind.

The bond between these men requires some explanation. To be sure, they had some political unity, although Arbuthnot and Swift were far more active Tories than Pope and Gay; later, of course, Gay sought the favors of a far different court, and Pope professed impartiality. There was considerable difference in age: Swift and Arbuthnot were born in 1667, Parnell in 1679, Gay in 1685, Pope in 1688. Pope's Catholicism meant that there was no religious unity. Even in literature, at this point, the five writers had worked in a wide variety of forms and styles. What actually brought them together, I suspect, was not common interests, but common dislikes, often a more effective bond. They despised ignorance, incompetence, and unreason—qualities which they saw all too frequently in the poetry and prose then being published at a dramatically increasing rate. When Martinus Scriblerus was brought out of retirement to write the notes for the *Dunciad*, he explained that the poet

> lived in those days, when (after providence had permitted the Invention of Printing as a scourge for the Sins of the learned) Paper also became so cheap, and printers so numerous, that a deluge of authors cover'd the land: Whereby not only the peace of the honest unwriting subject was daily molested, but unmerciful demands were made of his applause, yea of his money, by such as would neither earn the one, or deserve the other.
>
> (TE V, 49)

Scriblerus is lamenting here a technological and economic development: the easy access to the press newly enjoyed by men with neither education nor gentility; the Scriblerians, who were educated gentlemen, saw the standards they treasured being threatened by the resulting "deluge of authors."

They also shared an antipathy to some authors who were by no means ignorant, such as the "slashing" textual critic Bentley, whose work struck them as pedantic and irrelevant. Finally, as the *Peri Bathos* shows, they were offended by florid writers, who used needlessly complex and obfuscatory rhetoric to hide their obvious and even stupid ideas. Their ideal was a lucid style which would clearly communicate ideas of substance, and the failure of the writers in the daily prints to approach this ideal was, for the Scriblerians, not merely a failure of skill but the betrayal of an essential quality of civilization. Gentlemen were to think and write clearly, absorb the humanism of the classics without undue fuss about iota subscripts, and get the point of a good joke.

There was a holiday spirit about the Scriblerians. All of their projects began as bagatelles; the group doggerel in which they used to invite Oxford to join them is outrageous; their letters to each other are filled with allusions, parodies, and in-jokes. Significantly, they felt free to parody each other and themselves. Here, for example, is a joint letter from Pope and Parnell, sent in 1714 to Charles Ford, who was from time to time associated with the group:

From the Romantic World.
May 19. By Sunshine.

Now is the Evening Sun, declining from the Hemisphere he had painted with Purple, & intermingled Streaks of Gold; rolling his rapid Chariot toward the Surface of the Ocean, whose waves begin to Sparkle at his beams; while the silver-footed Thetis, and all her Water Nymphs around, are preparing their Crystal Palaces for his Reception. It seems to us Mortalls, as if his glorious Orbe were prop'd under the Chin by the Tops of the distant Mountains, whose lovely Azure appears sprinkled with the loose Spangles he shakes from his Illustrious Tresses. The lengthening Shadows extend themselves after him, as if they endeavoured to detain him with their long black Arms; or rather (if we consider their Position is directly contrary) they seem the

Long Arrows of far-darting Phoebus, which he shoots backward, like a Parthian, as he retreats. The Green Mantle of the Earth is trimm'd with Gold, and the Leaves of the Trees turn'd up with the same. But the God, better pleasd with the Water-Tabby of the Ocean, is resolved to enrich it with all his Spangles. & now he sinks beneath our Horizon leaving some illustrated tracks of his former beauty behind him, which as they insensibly wear away are suceeded by the silver gleams of his palefacd delegate. From the dark tops of the hills She emerges into Sight to run her inconstant race over the Azure firmament. The Starrs wait around her as a numerous train of Inamorato's who confess the flames of love at the Sight of the celestiall Goddess; the fixed Starrs seem to stand amazd to behold her, while the Planets dance in her presence & wink upon her as a sett of more familiar gallants. But now while I look behold a new & more melancholy scene, a darkning cloud intercepts her streaming glorys, She goes behind it as a matron mounting up into a Mourning Chariot, & now & then peeps through it as a pretty young widdow looking through her crapes. Darkness has now spread its veil over the variety of this terrestriall creation for which rejoyce ye quarrelling Oyster wenches whom it parts & ye fondling Lovers who are to meet in it but what will ye do ye Mooncalves who have stayd late in company in hopes to go home by the light of this second luminary.

By this time it is evident that we have written the day down & the night allmost through which makes it no feignd excuse but a reall reaaon for us upon the account of want of time to conclude with professing our selves Your Most Affectionate Friends & Humble Servants
ɔqoꝓarnell

By Moonshine. May 19.

(I, 223-4)

In the surviving manuscript of this brilliant letter, the first half is in Pope's hand, the remainder in Parnell's; the homo-

geneity of the style, however, suggests that the text is a coopera-
tive effort.   Having no real news to write, the two travelers
concoct an absurd description of three normal events: sunset,
the rising of the moon, and the moon's being covered by a cloud.
For details of their description, they draw on Pope's own
characteristic descriptive modes.   The bright colors ("Purple,
Gold, Azure, Green") are those Pope had used effectively in
Windsor Forest, most memorably in the lines on the dying
pheasant:

> Ah! what avail his glossie, varying Dyes,
> His Purple Crest, and Scarlet-circled Eyes,
> The vivid Green his shining Plumes unfold;
> His painted Wings, and Breast that flames with Gold?
>
> (115-8)

The epic details ("silver-footed Thetis," "far-darting Phoebus")
reflect Pope's ongoing labor on the *Iliad* translation.   Bits of
conventional "poetic diction" ("lengthening Shadows," "flames
of love," "melancholy scene," "darkning cloud") provide a
context in which the absurdly inappropriate similes ("as if his
glorious Orbe were prop'd under the Chin by the Tops of the
distant Mountain") seem even more absurd.   The insertion into
the self-consciously "poetic" texture of ordinary and deflating
elements of the real world ("a numerous train of Inamorato's,"
"a matron mounting up into a Mourning Chariot," even "quarrelling Oyster wenches") is a technique Pope had perfected in
The Rape of the Lock, which had been published in its expanded
version just two months earlier.   Like that poem, this letter
assumes a reader with the background and skill to appreciate the
many levels of parodic language.[21]   One hopes Mr. Ford was
such a reader.
   Certainly Dr. Arbuthnot was, and Pope sent to him, in the
summer of 1714, a report of a visit he and Parnell made to Swift,
who had exiled himself from London to Letcomb in disgust and
apprehension about the disarray of the Tory government.
Pope's letter, with its coy insinuations and uncertainties, is
meant as a parody of contemporary polical news reporting:

This Day the Envoys deputed to Dean S——— on the Part
of his late Confederates, arrived here, during the Time of
divine Service. They were receivd at the Back Door, and
having paid the usual Compliments on their part, & receivd
the usual Chidings on that of the Dean, were introduced to
his Landlady, & entertaind with a Pint of the Lord Bolingbroke's Florence. The Health of that great Minister was
drank in this Pint, together with the Lord Treasurer's
(whose wine we also wished for). After which were com-
memorated Dr. Arbuthnot, & Mr Lewis, in a sort of Cyder,
plentiful in these parts, & not altogether unknown in the
Taverns of London. There was likewise a Side Board of
Coffee which the Dean roasted with his own hands in an
Engine for the purpose, his Landlady attending, all the
while that office was performing. He talked of Politicks
over Coffee, with the Air & Stile of an old Statesman, who
had known something formerly; but was shamefully ignorant of the Three last weekes. When we mentioned the
wellfare of England he laughd at us, & said Muscovy would
become a flourishing Empire very shortly. He seems to
have wrong notions of the British Court, but gave us a Hint
as if he had a Correspondence with the King of Sweden.

As for the methods of passing his time, I must tell you
one which constantly employs an hour about noone. He
has in his window an Orbicular Glass, which by Contrac-
tion of the Solar Beams into a proper Focus, doth burn,
singe, or speckle white, or printed Paper, in curious little
Holes, or various figures. We chanced to find some Experiments of this nature upon the Votes of the House of Com-
mons. The name of Tho. Hanmer Speaker was much singed,
and that of John Barber entirely burn'd out; There was a
large Gapp at the Edge of the Bill of Schisme, and Several
Specks upon the Proclamation for the Pretender. I doubt
not but these marks of his are mysticall, & that the Figures
he makes this way are a significant Cypher to those who
have the Skill to explain 'em—

That I many not conclude this Letter without Some Verses,
take the following Epigram which Dr Parnelle & I composed

as we rode toward the Dean in the mist of the morning, & is after the Scriblerian Manner. I am with the truest Esteem, Sir—Your most oblig'd Servant

A. Pope.

> How foolish Men on Expeditions goe!
> Unweeting Wantons of their wetting Woe!
> For drizzling Damps descend adown the Plain
> And seem a thicker Dew, or thinner Rain;
> Yet Dew or Rain may wett us to the shift
> We'll not be slow to visit Dr. Swift.

(I, 234-5)

Arbuthnot could be counted on to notice another kind of parody in this skillful letter: he would remember the importance of gaps, specks, and mystical ciphers in Swift's *Tale of a Tub*; he would recognize the pseudo-scientific language ("Engine," "Orbicular Glass," "Experiments") as imitative of Swift's own strictures on the "learned *Aeolists*" or on the quack astrologer Partridge; he would recognize the deadpan manner of the speaker as very like one of Swift's most frequent and effective *personae*. He would realize, in sum, that Pope was describing Swift in Swift's own mode. With the death of the Queen in the next month, the skills of the Scriblerians in interpreting each other's writing began to be put to a more serious purpose: Swift at least had reason to believe that his mail was being routinely opened by the government, and found it necessary to use hints and periphrases when writing to Pope and the others about politics or publication. His letters became what Pope comically alleged his burnings were, "a significant Cypher to those who [had] the Skill to explain 'em."

Even had there been no political danger, I suspect the letters the Scriblerians exchanged would still have been allusive and tricky. Not only did they have fun writing and deciphering such letters, but that sort of correspondence affirmed their conception of themselves as the last true wits, allied against learned pedantry and ignorant pomposity in a valiant but vain cause. They wrote to each other as if they were a saving and scattered remnant, about to be overwhelmed by the forces of unreason, uncertain whether to laugh or cry, taking comfort in a mixture of mockery and despair.   Swift's outrage at man's failings, powerfully expressed in the voyage to the Houyhnhms, is an attitude often present in these letters; it emerges in such wry comments as his admission to Gay, "I now hate all people whom I cannot command" (19 November 1730; III, 151).   Similarly, Pope's terrifying vision of Universal Darkness burying the values he treasured and shared with the others is adumbrated in his letters to them; just three years after the first version of the *Dunciad*, he writes Gay, "the whole age seems resolv'd to justify the Dunciad, and it may stand for a publick Epitaph or monumental Inscription, like that at Thermopylae, on a *whole people perish'd!*" (23 October 1730; III, 142-3).   Gay's final political cynicism, which produced the ill-fated *Polly*, shows in his letters to Swift; speaking of chair-hire, he says, "I persuade myself that it is shilling weather as seldom as possible and have found out that there are few Court visits that are worth a shilling. . . . I envy no man, but have the due contempt for the voluntary slaves of Birth and fortune" (20 March 1730/1; III, 186).   Each man wrote to the others with a special confidence; he knew they would both understand and sympathize.   The many-leveled irony they all enjoyed was not merely a pragmatic defense against prying eyes; it was more importantly a psychological defense against their shared sense of impending doom.   Each recognized aspects of society and human nature as both tragic and funny; irony was the best way to describe these things, and the Scriblerians found in each other willing and sophisticated appreciators of irony.

The shared antipathies, attitudes, and skills I have been enumerating led to a powerful love among these men—and to a very different kind of letter, in which love is communicated without artifice. Here, for example, is Pope, writing to Gay when both Gay and Pope's mother were seriously ill:

> God preserve your life, and restore your health.   I really beg it for my own sake, for I feel I love you more than I thought, in health, tho' I always lov'd you a great deal. If I am so unfortunate as to bury my poor Mother, and yet have the good fortune to have my prayers heard for you,

I hope we may live most of our remaining days together. If, as I believe, the air of a better clime as the Southern Part of *France* may be thought useful for your recovery, thither I would go with you infallibly; and it is very probably we might get the Dean with us, who is in that abandon'd state already in which I shall shortly be, as to other Cares and Duties.

([1728/9]; III, 1)

The plan to move to France was, of course, impossible, as Pope could never have managed a sea voyage. That he had such a dream is indicative of the intensity of his feelings for Gay and Swift, an intensity which manifests itself in sudden break-throughs of radical honesty in his letters. When Swift departed suddenly from Twickenham in 1727, embarrassed by his deaf-ness and giddiness, and determined not to be a burden to Pope, he left an explanatory letter for Pope at Gay's lodgings. Pope replied:

It is a perfect trouble to me to write to you, and your kind letter left for me at Mr. Gay's affected me so much, that it made me like a girl. I can't tell what to say to you; I only feel that I wish you well in every circumstance of life: that 'tis almost as good to be hated, as to be loved, considering the pain it is to minds of any tender turn, to find themselves so utterly impotent to do any good, or give any ease to those who deserve most from us. I would very fain know, as soon as you recover your complaints, or any part of them. Would to God I could ease any of them, or had been able even to have alleviated any! I found I was not, and truly it grieved me. I was sorry to find you could think your self easier in any house than in mine, tho' at the same time I can allow for a tenderness in your way of thinking, even when it seem'd to want that tenderness. I can't explain my meaning, per-haps you know it: But the best way of convincing you of my indulgence, will be, if I live, to visit you in Ireland, and act there as much in my own way as you did here in yours. I will not leave your roof, if I am ill.

(2 October 1727; II, 447-8)

This is naked prose, not at all self-concealing about Pope's being hurt by Swift's departure, firm in its promise of continued affection. Similarly bare in its depression is a letter from Swift to Gay three years later:

> Mr Pope complains of seldom seeing you, but the evil is unavoidable, for different circumstances of life have always separated those whom friendship would joyn, God hath taken care . . . of that to prevent any progress towards real happyness here, which would make life more desirable & death too dreadfull.
>
> (10 November 1730; III, 148)

To see these great comic writers thus confessing to one another, without irony or defense, is to begin to understand the special qualities of the friendship of the Scriblerians. That friendship began as an alliance of young wits against the Dunces; as the young wits grew older, suffered disappointments, and saw the Dunces multiply, the intensity of their friendship deepened.

With John Gay, the improvident poet and flutist who endeared himself to so many of the great men of his time, Pope began a special relationship early. In his first preserved letter to Gay, he solicits aid in patching up a quarrel with Cromwell:

> Our Friend Mr. *Cromwell* too has been silent all this year; I believe he has been displeas'd at some or other of my Freedoms; which I very innocently take, and most with those I think most my friends. But this I know nothing of, perhaps he may have open'd to you: And, if I know you right, you are of a Temper to cement Friendships, and not to divide them. I really much love Mr. *Cromwell*, and have a true affection for your self, which if I had any Interest in the world, or Power with those who have, I shou'd not be long without manifesting to you.
>
> (13 November 1712; I, 153)

Gay was indeed "of a Temper to cement Friendships," and his friendship with Pope was cemented by joint rambles to the country, gallantries with the Maids of Honor, and such coopera-

tive literary efforts as the farce *Three Hours After Marriage*, in
which Arbuthnot also had a hand. The sunlit quality of that
friendship is abundantly demonstrated by the high spirits of a
letter Pope wrote Gay on 23 September 1714, welcoming him
back from Hanover, where he had hurried after Queen Anne's
death in the vain hope of securing a position from the new
monarch:

> The late universal Concern in publick affairs, threw us
> all into a hurry of Spirits; even I who am more a Philosopher
> than to expect any thing from any Reign, was born away
> with the current, and full of the expectation of the Suc-
> cessor: During your Journeys I knew not whither to aim a
> letter after you, that was a sort of shooting flying: add to
> this the demand *Homer* had upon me, to write fifty Verses
> a day, besides learned Notes, all which are at a conclusion
> for this year. Rejoice with me, O my Friend, that my Labour
> is over; come and make merry with me in much Feasting,
> for I to thee and thou to me. We will feed among the Lillies.
> By the Lillies I mean the Ladies, with whom I hope you
> have fed to satiety: Hast thou passed through many Coun-
> tries, and not tasted the delights thereof? Hast thou not
> left of thy Issue in divers Lands, that *German Gays* and
> *Dutch Gays* may arise, to write Pastorals and sing their
> Songs in strange Countries? Are not the *Blouzelinda*'s of
> the *Hague* as charming at the *Rosalinda*'s of *Britain*? or
> have the two great Pastoral Poets of our Nation renounced
> Love at the same time? for *Philips*, immortal *Philips*,
> *Hanover Philips*, hath deserted, yea and in a rustick manner
> kicked his *Rosalind*. — Dr. *Parnelle* and I have been in-
> seperable ever since you went. We are now at the *Bath*,
> where (if you are not, as I heartily hope, better engaged)
> your coming would be the greatest pleasure to us in the
> world. Talk not of Expences: *Homer* shall support his
> Children. I beg a line from you directed to the Posthouse
> in *Bath*. Poor *Parnelle* is in an ill state of health.
> Pardon me if I add a word of advice in the Poetical way.
> Write something on the King, or Prince, or Princess. On
> whatsoever foot you may be with the Court, this can do no

harm — I shall never know where to end, and am confounded
in the many things I have to say to you, tho' they all amount
to this, that I am entirely, as ever, Your, &c.

(I, 254-5)

The succession of topics here shows many of the interests the two
men shared: Biblical parody ("make merry with me in much
Feasting") leads to a comic exegesis ("By the Lillies I mean the
Ladies"), which leads to some envious joking about Gay's amorous tendencies, with an incidental reference to pastoral, which
provides an excuse to introduce a jocular reference to a common
enemy (Ambrose Philips), followed by concern for a common
friend (Parnell), an invitation to join both Pope and Parnell
at Bath, and a bit of tactful practical advice. The conversational
ease of the progression bespeaks the closeness of the correspondents; the only logic of the paragraph is the logic of a loose
train of associations. Pope is really writing here in the way he
often *claimed* to write—tossing off ideas as they occur to him.
But for most of his correspondents, he made such remarks to
hide or downplay the relatively careful ordering of his letters.
With Gay, he could relax and banter.

As he insinuates here in his friendly offer to support Gay at
Bath, Pope's Homeric translations were making him financially independent. Gay never secured such independence. He
hovered about the court, charming everyone, always in hope of
advancement, never finding a permanent place. His hopes of
a high position were dashed when he was offered the post of
Gentleman Usher to the two-year-old Princess Louisa in 1727.
Both Pope and Swift praised Gay for refusing this demeaning
offer, Pope in a strong letter which concludes with a promise
of support:

Dear *Gay*, adieu. I can only add a plain, uncourtly Speech:
While you are no body's Servant, you may be any one's
Friend; and as such I embrace you, in all conditions of life.
While I have a shilling, you shall have six-pence, nay eight
pence, if I can contrive to live upon a groat. I am faithfully
Your, &c.

(16 October 1727; II, 454)

Gay found a wealthier defender. His best work, *The Beggar's
Opera* (1728), was resented by Walpole but appreciated by the
Dutchess of Queensberry. When his next ballad opera, *Polly*,
was forbidden performance, he had it printed, and the Dutchess
of Queensberry organized a subscription for it—an action which
led to her own effective banishment from court. For most of the
rest of his life, Gay lived with the Queensberrys at their estate,
a comfortable situation, but a depressing one for Gay, used to
the glitter and hurry of city and court. His letter to Pope on the
occasion of his removal is a sad one:

> Dear Mr. Pope,—My Melancholy increases, and every Hour
> threatens me with some Return of my Distemper; nay, I
> think I may rather say I have it on me. Not the divine Looks,
> the kind Favours and Expressions of the divine Dutchess,
> who hereafter shall be in Place of a Queen to me, (nay, she
> shall be my Queen) nor the inexpressible Goodness of the
> Duke, can in the least chear me. The Drawing-Room no
> more receives Light from those two Stars. There is now
> what *Milton* says is in Hell, Darkness visible.—O that I had
> never known what a Court was! Dear *Pope*, what a barren
> Soil (to me so) have I been striving to produce something out
> of! Why did I not take your Advice before my writing Fables
> for the Duke, not to write them? Or rather, to write them for
> some young Nobleman? It is my very hard Fate, I must get
> nothing, write for them or against them. I find myself in
> such a strange Confusion and Depression of Spirits, that
> I have not Strength even to make my Will; though I per-
> ceive, by many Warnings, I have no continuing City here.
> I begin to look upon myself as one already dead; and desire,
> my dear Mr. *Pope*, (whom I love as my own Soul) if you
> survive me, (as you certainly will) that you will, if a Stone
> should mark the Place of my Grave, see these Words put
> on it:
>   Life is a Jest, and all Things show it;
>   I thought so once, but now I know it.
> With what more you may think proper.
>   ([February-March 1728/9]; III, 19-20)

Even in his depression, Gay remains a Scriblerian: he is allusive, metaphorical, poetic.   But the allusion to Milton's Hell is far from playful, and the metaphor describing the court as "a barren Soil" is a harsh one; even the couplet for his tombstone, in this context, seems grim.

Gay was not alone in his sadness at the turn of events. Pope's depression over Gay's absence was serious, and never more movingly expressed than in this letter of October 1730:

> It is true that I write to you very seldom, and have no pre-
> tence of writing which satisfies me, because I have nothing
> to say that can give you much pleasure: only merely that I
> am in being, which in truth is of little consequence to one
> from whose conversation I am cut off, by such accidents
> or engagements as separate us. I continue, and ever shall,
> to wish you all good happiness: I wish that some lucky
> event might set you in a state of ease and independency all
> at once! and that I might live to see you as happy, as this
> silly world and fortune can make any one. Are we never to
> live together more, as once we did? I find my life ebbing
> apace, and my affections strengthening as my age encreases:
> not that I am worse, but better, in my health than last winter:
> but my mind finds no amendment nor improvement, nor
> support to lean upon, from those about me: and so I feel
> my self leaving the world, as fast as it leaves me. Com-
> panions I have enough, friends few, and those too warm
> in the concerns of the world for me to bear pace with; or
> else so divided from me, that they are but like the dead
> whose remembrance I hold in honour. Nature, temper, and
> habit, from my youth made me have but one strong desire;
> all other ambitions, my person, education, constitution,
> religion, &c. conspir'd to remove far from me. That desire
> was to fix and preserve a few lasting, dependable friendships:
> and the accidents which have disappointed me in it, have put
> a period to all my aims. So I am sunk into an idleness, which
> makes me neither care nor labour to be notic'd by the rest of
> mankind; I propose no rewards to myself, and why should
> I take any sort of pains? here I sit and sleep, and probably
> here I shall sleep till I sleep for ever, like the old man of

Verona. I hear of what passes in the busy world with so little attention, that I forget it the next day: and as to the learned world, there is nothing passes in it. I have no more to add, but that I am with the same truth as ever, Yours, &c.

(III, 138)

As usual, Pope exaggerates: he was not actually so removed from interest in worldly affairs as this letter claims, nor was his life actually "ebbing apace." Still, the complaint that "my mind finds no amendment nor improvement, nor support to lean upon, from those about me" indicates some of the reasons why Pope missed Gay. His aging mother and his faithful Patty, devoted companions though they were, could not provide all the kinds of companionship Pope needed. Similarly, while Pope's "person, education, constitution, religion, &c." had *not* "conspir'd to remove" all ambitions from him, those aspects of his life had made him vulnerable; he needed "lasting, dependable friend-ships" of the kind that, in 1714, the Scriblerians seemd to provide. The scattering of the group in later years, especially Gay's removal from London, left Pope feeling isolated.

Gay's sudden death in 1732 was a severe blow. In a letter Swift left unopened for five days, suspecting that it held bad news, Pope's grief is acute:

> Good God! how often are we to die before we go quite off this stage? in every friend we lose a part of ourselves, and the best part. God keep those we have left! few are worth praying for, and one's self the least of all.
>
> I shall never see you now I believe; one of your principal Calls to England is at an end. Indeed he was the most amiable by far, his qualities were the gentlest, but I love you as well and as firmly.
>
> (5 December 1732; III, 335)

In the next April, in another letter to Swift, the grief is more quietly expressed, but no less moving:

> You say truly, that death is only terrible to us as it separates us from those we love, but I really think those have the worst

of it who are left by us, if we are true friends. I have felt more
(I fancy) in the loss of poor Mr. Gay, than I shall suffer in
the thought of going away myself into a state that can feel
none of this sort of losses. I wish'd vehemently to have seen
him in a condition of living independent, and to have lived
in perfect indolence the rest of our days together, the two
most idle, most innocent, undesigning Poets of our age.
I now as vehemently wish, you and I might walk into the
grave together, by as slow steps as you please, but content-
edly and chearfully: Whether that ever can be, or in what
country, I know no more, than into what country we shall
walk out of the grave.

(III, 365)

The renewed wish for Swift's companionship, which leads in
the end of this letter to a request that Swift come to England so
that "we may go all together into France," indicates how isolated Pope felt by Gay's death. That the fantasy about going
to France had originally included Gay, whether or not Pope
subconsciously remembered the earlier letter, increases the pathos
of its introduction here.

The attending physician during Gay's last illness was, naturally enough, Dr. Arbuthnot. His own death two years later was
another severe blow for Pope, who had lost his mother in the
interim. During Arbuthnot's long and painful final illness, Pope
wrote of him to Swift:

He himself, poor man, is much broke, tho' not worse than
for these two last months he has been. He took extremely
kindly your letter. I wish to God we could once meet again,
before that separation, which yet I would be glad to believe
shall re-unite us: But he who made us, not for ours but his
purposes, knows whether it be for the better or the worse,
that the affections of this life should, or should not continue
into the other: and doubtless it is as it should be. Yet I am
sure that while I am here, and the thing that I am, I shall
be imperfect without the communication of such friends
as you; you are to me like a limb lost, and buried in another

country; tho' we seem quite divided, every accident makes
me feel you were once a part of me.

(19 December 1734; III, 444-5)

Pope's physical image of his friends as amputated parts of his
body is an expressive one; Swift was to use an even starker image
when Arbuthnot died:

The Death of Mr. Gay & the Doctor hath been terrible
wounds near my heart.

(12 May 1735; V, 14)

Pope's devotion for Arbuthnot, beginning with their literary
collaborations during the days of the club, lasted unbroken until
the doctor's death. Arbuthnot was a dependable ally and defender. On one occasion, he is thought to have caned James
Moore-Smythe for a libel on Pope.[22] As a physician, he was
acutely aware of how devastating a physical attack would be
for Pope, and concerned that he protect himself. In his last
letter to Pope, he made this a formal request:

As for you, my good Friend, I think since our first acquaintance there has not been any of those little Suspicions
or Jealousies that often affect the sincerest Friendships; I
am sure not on my side. I must be so sincere as to own, that
tho' I could not help valuing you for those Talents which
the World prizes, yet they were not the Foundation of my
Friendship: They were quite of another sort; nor shall I at
present offend you by enumerating them: And I make it my
Last Request, that you continue that noble *Disdain* and
Abhorrence of Vice, which you seem naturally endu'd with,
but still with a due regard to your own Safety; and study
more to reform than chastise, tho' the one often cannot be
effected without the other.

(17 July 1734; III, 416-17)

Pope's reply took three forms. On 2 August [1734] he responded
briefly:

I thank you dear Sir for making That your Request to
me which I make my Pride, nay my Duty; "that I should
continue my Disdain & abhorrence of Vice, & manifest it
still in my writings." I would indeed do it with more restrictions, & less personally; it is more agreeable to my nature,
which those who know it not are greatly mistaken in: But
General Satire in Times of General Vice has no force, & is
no Punishment: People have ceas'd to be ashamed of it when
so many are joind with them; and tis only by hunting One
or two from the Herd that any Examples can be made. If
a man writ all his Life against the Collective Body of the
Banditti, or against Lawyers, would it do the least Good,
or lessen the Body? But if some are hung up, or pilloryed,
it may prevent others. And in my low Station, with no
other Power than this, I hope to deter, if not to reform.
                                                              (III, 423)

But at some later point, perhaps after Arbuthnot's death, the
issue of how he ought to satirize so fascinated him that he
expanded these ideas into a long and eloquent letter, which he
published in the 1737 *Letters* under the date of 26 July 1734.
In that version, the expanded paragraph reads:

What you recommend to me with the solemnity of a Last
Request, shall have its due weight with me. That disdain
and indignation against Vice, is (I thank God) the only
disdain and indignation I have: It is sincere, and it will be
a lasting one. But sure it is as impossible to have a just
abhorrence of Vice, without hating the Vicious, as to bear
a true love for Virtue, without loving the Good. To reform and not to chastise, I am afraid is impossible, and
that the best Precepts, as well as the best Laws, would prove
of small use, if there were no Examples to inforce them.
To attack Vices in the abstract, without touching Persons,
may be safe fighting indeed, but it is fighting with Shadows.
General propositions are obscure, misty, and uncertain,
compar'd with plain, full, and home examples: Precepts only
apply to our Reason, which in most men is but weak: Examples are pictures, and strike the Senses, nay raise the

Passions, and call in those (the strongest and most general of all motives) to the aid of reformation. Every vicious man makes the case his own; and that is the only way by which such men can be affected, must less deterr'd. So that to chastise is to reform. The only sign by which I found my writings ever did any good, or had any weight, has been that they rais'd the anger of bad men. And my greatest comfort, and encouragement to proceed, has been to see, that those who have no shame, and no fear, of any thing else, have appear'd touch'd by my Satires.

(III, 419)

Pope probably meant no disservice to Arbuthnot by publishing this improved version. To be sure, it is a fabrication, but he probably considered it something of an honor to his dead friend to print as a letter to him this closely reasoned, carefully written essay on the original theme. He probably did not see this publication as particularly different in purpose or effect from the *Epistle to Dr. Arbuthnot*, published before his friend's death, which raises many of the same issues. In fact, one part of the Advertisement for the poem may have reminded Arbuthnot of his request:

> *Many will know their own Pictures in it, there being not a Circumstance but what is true; but I have, for the most part spar'd their* Names, *and they may escape being laugh'd at, if they please.*
> *I would have some of them know, it was owing to the Request of the learned and candid Friend to whom it is inscribed, that I make not as free use of theirs as they have done of mine. However I shall have this Advantage, and Honour, on my side, that whereas by their proceeding, any Abuse may be directed at any man, no Injury can possibly be done by mine, since a Nameless Character can never be found out, but by its* Truth *and* Likeness.

(TE IV, 95)

With typical precision, Pope selected for this passage those qualities in Arbuthnot which were fundamental to their relationship, his learning and candor. Arbuthnot's wide-ranging learning, both scientific and literary, made him a fascinating companion and an astute and receptive reader. Swift's joking remark to Gay at the time of the success of the *Beggar's Opera* ("How is the Doctor, does he not chide that you never called upon him for hints")[23] is one of many references which indicate Arbuthnot's continuing interest in reading and "improving" the productions of his old friends. Pope found him a valuable reader, not only because he was skillful, but because he was as candid in his literary criticism as in his advice to his patient about his physical health.

CHAPTER 5

With Great Unreservedness: Letters to Swift

JONATHAN SWIFT FELT FREE to be at least as candid as the other Scriblerians in his remarks about Pope's works. When the first volume of the *Iliad* came out, he commented:

> I borrow'd your Homer from the Bishop (mine is not yet landed) and read it out in two evenings. If it pleases others as well as me, you have got your end in profit and reputation: Yet I am angry at some bad Rhymes and Triplets, and pray in your next do not let me have so many unjustifiable Rhymes to *war* and *gods*. I tell you all the faults I know, only in one or two places you are a little obscure; but I expected you to be so in one or two and twenty. I have heard no soul talk of it here, for indeed it is not come over; nor do we very much abound in judges, at least I have not the honour to be acquainted with them. Your Notes are perfectly good, and so are your Preface and Essay.
>
> (28 June 1715; I, 301)

Swift's complaint about the rhymes was justified; in the first book alone, Pope rhymes "war" with "spare" and "dare," and "god(s)" with "bestow'd," "Abodes," and "ow'd."[1] The important point about the complaint, however, is the confidence with which Swift could make it. He wrote as one successful professional writer addressing another; he wrote as a man twenty-one years Pope's senior, who had thrown his reputation and power behind the young poet's career; and he wrote in the full confidence that his bluntness would neither threaten nor offend

Pope, who was so far from being offended that he himself published the letter.

Everything I have said about the closeness of the Scriblerians,
their sense of alliance against the forces of unreason, applies
doubly to the relationship between Pope and Swift. In 1723,
lamenting his separation from the whole group, Swift wrote
to Pope:

> I have often endeavoured to establish a Friendship among
> all Men of Genius, and would fain have it done. they are
> seldom above three or four Cotemporaries and if they could
> be united would drive the world before them.
>
> (II, 199)

At this point, Swift's Irish "exile" was already eight years old.
It was beginning to appear unlikely that political realities
would change in a way which would allow him to return to
England and the daily intercourse with his fellow writers (especially Pope) which would enable them, in his oddly martial
phrase, to "drive the world before them." Like a sulking Achilles,
he itched for action. His frustration took the form of the conviction that he and Pope united could take on and defeat the
world—a sentiment not unlike the violent wish in which Achilles
expresses his love for Patroclus:

> Oh! would to all th'immortal Pow'rs above,
> *Apollo, Pallas*, and the almighty *Jove*!
> That not one *Trojan* might be left alive,
> And not a *Greek* of all the Race survive;
> Might only we the vast Destruction shun,
> And only we destroy th'accursed Town!
>
> (Pope's *Iliad*, XVI, 122-7)

In commenting on this passage, Pope takes a sympathetic view
of the psychological state which drives Achilles to his outburst:

> What a little qualifies this bloody Wish, is that we may

suppose it spoken with great Unreservedness, as in secret,
and between Friends.

(TE VIII, 241)

Pope's understanding of Achilles may well have been enriched
by the "unreservedness" which was a part of his relationship with
Swift. To be sure, they shared a number of attitudes, and a professional commitment to writing well. But the forces dividing
them—age, religion, and the Irish Sea—were at least as powerful. Yet they carried on a correspondence for twenty-seven years,
from the death of Queen Anne to Swift's living death, during
a separation broken only by Swift's visits to England in the
summers of 1726 and 1727. They were both proud men, and
they disagreed about issues as trivial as grammar and as important as the nature of man. That they nonetheless remained
friends and correspondents may partly be a result of the "unreservedness" with which each felt he could address the other.
Rather than pretend that they had no differences, they wrote
about the differences with all their skill, and the delight each
man took in the other's skill made a continuing relationship
possible despite the disagreements. Throughout the long years
of their correspondence, despite frequent protests by each man
that he "never leaned on his elbow" to consider his phrasing,
both of them evidently worked at writing well, with considerable success. Each man considered the other a particularly
well-equipped reader, to whom he wished to give the pleasure
of his best wit; and each man enjoyed the chance to flex his
own muscles as a maker of phrases and metaphors.[2] Nor was
possible publication the only impetus: one of Pope's best and
most carefully constructed letters to Swift, the brilliantly comic
refusal to accept twenty guineas to change his faith (8 December 1713; I, 198), could never have been published while he was
alive. Yet Pope, who probably already had "schemes of Epistolary fame" at this early date, and who must have known that
the wit of this particular letter was not to be for public consump-
tion, was satisfied with the letter only when he had brought it
to polished perfection.

The letter links ironic statements in a pseudo-logical progression sure to delight Swift, and very much in the Scriblerian manner. Pope proposes that he organize "a Change of my Faith by Subscription" and proceeds to list others he would like saved as well, with estimates of the cost. At the end of the list comes Swift himself:

> There is but One more, whose Salvation I insist upon, and then I have done: But indeed it may prove of so much greater Charge than all the rest, that I will only lay the Case before you, and the Ministry, and leave to their Prudence and Generosity what Summ they shall think fit to bestow upon it.
>
> The Person I mean is Dr Swift, a dignified Clergyman, but One who, by his own Confession, has composed more Libels than Sermons. If it be true, what I have heard often affirmed by innocent People, that too much Wit is dangerous to Salvation, this unfortunate Gentleman must certainly be damned to all Eternity. But I hope his long Experience in the World, and frequent Conversation with Great Men, will cause him (as it has some others) to have less and less Wit every Day. Be it as it will, I should not think my own Soul deserved to be saved, if I did not endeavour to save his, for I have all the Obligations in Nature to him. He has brought me into better Company than I cared for, made me merrier, when I was sick, than I had a Mind to be, put me upon making Poems on Purpose that he might alter them, &c. I once thought I could never have discharged my Debt to his Kindness, but have lately been informed, to my unspeakable Comfort, that I have more than paid it all. For Monsieur de Montayne has assured me, that the Person, who receives a Benefit, obliges the Giver; for since the chief Endeavour of one Friend is to do Good to the other, He, who administers both the Matter, and Occasion, is the Man that is Liberal. At this Rate it is impossible Dr Swift should be ever out of my Debt, as matters stand already; and for the future he may expect daily more Obligations

from His most Faithful, Affectionate, Humble Servant
A. Pope.

(I, 200-201)

Timing his surprises skillfully, Pope delays introducing Swift's
name as long as he can, and effects a curiously comic division in
his reader by first proposing to "lay the Case before you," and
then discussing the person involved in the third person, as "Dr
Swift, a dignified Clergyman." He bases a series of arguments
on a fraudulent hypothesis ("that too much Wit is dangerous
to Salvation"), which he deftly discredits by noting its acceptance
by "innocent people." From the hypothesis, it follows that
Pope should hope that Swift will have "less and less Wit every
Day." The way to become less witty is, of course, "frequent
Conversation with Great Men."

By now, the series of ironies is almost hopelessly tangled.
Swift ("you") is supposed to be considering the case of an
"unfortunate Gentleman" (named Swift) who is in danger of
being damned for too much wit. His friend Pope, taking comfort in those aspects of Swift's career which are likely to deprive
him of wit, explains his zeal to have Swift saved. And here a
curious thing happens: in the middle of this tangle, Pope makes
a series of evidently sincere statements about Swift's kindness to
him. To be sure, they are made in the third person, surrounded
by ironies, and even interrupted by a little joke about Swift's
fondness for correcting poems, but they are a true record nonetheless of what Pope appreciated about his older friend. Swift
had introduced Pope to people who had helped him, visited
him during his illnesses, and suggested subjects for poetry;
Pope was less embarrassed about recording his real gratitude
for those friendly acts in this comic mode than in a straightforward and effusive epistle of thanks, and perhaps Swift was
less embarrassed about receiving thanks in such a mode.

After the list of favors, without even a full stop, the irony
continues, with Montaigne's maxim about benefits used to
allege that it is Swift who is actually in Pope's debt, not Pope
in Swift's—a final reversal which leads gracefully to the close.

It is difficult to know how serious Swift's financial offer to Pope was, but Pope's choice of the comic mode as a way to answer the offer made it possible for him to refuse the offer with wonderful gracefulness, while simultaneously assuring Swift of his continuing friendship.   The prose has the brilliance of Mozart's music; the effortlessness with which it reads, the rapid and fluent motion, so impress the reader that he fails to notice, at least as first, the economy and skill with which it is constructed and the serious purposes which it serves.

Something about writing to Swift called forth this kind of prose from Pope.   There are set-pieces in these letters in which Pope's prose makes its closest approach to his poetry.   Consider, for example, the couplet-like rhetoric of this passage:

> I can't help thinking, (when I consider the whole, short List of our friends) that none of 'em except you and I are qualify'd for the Mountains of Wales.   The Dr. goes to Cards, Gay to Court; one loses money, one loses his time. Another of our friends labours to be unambitious, but he labours in an unwilling soil.   One Lady you like has too much of France to be fit for Wales: Another is too much a subject to Princes and Potentates, to relish that wild Taste of liberty and poverty.   Mr. Congreve is too sick to bear a thin air; and she that leads him too rich to enjoy any thing. Lord Peterborow can go to any climate, but never stay in any.   Lord Bathurst is too great an husbandman to like barren hills, except they are his own to improve.   Mr. Bethel indeed is too good and too honest to live in the world, but yet 'tis fit, for its example, he should.   We are left to ourselves in my opinion, and may live where we please, in Wales, Dublin, or Bermudas.
>
> (3 September 1726; II, 395)

Many of the characteristic techniques of Pope's couplets are present here.   Verbs are forced to do double duty by zeugma or by repetition, with comic results.   When "loses," for example, can describe both Arbuthnot's gambling misfortunes and Gay's loss of his whole life in hopeless place-seeking, the disparity between the seriousness of the losses involved is sharpened by the use of one common word. Such famous lines as

. . . . Or stain her Honour, or her new Brocade
(*Rape of the Lock*, II, 107)

depend upon the same technique. In fact, one can easily imagine this sentence of the letter, with a minimum of alteration, becoming a couplet:

The Doctor goes to Cards, Gay goes to Court;
One loses Time, one Money at his sport.

Or consider the timing of the next sentence, doubtless about Bolingbroke, in which the sudden concreteness of the word "soil," coming at the very end, turns statement into metaphor: suddenly Bolingbroke's "labour" is made immediate as a kind of plowing, with the added irony that the soil he cannot work into a state of unambition is himself.[3] Each of the remaining "characters" is described by means of some neat rhetorical twist, some balancing antithesis: to describe Lady Bolingbroke, Pope opposes France and Wales; for Mrs. Howard (mistress of the Prince of Wales), "Princes and Potentates" outweigh "liberty and poverty"; Congreve is "too sick," but his lady friend, the Duchess of Marlborough, is "too rich"; Peterborow can go, but cannot stay. Out of just such antitheses, Pope made his couplets; the more complicated twists in the descriptions of Bathurst and Bethel also have parallels in the poetry. The most impressive thing about the paragraph as a whole is its economy: by declaring the reasons their various friends are unfit for Wales, Pope gives Swift pertinent news about them, with a thriftiness about words analogous to that thrift Swift praised in his poetry:

In POPE I cannot read a Line,
But with a sigh, I wish it mine:
When he can in one Couplet fix

More sense than I can do in Six:
It gives me such a jealous Fit,
I cry, Pox take him, and his Wit.[4]

Perhaps Swift was occasionally jealous of Pope's poetic wit, but he had no reason to be jealous of Pope's letter-writing skill; he was a brilliant letter writer himself. The letter gave Swift the opportunity to exercise his skill at shifting *personae*, over-throwing logic, and turning his ready wit upon his correspondents and himself. One marvelous early example is this paragraph, ostensibly twitting Pope on his pretensions of political neutrality, his religion, and his failure to write effusive dedications:

> I had the favour of yours by Mr. F[ord] of whom, before any other question relating to your health, or fortunes, or success as a poet, I enquired your principles in the common form, "Is he a Whig or a Tory?" I am sorry to find they are not so well tally'd to the present juncture as I could wish. I always thought the terms of *Facto* and *Jure* had been introduced by the Poets, and that Possession of any sort in Kings was held an unexceptionable title in the courts of Parnassus. If you do not grow a perfect good subject in all its present latitudes, I shall conclude you are become rich, and able to live without dedications to men in power, where-by one great inconvenience will follow, that you and the world and posterity will be utterly ignorant of their virtues. For, either your brethren have miserably deceiv'd us these hundred years past, or Power confers virtue, as naturally as five of your Popish sacraments do Grace.—You sleep less and drink more.—But your master Horace was *Vini somnique benignus*: and as I take it, both are proper for your trade. As to mine, there are a thousand poetical texts to confirm the one; and as to the other, I know it was an-ciently the custom to sleep in temples for those who would consult the Oracles, "Who dictates to me slumbring", &c.
>   (30 August 1716; I, 358)

In the opening of this paragraph Swift pretends to be a political zealot, more interested in Pope's party alignment than in his "health, or fortunes, or success as a poet." This speaker melts into one so (falsely) naive as to believe "that Possession of any sort in Kings was held an unexceptionable title in the courts of Parnassus," i.e., that all poets (including Pope) necessarily praise all kings (including that dullard George I). Pope's failure to flatter the King and Court, according to this logic, can only be taken as proof of wealth, so (alas) posterity will lack a description of the virtues of these fine men. The next sentence seems to glance disparagingly at Pope's Catholicism, suggesting that the efficacy of its sacraments is analogous to the truth of the notion that "Power confers virtue," a notion thoroughly discredited by what has come before. But these clauses, after all, are part of a mutually exclusive proposition: "Either your brethren [the poets] have miserably deceiv'd us these hundred years past, or . . . " In fact, as Pope would realize, the final implication of the paragraph is a compliment: Swift is praising Pope for his refusal to flatter. Pope is not like the poets of the preceding century, including Dryden, who rushed to celebrate each succeeding regime. His commitments are actually more lasting, even brave, and he has shown courage in such actions as complimenting the fallen Bolingbroke in the Preface to his *Iliad*.[5] Finally, Swift seizes on a remark in Pope's last letter ("I learn to sleep less and drink more, whenever you are named among us")[6] in order to shift to yet another of his favorite *personae*, the pedant. He quotes Horace and Milton and alludes to mythological precedent, all in support of the notion that wine and sleep are appropriate for both poets and clergymen. Again, behind all the disguises, the final import is far from critical: Swift implies that wine and sleep are useful in both men's trades, and that poetry is as sacred a calling as the cloth.

For both men, the habit of wit extended to details. In a letter of introduction for an aspiring lady poet named Mrs. Sykins, Swift playfully apologizes for sending her to Pope:

I give her this Passport to have the honor and happyness

of seeing you, because She hath already seen the Estrich, which is the only rarity at present in this Town, and her ambition is to boast of having been well received by you, upon her return; and I do not see how you can well refuse to gratify her, for if a Christian will be an Estrich, and the only Estrich in a Kingdom he must suffer himself to be seen, and what is worse, without money.

(6 February 1729/30; III, 89-90)

Pope, having missed the lady's visit, replied wryly, "She has seen no greater monster, yet, than the Estrich" ([9 April 1730]; III, 101). Even the tiniest phrase could contain a private joke. Asking Swift to subscribe to Samuel Wesley the Elder's commentary on Job, Pope writes:

Lord Bolingbroke is a favourer of it; and allows you to do your best to serve an old Tory, and a sufferer for the Church of England, tho' you are a Whig, as I am.

([4 March 1729/30]; III, 95)

The jest, of course, is that Pope was as much a Whig as Swift, i.e., not at all.

In such letters, Pope and Swift use their characteristic skills not only to delight each other, but to celebrate their affection for one another. There are also many moments in the correspondence when that affection is celebrated without flashiness or disguise. When Pope was ill during one of Swift's visits, Swift's concern was immediate and serious:

My Lord Peterborow spoiled every body's dinner, but especially mine, with telling us that you were detained by sickness. Pray let me have three lines under any hand or pothook that will give me a better account of your health; which concerns me more than others, because I love and esteem you for reasons that most others have little to do with, and would be the same although you had never touched a pen, further than with writing to me.

(4 [August] 1726; II, 384)

Later, having returned to Dublin, Swift wrote again of his concern for Pope's health:

> I must needs confess, that the pleasure I take in thinking of
> you is very much lessened by the pain I am in about your
> health: You pay dearly for the great talents God hath given
> you; and for the consequences of them in the esteem and
> distinction you receive from mankind, unless you can provide
> a tolerable stock of health; in which pursuit I cannot much
> commend your conduct, but rather entreat you would mend
> it by following the advice of my Lord Bolingbroke and
> your other Physicians.
>
>   ([August 1726]; II, 393)

And in 1737, when they had not seen each other once in ten years,
Pope still hoped Swift might be persuaded to come over to
England:

> Would to God you would come over with Lord Orrery,
> whose care of you in the voyage I could so certainly depend
> on; and bring with you your old housekeeper and two or
> three servants. I have room for all, a heart for all, and
> (think what you will) a fortune for all. We could, were
> we together, contrive to make our last days easy, and leave
> some sort of Monument, what Friends two Wits could be
> in spite of all the fools of the world. Adieu.
>
>   (23 March 1736/7; IV, 63-4)[7]

Pope's contention that he and Swift could show, if they lived
and worked together, "what Friends two Wits could be" is
as touching as it is unrealistic. In fact, on his second visit, in 1727,
Swift was embarrassed by his own recurring giddiness and
deafness, and complained to Sheridan, before departing abruptly
from Twickenham, that Pope was "too sickly and complai-
sant" (II, 442). Later, in a kind letter explaining his departure
to Pope, he explained that "Two sick friends never did well
together" (II, 452), and he was no doubt correct. Still, the
concern each man felt about the other's health was based on

the cruel reality that illness, given the state of medical practice, could arrive one day and produce death the next.

Had the two wits lived together for any length of time, their physical ailments might not have been the only factors making their relationship difficult. In fact, there were so many differences between the two in personality and philosophy that their geographical separation may have been an important factor in their managing to remain friends. These differences emerge in the correspondence, but usually in far from explicit ways. Typically, when Swift wishes to disagree with Pope, he employs a kind of peevish undertone, which Pope affects to disregard, while often answering in a similarly disguised way.

Disguise and innuendo were habits Swift and Pope had learned not merely as an exercise of wit, but because of the necessity for self-protection from unintended readers. Swift often ends letters with this sort of substitute for a signature:

> I have an ill name and therefore shall not Subscribe it. but you will guess it comes from one who esteems and loves you about half as much as you deserve. I mean as much as he can
>
> (29 September 1725; II, 327)[8]

Swift means by this circumlocution that he wishes to conceal himself from the post office clerks, agents of a hostile ministry, who were notorious for opening mail. Since they could not always send letters by private hands, Swift and Pope became highly skilled at hinting to each other when a direct statement of facts might have played into the hands of their literary or political enemies. When Pope's parody of the first Psalm was surreptitiously published, for example, he wrote about it to Swift in carefully ambiguous words:

> I have begun to take a pique at the Psalms of David (if the wicked may be credited, who have printed a scandalous one in my name.)
>
> (20 June 1716; I, 342)

At the close of the letter, he added another signal sure to alert Swift to the deceptive quality of what had come before:

> Truth is a kind of contraband commodity which I would not venture to export, and therefore the only thing tending that dangerous way which I shall say, is, that I am and always will be with the utmost sincerity, Yours, &c.

Swift recognized the message as the admission of authorship it was designed to be, and answered in a similarly slippery way:

> I never saw the thing you mention as falsely imputed to you; but I think the frolicks of merry hours, even when we are guilty, should not be left to the mercy of our best friends, till Curl and his resemblers are hanged.
>
> (30 August 1716; I, 359)

Having learned by necessity to communicate by implication, Swift and Pope found many uses for such writing. Not only did they need to hide potentially dangerous information from the prying eyes of Walpole's agents, but they also wished to have a private level of communication even in those letters they knew would be showed about. Swift, who often included messages for Gay and Bolingbroke in his letters to Pope, might nonetheless want to include private communications; given Pope's skill as a reader, he knew he could accomplish this by undertone, exaggeration, periphrasis, or irony.[9]

Certainly these forms of indirection were Swift's habitual modes for expressing his disagreements with Pope. One continuing disagreement was about outspoken political comment: Swift, whose hopes had been dashed by the fall of the Tories and the death of the queen (and later by Walpole's long tenure), favored a stance of open contempt for the Hanoverians and the Whigs; but Pope, always conciliatory, was reluctant to give direct offense to friends who did enjoy the favor of the regime, such as Burlington and Fortescue. Swift's way of dealing with this disagreement was to suggest, instead, a joint posture of defiance:

If you will give me leave to join us, is not your life and mine
a state of power, and dependance a state of slavery? We
care not three pence whether a Prince or Minister will see
us or no: We are not afraid of having ill offices done us,
nor are at the trouble of guarding our words for fear of
giving offence.

(5 December 1726; II, 419)

The confidence of the first person plurals (*"We* care not . . .
We are not afraid") is a trifle undercut by the first phrase (*"If*
you will give me leave to join us"), but Swift's purpose is clear:
he suggests that Pope should become more like him, less conscious of the dangers of opposing the government. Pope's
next letter, however, picks up the theme of togetherness by
talking of the most recent volume of their *Miscellanies*:

Our Miscellany is now quite printed. I am prodigiously
pleas'd with this joint-volume, in which methinks we
look like friends, side by side, serious and merry by turns,
conversing interchangeably, and walking down hand in
hand to posterity; not in the stiff forms of learned Authors,
flattering each other, and setting the rest of mankind at
nought: but in a free, un-important, natural, easy manner;
diverting others just as we diverted outselves.

([17 February 1726/7]; II, 426)

Pope's assertion that the two friends are not like "learned
Authors . . . setting the rest of mankind at nought" seems
intended as an answer to Swift, Pope implying that a benevolent
attitude toward mankind, even (perhaps) toward those in power,
is what the "serious and merry" authors of the *Miscellanies*
ought to share. Later in the same letter, he replies a little more
directly:

You see how much like a Poet I write, and yet if you were
with us, you'd be deep in Politicks. People are very warm,
and very angry, very little to the purpose, but therefore the
more warm and the more angry: *Non nostrum est, Tantas
componere lites.* I stay at Twitnam, without so much as

reading news-papers, votes, or any other paltry pamphlets: Mr. Stopford will carry you a whole parcel of them, which are sent for your diversion, but not imitation.

Again, implications are probably important, and this passage may imply that Swift should *not* be "deep in Politicks." Being "very warm, and very angry" (a habitual stance for Swift) is called "very little to the purpose." In that case, the Latin tag, adapted from Virgil's third Eclogue, has a double significance. In the original it is spoken by Palaemon, who is refusing to make a judgment, declaring the singing march between Menalcas and Damoetas a tie; by applying the refusal to judge to the political situation, Pope is perhaps indicating that there is as little difference between factions as between pastoral singers.[10] Perhaps it is also significant that he chooses a tag with a first person plural pronoun, literally translated: "It is not *our* task to settle such controversies." We, the poets, Pope implies, can ignore these things quietly; we need not trumpet our contempt. Then, with a broader humor, he cautions Swift against imitating political pamphlets.

However, Swift proceeded to publish, in 1730, *A Libel on D[octor] D[elany]*, in which he praised Pope for detesting the court:

> Hail! happy *Pope*, whose gen'rous Mind,
> Detesting all the Statesmen kind,
> Contemning *Courts*, at *Courts* unseen,
> Refus'd the Visits of a Queen;
> A Soul with ev'ry Virtue fraught
> By *Sages, Priests*, or *Poets* taught;
> Whose filial Piety excels
> Whatever *Grecian* Story tells:
> A Genius for all Stations fit,
> Whose *meanest Talent* is his *Wit*:
> His Heart too Great, though Fortune little,
> To lick a *Rascal Statesman's* Spittle.
> Appealing to the Nation's Taste,
> Above the Reach of Want is plac't:
> By *Homer* dead was taught to thrive,

Which *Homer* never cou'd alive.
And, sits aloft on *Pindus* Head,
Despising *Slaves* that *cringe* for Bread.[11]

Pope quickly wrote to Fortescue:

> I've had another Vexation, from the sight of a paper of
> verses said to be Dr Swift's, which has done more by prais-
> ing me than all the Libels could by abusing me, Seriously
> troubled me: As indeed one indiscreet Friend can at any time
> hurt a man more than a hundred silly Enemies. I can hardly
> bring myself to think it His, or that it is possible his Head
> should be so giddy.
>
> (20 February [1729/30]; III, 91)

Probably he knew perfectly well that the poem was Swift's, but
suggesting that it might be spurious suited his purposes in
affecting dismay over its contents. In fact, in order to sharpen
his reprimand when he complained to Swift at the same time,
he pretended again to believe that the *Libel* was not Swift's

> We have here some verses in your name, which I am angry
> at. Sure you wou'd not use me so ill as to flatter me? I
> therefore think it is some other weak Irishman.
>
> ([4 March 1729/30]; III, 95)

Actually, as Pope knew (and was perhaps indicating to Swift) it
was easier to be bold in Dublin than in London, particularly when
many of your best friends were involved in the regime. Swift,
isolated and not a little out of touch, was still fighting battles
which were long over, and in the process making it harder for
Pope to survive to fight new battles—as he was already doing
in his more subtle ways with the Horatian series he was then
beginning. Two years later, when Pope chose, for the same
reasons, to omit the poem from a volume of the *Miscellanies*,
the two friends again corresponded about it, Pope affecting pain
at the necessity of leaving it out, Swift twitting Pope on his
"charity," with the implication that it was actually cowardice.[12]
    This minor disagreement about politics, playfully dramatized

in the letters, is indicative of some of the larger differences between Pope and Swift, differences most dramatically apparent in their famous exchange about the nature of man, just before the publication of *Gulliver's Travels*. Swift told Pope that he was seeking, in that work, to assert the validity of one definition of man against another:

> I have ever hated all Nations professions and Communityes and all my love is towards individualls for instance I hate the tribe of Lawyers, but I love Councellor such a one, Judge such a one for so with Physicians (I will not Speak of my own Trade) Soldiers, English, Scotch, French; and the rest but principally I hate and detest that animal called man, although I hartily love John, Peter, Thomas and so forth. this is the system upon which I have governed my self many years (but do not tell) and so I shall go on till I have done with them I have got Materials Towards a Treatis proving the falsity of that Definition *animal rationale*; and to show it should be only *rationis capax*. Upon this great foundation of Misanthropy (though not Timons manner) The whole building of my Travells is erected: And I never will have peace of mind till all honest men are of my Opinion: by Consequence you are to embrace it immediately and procure that all who deserve my Esteem may do so too The matter is so clear that it will admit little dispute. nay I will hold a hundred pounds that you and I agree in the Point.
> (29 September 1725; II, 325)

But was Pope supposed to believe Swift's description of his most brilliant fiction as "Materials Towards a Treatis"? Was he supposed to believe that Swift's method was a logical proof, built "Upon this great foundation of Misanthropy"? The real difficulty in interpreting such letters is knowing to what degree energetic role-playing casts suspicion upon what is asserted. For example, it is clear than in this letter Swift *plays* the enthu-siast, the man who "will never have peace of mind till all honest men are of my Opinion," who says peremptorily to his friend, "you are to embrace it immediately and procure that all who deserve my Esteem may do so too."[13] It seems reasonable to conclude that by playing this role he is poking fun at the misanthropy he professes earlier on. If so, Pope (and we) might wonder how seriously to take the proposed definition of man as "only *rationis capax*," since it is argued for in such a humorously overwrought way.

But *Gulliver's Travels* is also humorous, and also requires a reader sensitive to shifting *personae*, and I would contend that its fundamental assertion *is* that man is only *capable* of reason. Similarly, I would contend that a qualified sort of misanthropy was a genuine part of Swift's personality. He had reasons to be angry: he had seen his hopes to be a bishop or a powerful politician vanish into the reality of an Irish "exile." In a moment of despair, he wrote to Bolingbroke: "It is time for me to have done with the world, and so I would if I could get into a better before I was called into the best, and not die here in a rage, like a poison'd rat in a hole" (III, 99). In his letters to Pope, Swift often undercut his misanthropy by exaggerating it, but the exaggeration was not a complete fiction; it was based on something real.

Mutatis mutandis, the same kind of statement can be made about Pope's role-playing. In answering Swift's letter, Pope used a fantasy he had developed to cope with the problem of separation, an imagined reunion of the old friends of the Scriblerus Club, all with changed minds and (especially for him) changed bodies:

> I have often imagined to myself, that if ever All of us met again, after so many Varieties and Changes, after so much of the Old world, and of the Old man in each of us, had been alter'd; after there has been a New Heaven, and a New Earth, in our Minds, and bodies, that Scarce a single thought of the one any more than a single atome of the other, remains just the same: I've fancy'd, I say, that we shou'd meet like the Righteous in the Millennium, quite in peace, divested of all our former passions, smiling at all our own designs, and content to enjoy the Kingdome of the Just in Tranquillity. But I find you would rather be employ'd as an Avenging Angel of wrath, to break your Vial of Indignation over the heads of the wretched pityful creatures of this World;

nay would make them *Eat your Book,* which you have made
as bitter a pill for them as possible.

(15 October 1725; II, 332-3)

The heavenly imagery is playful, but not merely playful. Pope
seeks to employ the notion of old friends reuniting in heaven,
"divested of all [their] former passions," as a dramatization of
his own more benevolent attitude toward mankind. He contrasts
that attitude with Swift's need to be "an Avenging Angel of
wrath, [breaking his] Vial of Indignation over the heads of
the wretched pityful creatures of this World." Again, both exag-
gerations serve to dramatize something real. Swift, while hardly
an "Avenging Angel," did have much more of the wrath of the
medieval Christian than did Pope. And Pope, who wished more
than anything else to be thought of as the Good Man, so much
so that he exaggerated his own benevolence, was in fact a
fundamentally benevolent man. Some of his deplorable failings,
such as his inability to tell unpleasant truths to Hill or Caryll,
sprang from his overwhelming need to be civil, polite, complimentary. In this very letter, that need leads him to claim to agree
with Swift's principles:

> I really enter as fully as you can desire, into your Principle,
> of Love of Individuals: And I think the way to have a Pub-
> lick Spirit, is first to have a Private one: For who the devil
> can believe any man can care for a hundred thousand peo-
> ple, who never cared for One? No ill humoured man can
> ever be a Patriot, any more than a Friend.

Of course, this is not precisely what Swift had said: Pope emphasized the "Love of Individuals," the part of Swift's attitude with
which he could concur; he quietly avoids agreeing to detest
mankind. In fact, in the last sentence, he implies that Swift does
not really detest mankind either; despite Swift's dramatization
of himself as ill-humored, Pope knows that he is, and wants to
be, a friend.

It was only toward the end of Pope's life that he began to move
toward Swift's more generalized pessimism. The *Dunciad* of 1728,

at least as Pope described it, was conceived of as a way to rid the
poet of his enemies ("these insects," as he called them) and bring
about their reformation. Pope allowed himself the comfort of
pretending that the Dunces would change their ways when
forced to recognize how ridiculous they were. By the end of
his career, he had learned differently. The presses continued
to spew forth, in ever increasing quantity, what Marshall
McLuhan has called "the accumulating backwash of private
self-expression."[14] Pope's response, the *Dunciad* of 1743, with
the generalized and philosophical satire of the new fourth book,
and the dark sense of defeat, is demonstrably a more Swiftian
production than the first version. Ironically, Swift never read
it; his eyes and his mind were too far gone by the time it was
published.[15]

We have Pope to thank for our knowledge of the fascinating
correspondence he carried on with Swift, for it was he who
recognized its interest and arranged its publication. At the same
time, many of the difficulties we have in understanding the
correspondence can be blamed on Pope: it was he who selected,
from an available group of letters, the ones which appeared in
1741 (and many were omitted); it was he who edited the ones
which did appear (in some cases omitting a great deal); and it
was his need to avoid detection as the publisher of the letters
which led him into a series of deceptions which compromised
the very friendship he meant to celebrate.

The story of Pope's plans to publish his correspondence with
Swift begins at least as early as the publication of the Wycherley
letters. Pope announced that publication to Swift in ambiguous
terms (see above, Ch. 1, p. 28), in a letter which also glances at
the possible interest of their own letters. Pope claims that the
letters he and Swift have exchanged, since they are written
"openly" and "negligently," would be of little value to a publisher:

> I smile to think how Curl would be bit, were our Epistles
> to fall into his hands, and how gloriously they would fall
> short of ev'ry ingenious reader's expectations?
>
> (28 November 1729; III, 79)

Later in the same letter, after explaining the publication of the early letters to and from Wycherley, he reopens the same possibility:

> I will not be asham'd of any thing . . . that is not immoral but merely dull (as for instance, if they printed this letter I am now writing, which they easily may, if the underlings at the Post-office please to take a copy of it.)
>
> (III, 80)

In fact, this long letter, like most of the letters the friends had exchanged, is far from dull. It seems plausible that Pope was testing Swift's reponse to the notion of publishing some of their letters.

If so, he got a quick negative reponse. Swift's next letter, which Pope never printed, shows firm opposition to letters (even good ones) written "with a view of publishing":

> I find you have been a writer of Letters almost from your infancy, and by your own confession had Schemes even then of Epistolary fame. Montaigne says that if he could have excelled in any kind of writing, it would have been in Letters; but I doubt they would not have been naturally, for it is plain that all Pliny's Letters were written with a view of publishing, and I accuse Voiture himself of the same crime, although he be an Author I am fond of. They cease to be Letters when they become a jeu d'esprit.
>
> (26 February 1729/30; III, 92)

Perhaps, as I have already suggested, Swift had concluded that Pope was responsible for the Wycherley volume and was twitting him on his youthful and present vanity (see above, Ch. 1, p. 29 and note). Pope's reply denies such vanity, claiming that his interest in letters springs only from friendship:

> I am pleased to see however your partiality, and 'tis for that reason I've kept some of your Letters and some of those of my other friends. These if I put together in a Volume, (for

my own secret satisfaction, in reviewing a Life, past in
Innocent amusements & Studies, not without the good will
of worthy and ingenious Men) do not therefore say, I aim
at Epistolary Fame: I never had any Fame less in my head;
but the Fame I most covet indeed, is that, which must be
deriv'd to me from my Friendships.

([9 April 1730]; III, 101)

Pope, as his later actions would show, was protesting too much
with his talk of "secret satisfaction," but he was proud of his
friendships, particularly of his friendship with Swift. That
pride, combined with a vanity that recognized the interest
inherent in their letters, kept him thinking about a way to
publish them.

Clearly, the correspondence with Swift was still on his mind
during Pope's intrigues at the time of publication of the 1735
Letters. Writing to Curll, as R. S., during those machinations,
he alluded to "much more important Correspondence that will
follow, *viz.* with SWIFT." And when, thanks to his intrigues,
he found himself "constrained" to publish his "official" edition,
he obviously thought of including some of the Swift letters.
Affecting concern lest they fall into unscrupulous hands, he
wrote to Swift (either in a lost letter or in a passage he later
suppressed) requesting the return of his letters. Then he announced that action to the Earl of Orrery, who was also in
Ireland:

The fear which has a good while been before my eyes, of
any Ill use which may be made of My Letters, which he
[Swift] told me he had (too partially) kept by him, made
me beg he would transmit them into Safe hands for me; I
wish those hands, my Lord, were your own; in which I
could trust any thing; even my Life: and (to be plain) I
think few hands in Ireland safe.

(2 April [1736]; IV, 8)

These requests only elicited a promise from Swift that his
executors would return Pope's letters when Swift died, and

an assurance that they were safe from prying eyes. In the same letter (22 April 1736), Swift reiterated a request he had been making for some time, that Pope adorn him by dedicating a poetic epistle to him. Pope avoided a direct reply, but did tell Swift, "I . . . will preserve all the memorials I can, that I was of your intimacy" (17 August 1736; IV, 28).

A few months later, in a mysterious way, some memorials of that intimacy became public. Curll, who had been routinely issuing other people's letters and assorted leftovers as new "volumes" of *Mr. Pope's Literary Correspondence*, issued something more significant. It was a pamphlet entitled *New Letters of Mr. Pope*, advertised for sale on 11 November 1736, which contained a letter written jointly by Pope and Boling-broke to Swift in 1723, printed as two letters (see II, 183-9). Curll claimed that he was printing "from the Original Manuscripts, transmitted from Ireland," although in 1741 he said instead that the letters had been given him by "a Gentleman of Essex." We have no evidence whatsoever as to the facts. Three hypotheses are possible:

(1) Pope secretly saw that Curll got a text, having for some reason kept a copy (not his usual practice), hoping to use the resulting publication to encourage Swift to return his letters.[16]

(2) Swift, not immune himself to "Schemes of Epistolary fame," secretly sent Curll a copy, hoping to test Pope's response.

(3) The letter really was stolen, by someone in Swift's household, or someone who had been allowed to make a copy, and sold to Curll.

Sherburn is inclined to accept hypothesis (1), but does note the evidence pointing to (2), particularly the Dublin printer Faulkner's memory that Swift had once offered him an opportunity to print some letters (see III, 492n). Nor should hypothesis (3) be discounted, as there were plenty of people who could and would have stolen and sold letters. Still, the fact that the letters appeared suited Pope's purposes admirably: it provided "proof" that the letters were in danger from unscrupulous agents, an argument Pope would use in begging for their return. Since Pope had done similar things before, it is hard to believe that he was not behind Curll's pamphlet.

However Curll got the letters, Pope's response was rapid. He cancelled a section of "Thoughts on Various Subjects," which was to have stood at the end of the official folio, and reprinted the letters Curll had published; significantly, he added another letter from Swift (see II, 198) and one from himself to Swift (II, 348). Another unanswered question is where the text for that second addition came from: had Pope kept a copy? The type for these additional letters was set rapidly; the printer misprinted a page number in his haste (234 for 324). By including these letters in the official edition of 18 May 1737 (and in the Roberts octavo of a month later), Pope was publicly acknowledging that they were genuine. Perhaps he was also hoping to whet the public's appetite for more of these letters.

But while he was reprinting the Swift letters, Pope was deploring their theft to Orrery:

> Within this month, the same Villain that publishd my other Letters, has printed two to the dean: one from Lord Bo: the other from me: the Copies whereof (he says in his advertisements) came from Ireland, as indeed they must, for I had none: It could have come about only by the Deans lending them out of his hands. The Dean's answer to those Letters I have by me, very safe. No doubt this fate will befall every Scrap he has, & he tells me he has ev'ry Scrap I ever writ to him. . . . I am overruled by my friends here, as to the Miscellaneous Prose pieces, which they would omit, & make the Volume consist wholly of Letters; with a view of enlarging it hereafter with Other Letters, which may come in order. . . . Would the Dean send me those Letters, & mark over every sentence he would leave out, I would copy, & return them to him: That point, if you have any opportunity, I wish you could bring him to: Indeed it is a mortifying prospect, to have one's most secret opinions, deliverd under the Sacredness of Friendship, betrayed

to the whole World, by the unhappy Partiality of one's own
best Friends in preserving them.

> (14 January [1736/7]; IV, 52-3)

No doubt, Pope expected Orrery to show or read this letter to
Swift. Since Swift was no fool, he would easily conclude that
Pope planned another volume of letters to match the 1737 folio,
and that he hoped to include some of the Swift correspondence,
offering Swift a chance to do some editing. Perhaps Swift also
knew Pope well enough to guess that Pope would create a pretext for such a volume by leaking the letters to Curll or someone
like him, in much the way he had operated in 1735. Pope was
also writing directly to Swift at this time, but here the story is
difficult to trace. It is clear from the letters which survive that
many letters Pope wrote to Swift at this time, letters to which
Swift refers in his replies, have disappeared altogether, and in
the letters Pope did eventually print, it seems likely that some
urgent requests for the return of his letters have been edited out.

Replying to these letters, and to the messages Pope was sending through Orrery, Swift gave a series of contradictory answers.
On 17 May 1737, Orrery wrote to Pope:

> The Dean assures me, "You shall have every Line You ever
> wrote to him, return'd to You by my Hands."
>
> (IV, 69)

But on 31 May, Swift wrote directly:

> All the letters I can find of yours, I have fastned in a folio
> cover, and the rest in bundles endors'd; But, by reading
> their dates, I find a chasm of six years, of which I can find
> no copies; and yet I kept them with all possible care: But,
> I have been forced, on three or four occasions to send all
> my papers to some friends, yet those papers were all sent
> sealed in bundles, to some faithful friends; however, what
> I have, are not much above sixty. I found nothing in any
> of them to be left out: None of them have any thing to do
> with Party, of which you are the clearest of all men, by

your Religion, and the whole Tenour of your life; while I am raging every moment against the Corruptions in both kingdoms, especially of this; such is my weakness.

(IV, 72)

By saying that he found nothing to be left out, Swift showed pretty clearly that he knew what Pope was up to, but the news of a chasm must have been disturbing to Pope, especially since Orrery, in a letter of 2 June, suggested that the missing letters might be in unscrupulous hands:

They are either stolen by People who have had Admission into his Closet, or else are not return'd by Those with whom he entrusted his Papers on some certain occasions. The latter is most probable. I will try to find out, if possible, where they are: tho' the Persons who were knavish enough not to restore Them, will I fear be cunning enough still to conceal Them.

(IV, 73)

On 14 June, Orrery explained that his efforts to locate the missing letters had failed, and described the "Chasm" as beginning "in the year 1722" (IV, 75). But when Swift wrote next, he promised that Orrery would bring with him

all the letters I preserved of yours, which are not above twenty-five. I find there is a great chasm of some years, but the dates are more early than my two last journeys to England [i.e., before 1726], which makes me imagine, that in one of those journeys I carry'd over another Cargo.

(IV, 76)

One can imagine Pope's confusion. Did Swift have sixty letters or only twenty-five? Were the missing years 1722-28 or 1716-22? Was Swift so senile that he forgot himself? Was Orrery's account of the Dean's poor health exaggerated? Orrery's arrival in July did not provide complete answers to these questions. Orrery did deliver about twenty-five letters, and Pope learned from examining them that the "chasm" was as Swift had described it, early in date. But he must still have wondered how many missing letters there were, and who had them, particularly when a letter from Swift, a year later, read as if the older man had forgotten sending the twenty-five letters by Orrery:

> I can faithfully assure you, that every letter you have favour'd me with these twenty years and more, are sealed up in bundles, and delivered to Mrs. W[hiteway], a very worthy, rational, and judicious Cousin of mine, and the only relation whose visits I can suffer: All these Letters she is directed to send safely to you upon my decease.
>
> (8-24 August 1738; IV, 115-16)

This was clearly impossible, but a postscript claiming to correct it was even more confusing:

> P.S. I will here in a Postscript correct (if it be possible) the blunders I have made in my letter. I shewed my Cousin the above letter, and she assures me that a great Collection of $\genfrac{}{}{0pt}{}{your}{my}$ letters to $\genfrac{}{}{0pt}{}{me}{you,}$ are put up and sealed, and in some very safe hand.

Pope's difficulties in interpreting these statements were severe; ours are more so. Because we depend on Pope's published versions for most of these letters, we cannot know what is missing from the texts or whether the texts have been altered. Further, it is plausible to argue that Pope and Swift would never have written to each other about a plot to publish their letters in a straightforward way: they would have used their habitual circumlocutions to keep their communication safe from the prying eyes of the postal clerks. Modern readers, alas, are more or less in the position of the postal clerks. The Victorians, always ready to think the worst of Pope, concluded that Swift really was senile and erratic, and that Pope took advantage of his friend's weakened state to publish the letters. But it is not necessary to assume that the contradictions in Swift's answers are absent-minded or senile. Swift's letters to all his correspondents for the years 1736-38, the period in question, are vigorous, coherent, and often funny. It seems more likely that Swift had concluded accurately that Pope was behind the 1735 *Letters*, responsible for Curll's 1736 "theft," anxious to print another fine volume of letters to match the 1737 folio, and particularly eager to fill that volume with Swift's letters. If he did so conclude, it would have been fully characteristic for Swift to have decided to have some fun with Pope by seeming to misunderstand his appeals for his letters. Archibald Elias's assertion that "In Swift's private communication with the poet, there may be a constant touch of anarchy—veiled playfulness, veiled mischief"[17] is clearly relevant to this episode. The problem, particularly in these difficult letters, is one of degree: is anything that Swift says genuinely forgetful, or is some of it mischievous? I suspect Pope was asking himself that question in 1738.

But he did have those twenty-five letters from himself to Swift, and we may assume that "paper-sparing Pope," who usually wrote rough drafts of his poetry on whatever was available, including letters to him, had spared Swift's letters and saved them; the discovery of careful transcripts in Oxford's library proves that Pope was certainly collecting Swift's letters after 1730.

Putting together the correspondence thus collected, and adding some of Swift's letters to Gay (which he had gotten possession of after Gay's death), and doubtless editing the whole, Pope had a small octavo volume privately printed, and sent it to Swift by Samuel Gerrard, who had been visiting in England in the spring of 1740. On 17 May, Pope wrote to Gerrard, who was in Bath about to depart, that he had nothing to send Swift, having just sent him "a very long & full Letter by a safe hand" (IV, 241). However, just before Gerrard took ship, some agent gave him a packet addressed to Swift, with an anonymous covering letter, which read:

> Sir,—The true Honour which all the honest and grateful Part of this Nation must bear you, as the most publick spirited of Patriots, the best of private Men, and the greatest

polite Genius of this Age, made it impossible to resist the Temptation, which has fallen in our Way, of preserving from all Accidents a Copy of the *inclosed Papers*, which at once give so amiable a Picture of your own excellent Mind, and so strong a Testimony of the Love and Respect of those who nearest know, and best can judge of it.

As there is Reason to fear they would be lost to Posterity after your Death, if either of your Two great Friends should be possessed of them (*as we are informed you have directed*) they are here collected and submitted to your own mature Consideration. Envy itself can find Nothing in them that either You, or They, need be ashamed of. But you, Sir, are the Person *most* concerned, and ought to be made the *only* Judge in this Case. You may be assured there is *no other Copy* of this Book in any Hands but your own: So that, while you live, it will be in the Power of no other, but yourself, to bestow it on the Publick. In so doing You shall oblige all Mankind in general, and *benefit any deserving Friend* in particular. But if during your Live, you suppress it, yet after your Death it is not fit that either You should be robbed of so much of your Fame, or We of so much of your Example;—We are, Worthy Sir, your Sincere Admirers, Obliged *Country-Men*, and Faithful, Affectionate Servants.

(IV, 242-3)

This letter seems designed to be used, as it later was, to prove that the printed volume had been produced by Irishmen, with its anonymous authors claiming to be Swift's *"Country-Men."* That Pope wrote the letter, had the volume printed, and sent the packet is further proved by his note to Ralph Allen, dated 27 May 1740, in which he admits to being "a little Impatient to know whether that Pacquet I sent for Mr. Gerrard reached him? In time before he went from Bath?" (IV, 245).

Swift was not fooled, as Orrery's letter to Pope on 6 October 1740 indicates:

These letters were brought from England by Mr. Gerrard, a gentleman you knew at Bath, the packet left for him there by an unknown hand, and the dean imagined they came from you. It is strange the dean should have such a surmise, or be desirous to have them reprinted here, because there are some things in them which, upon a cooler consideration, I believe he would not think ought to appear, especially as they now are.

(IV, 276)[18]

Swift, so far as we can reconstruct the history, looked over the volume, made some trifling editorial corrections, added some footnotes, perhaps added one long letter (really an essay of political self-defense, see II, 64-72),[19] and turned it over to Faulkner, the Dublin printer.

Faulkner was no Curll. He wrote Pope to tell him what he was doing, and this bit of honesty forced Pope to engage in more complicated machinations. He sent to Faulkner "the strongest Negation I could possibly" (IV, 264), with the result that Faulkner stopped printing and turned over the clandestine volume and the sheets he had started to Orrery, who was acting as Pope's agent in Ireland. Pope thanked Faulkner, and asked for a sight of the volume and the anonymous accompanying letter, pretending that he hoped to find out who was responsible. After some confusing delays and much correspondence, Orrery got all these materials from Faulkner and sent them to Pope. Orrery's own opinion, having read the letters, was that "they were never meant for print" (IV, 294). Pope pretended to concur in this opinion, but seized upon the fact that Swift had added notes to argue (probably accurately) that Swift wanted the letters published. He suggested as much to Orrery: "as it appears from several things . . . [including the footnotes] that he [Swift] takes a pleasure in these freedoms, I believe the printing them will give him more Satisfaction than the consequences can give him any pain" (3 December 1740; IV, 301). Finally, on 27 December 1740, Pope returned the clandestine volume to Orrery, without (significantly) the sheets Faulkner had begun printing, which included the new long letter and the valuable notes added by Swift.

The Works of Mr. Alexander Pope, in Prose. Vol. II was splendidly printed in London, in a format to match the official

1737 edition of the letters. It included, of course, the new material which could only have come from the sheets Pope did not return to Faulkner. "The Booksellers to the Reader" claimed that the Swift correspondence had been "copied from an Impression sent from *Dublin*, and said to be printed by the Dean's Direction" (I, xli). The implication, of course, was that the Dublin edition was first, which was not the case: the London edition was in fact issued on 16 April 1741; Faulkner's did not appear until 20 June, and he had time to add as a supplement letters which the London preface claimed were not in the Dublin edition. Next came Curll's predictable piracy and a small octavo *"Printed for T. Cooper"* which contained remainder sheets of the original clandestine volume.[20]

It is hard to sympathize with Pope's actions and statements about the publication of the Swift correspondence. He used Orrery as a tool and lied steadily to him. His stated suspicions of Mrs. Whiteway and others around Swift seem almost hysterical, even if their purpose was to keep suspicion away from himself. Pope sounds confused and helpless in some of these passages, frustrated in his efforts to communicate with Swift, whether because Swift was genuinely erratic by the time of the publication or because he was deliberately mystifying Pope. Much remains uncertain. Was Mrs. Whiteway, whose letters on the subject are strangely wrought up, always truthful in her accounts of her part in the negotiations? Why does Orrery portray Swift as befuddled, even at times when he was evidently capable of editorial work, and perhaps capable of trickery of his own? A final judgment of Pope's actions must depend upon answers to such difficult questions, and I doubt that enough new facts will ever come to light to answer them with confidence. Certainly, the nineteenth-century reading of the episode, which saw Pope as cruelly betraying his old friend, failed to take into account the fact that the kind of skillful hinting Pope once called "genteel equivocation" was a continuing element in that friendship. To be sure, Pope was vain, and his attempts to avoid the "imputation of vanity" were dishonest. But his basic motive in seeking to publish the letters was pride of a different sort—not simply vanity about his own prose but a touching pride in the fact that he was valued by a man as great as Swift. It is to Pope's credit that "the volume of letters contains more and better letters by Swift than by Pope."[21]   And without that volume, we should know very little about the remarkable friendship of the two greatest writers of the age.

Words were the stuff of which their friendship was built, and the "Monument" Pope erected to the friendship by publishing the letters was a monument of words. So it seems sad, however natural, that he had to recognize, at the outset of his last letter to Swift, that words were impotent to express his feelings:

> My Dear Friend, When the Heart is full of Tenderness, it must be full of Concern at the absolute Impotency of all Words to come up to it. You are the only Man now in the world, who cost me a Sigh every day of my Life, and the Man it troubles me most, altho' I most wish, to write to. Death has not used me worse in separating from me for ever, poor Gay, Arbuthnot &c, than Disease & Distance in separating You so many years. But nothing shall make me forget you, and I am persuaded you will as little forget me; & most things in this world one may afford to forget, if we remember, & are rememberd by, our Friends. I value and enjoy more, the memory of the Pleasures & Endearing Obligations I have formerly receivd from you, than the present Possession of any other. I am less anxious every day I live for present Enjoyments of any sort, & my Temper of Mind is calmer as to Worldly disappointments & accidents except the loss of Friends by Death, the only way (I thank God) that I ever have lost any. Think it not possible that my Affection can cease but with my last breath: If I could think yours was alienated, I should grieve, but not reproach you: If I felt myself ev'n hurt by you, I should be confident you knew not the Blow you gave, but had your hand guided by another: If I never more had a kind word from you, I should feel my heart the same it has ever been towards you. I must confess a late Incident has given me some pain: but I am satisfied you were persuaded it would not have given me

any: And whatever unpleasant circumstances the printing
our Letters might be attended with, there was *One* that
pleas'd me, that the strict Friendship we have born each
other so long, is thus made known to all mankind. As far
as it was Your Will, I cannot be angry, at what in all other
respects I am quite uneasy under. Had you ask'd me, before
you gave them away, I think I could have proposed some
better Monument of our Friendship or at least of *better
Materials*: And you must allow me to say, This was not of
my erecting, but yours. My Part of them is far too mean,
& how inferior to what you have every where in your Works
set up to Me? Can I see these without Shame? when I reflect
on the many beautiful, pathetic, & amiable Lines of yours,
which carry to Posterity the Name of a Man, who if he had
every good Quality which you so kindly ascribe to him,
would be so proud of none, as the Constancy, and the Justice, of his Esteem for you. Adieu. While I can write, speak,
remember, or think, I am Yours. A. Pope.

(22 March 1740/1; IV, 337-8)

There is some equivocation in this letter, and it is neither genteel
nor witty. Pope's continuing need to pretend to Orrery, with
whom he was writing, that he had nothing at all to do with the
publication of the letters, and his continuing inability to apologize, explain but hardly excuse his hypocrisy. His assertion
that words are impotent is a part of that hypocrisy, for a few
honest words could have admitted the truth. Still, the fact
that some of what Pope says here can be identified as hypocritical is no reason to impugn everything in the letter. He was,
I believe, entirely sincere in admitting being pleased that "the
strict Friendship we have born each other so long, is thus made
known to all mankind." In "all mankind," is included the idea
of posterity, as he had told Swift many years before:

> At all adventures, yours and my name shall stand linked
> as friends to posterity, both in verse and prose, and (as
> Tully calls it) in *consuetudine Studiorum*.

(23 March 1727/8; II, 480)

Pope achieved his goal: every account of eighteenth-century literature links his name with Swift's. The irony is that in assuring the continued fame of their friendship, he compromised it. But even in the final letter, he chose and ordered his words in a way which emphasizes the essentials of their remarkable friendship:

While I can write, speak, remember, or think, I am Yours.

Another man might have written, "While I live and breathe," but for Pope, writing, speaking, remembering, and thinking (more or less in that order) were the essential activities. Shortly after this letter, Swift lost the ability to perform these essential activities; his continued physical life was the last cruel twist of a fate that had dictated his prolonged separation from Pope and his other writing friends. I have spoken before of the Swiftian despair of the last version of the *Dunciad.* When he finished that poem, Pope had lost the friends with whom he shared the life of writing: Parnell, Gay and Arbuthnot were long dead, and Swift was a speechless hulk. Pope's own death was fast approaching. Perhaps the intensity with which the falling of Universal Darkness is realized in the final lines of the poem results not only from Pope's horror at the power of the forces of Unreason, but also from his complete isolation as the last functioning member of a group of men who saw writing well as the sign and purpose of life.

A Window in the Bosom

THE PROBLEMS MODERN READERS have in understanding Pope's letters—our ignorance of his allusions, our suspicion of his elegance, our curiosity about those aspects of his life which he kept private—can lead to frustration. Many readers must finish the Sherburn collection wishing for the more direct self-revelation of a Keats or a Virginia Woolf. A more sympathetic reading will recognize that Pope, despite his reticence, his artifice, and his role-playing, was actually a pivotal figure in the history of letter writing, whose major innovation, even in those carefully selected letters he chose to publish, is his interest in personality. His private letters, with their great range of style, tone, and matter, show how well he understood and responded to the personalities of his correspondents, and how rich and complex his own personality was. Pope realized that "Candour & Good nature . . . would draw out one's most naked Sentiments, without any Care about the cloathing them," and even claimed that "my style, like my soul, appears in its natural undress before my friend." But Pope's twisted body, in its "natural undress," was far from beautiful, and his social behavior, as he admitted to Bethel and Allen, sometimes fell short of his ethical principles. Pope's need for a more attractive physical appearance led him to dress in ways which concealed his physical malformation as much as possible,[1] and to sit for a series of carefully staged portraits which concealed it altogether.[2] A similar need for an attractive social and moral appearance led to the role-playing I have described in his letters—his use of rakish language in addressing women, his pretended aloofness to attacks from lesser writers, his elegant deference to aristocrats.

But with one of those very aristocrats, Oxford, "he used to dine
sometimes . . . privately, in a velvet cap."³ Even this dress, of
course, was not a complete stripping away of covering; Pope
did not dine bald. But the cap was a less elaborate defense than
the wigs Pope (and other eighteenth-century gentlemen) wore in
public. That kind of difference in degree of self-revelation shows
in Pope's letters to his closest friends, and in his most interesting
metaphor about self-revelation, from which this book takes its
title:

> The old project of a Window in the bosom, to render the
> Soul of Man visible, is what every honest friend has mani-
> fold reason to wish for.
>
> ([1720?]; II, 23)

That sentence opens a letter to Charles Jervas which Pope published in 1735; in an earlier letter to Lady Mary Wortley Montagu,
which he never published, Pope extended the metaphor somewhat further:

> If Momus his project had taken of having Windows in our
> breasts, I should be for carrying it further and making those
> windows Casements: that while a man showd his Heart to all
> the world, he might do something more for his friends, e'en
> take it out, and trust it to their handling.
>
> (18 August [1716]; I, 353)

Typically, the metaphor is not one Pope invented, but one he
remade to suit his purposes; the "old project" is described in
Lucian's *Hermotimus*. In both the mild version to Jervas and
the extravagant version to Lady Mary, Pope uses the metaphor
to suggest a distinction between "every honest friend" and the
general public. Pope obviously did not show "his Heart to all
the world"; the window he made in his bosom in his published
letters was carefully constructed to reveal only a few aspects of
his mind, selected and polished for public display. But even that
qualified kind of self-revelation was, as I have argued, a turning
point in the history of letter writing. For his friends, Pope tried

to do more. He recognized that self-revelation was "what every honest friend [had] manifold reason to wish for," but the restraint of that phrase suggests that he also recognized the impossibility of complete self-revelation—for himself or any man. Even while proposing to Lady Mary that a man should be able to trust his heart to the handling of his friends, Pope must have known that such openness could lead to painful wounds—although he may not have guessed that Lady Mary herself would handle his heart so roughly. Surrounded as he was by enemies and sycophants, Pope could hardly afford to expose himself completely to anyone. But he did manage to show parts of himself to some of his closest friends: to Bethel, he admitted his physical frailty as to no other man; to Swift, he sent some of his most cherished thoughts on their common craft; to Martha Blount, he confessed feelings he would have hidden from any male friend.

Modern readers, thanks largely to the care with which Pope's friends preserved his letters, enjoy an opportunity not one of his friends ever had—the chance to form a composite picture of Pope. We see a man who lived most of his life in physical pain, but who had the vitality to keep his withered frame alive and productive for fifty-six years; a man whose early hope that his wit might win him a wife ended in pain and frustration, but who had the foresight to gather about him old and trusted friends (including his faithful dogs) who were not self-conscious about his size and shape; a man whose enemies exploited both his body and his unpopular religion, but who had the imaginative brilliance and shrewd acument to make a great career in spite of his disadvantages of form and faith. We see, as well, a man who preferred equivocation to admitting that he had attacked Aaron Hill, or corresponded with Atterbury in the Tower, or propagated his own letters; who could lie not only to the public but to friends as trusted as Caryll and Swift; who was never less admirable than when seeking to appear admirable. Finally, we see a man who treated writing well as a sacred calling, who drew on every resource available to him—the literary tradition, his powerful imagination, and his human experiences (even the painful ones)—to create a poetry he knew would endure.

APPENDIX

A Timetable
of the 1735 Publication

I offer here one possible account of the events leading up to the publication of the 1735 *Literary Correspondence*. My account is frankly speculative, not only about dates and facts (which are murky at best) but about the motivations of both Pope and Curll.[1]

3 March 1734/35. Pope writes to Oxford, requesting "the bound Book of Copies of Letters, which I want to inspect for a day or two" (III, 453). Whether this book included what are now called the Harleian transcripts is unclear. Pretty certainly Pope's request had something to do with his plot to have his letters published. Perhaps he had already had some of the letters printed, and intended to use the transcripts to held him read proof.[2]

22 March 1735. Curll finds the E. P. and P. T. letters in a drawer, and sends to Pope the text of the still unplaced advertisement, in P. T.'s handwriting. Curll's covering letter announces his intention to reprint the Cromwell correspondence, but protests his "readiness to oblige" Pope, and proposes a meeting to "close all Differences." In his later account, Curll would claim a pure and admirable motive:

> Reflecting within my self that the Resentment between Mr *Pope* and me, tho' from the first ungenerously taken up by him, had continued much too long, being almost eight Years, I was willing to lay hold of an Opportunity for proposing an Accommodation.
>
> (*In. Corr.*, p. 12)

Pope's *Narrative*, with some basis, would allege instead that "the whole Design of *E. Curl* was to get [Pope] but to look on the Edition of *Cromwel's* Letters, and so to print it as *revis'd* by Mr. *Pope*" (*Nar.*, p. 13).[3] Perhaps Curll hoped the "Accommodation" might take the form of a payment for suppressing the proposed edition. Perhaps he merely wanted to discover whether Pope knew anything about the suspicious circumstance of that "large Collection" of stolen letters. Perhaps Pope himself, having his printed texts now almost ready to publish, saw to it that Curll was reminded of the earlier approach by P. T.[4] Whatever its motive or mixture of motives, Curll's letter was basically an attempt to get Pope to show his hand.

3 April 1735. Pope acts, publicly and privately, to forward his revived scheme. On the public front, he advertises in the *Daily Post-Boy*:

> Whereas *A. P.* hath received a Letter from *E. C.* Bookseller pretending that a Person, the initials of whose Name are *P. T.* hath offered the said *E. C.* to print a large Collection of Mr. *P.*'s Letters, to which *E. C.* requires an Answer, *A. P.* having never had, nor intending to have, any private Correspondence with the said *E. C.* gives it him in this Manner. That he knows no such Person as *P. T.* that he believes he hath no such Collection, and that he thinks the whole a Forgery, and shall not trouble himself at all about it.[5]

Pope does *not* threaten legal action, nor does he rush to announce a preventive "authorized edition." On the contrary, by placing this advertisement, he begins what amounts to a campaign of promotion for the unauthorized edition. For the first time, the public is aware that someone is offering to publish Pope's letters. They will soon hear more.

4 April 1735. The time is right for private action. As P. T., Pope writes to Curll accusing him of treachery in corresponding with Pope. Naturally enough, he does not rescind his offer, but now he offers a printed text, not the manuscripts as he had in 1733.

I see an Advertisement in the Daily Advertisements, which I take to relate to Me. I did not expect you of all Men would have betray'd me to Squire *Pope*; but you and he both shall soon be convinc'd it was no *Forgery*. For since you would not comply with my Proposal to advertise, I have printed them at my own Expence, being advis'd that I could safely do so.

> (*Nar.*, p. 20)

P. T. continues with a vague financial offer: he wishes to be reimbursed for costs and paid "handsomely" for the copyright. If Curll will advertise (again the insistence on seeing that list of correspondents and promise of originals in print), P. T. will meet with him. Pope at this stage in his career was supervising the printing of his own works, so access to a discreet printer was no problem, and delivering a printed version to Curll would conveniently deprive Curll of the chance to alter texts or add footnotes.

5 April 1735. Curll is sufficiently encouraged by hearing from P. T. to reply defiantly to Pope's public advertisement. He places a reply advertisement in the *Daily Post-Boy*:

Whereas A. P. Poet, has certified in the *Daily Post-Boy*, that he shall not trouble himself at all about the Publication of a large Collection of the said Mr *P___'s* Letters which *P. T.* hath offered *E. C.* to print. This is to certify, that Mr *C.* never had, nor intended ever to have, any private Correspondence with *A. P.* but was directed to give him Notice of these Letters. Now to put all *Forgeries*, even *Popish ones*, to flight; this is to give him Notice, that any Person, (or, *A. P.* himself) may see the ORIGINALS, in Mr *P___'s* own Hand, when printed. *Initials* are a *Joke*; Names at length are *real*.

> *No longer now like Suppliants we come,*
> E. C. *makes War, and* A. P. *is the* Drum.

The last sentence perhaps implies a degree of suspicion about

P. T.'s identity, but the promise to the public of authenticating originals indicates Curll's continuing confidence that he would be able to close a deal with P. T. An odder feature of the advertisement is the insistence that Curll "was directed to give [Pope] Notice of these Letters." By whom? The claim is particularly strange in view of Curll's later description of his action as an overture of reconciliation. Here he implies that someone else was the motivating force.[6]

6 or 7 April 1735. Pope, having publicly declared himself unconcerned, takes no public action, but he is well aware of Curll's growing concern about the mysteriousness of P. T., and he still wants Curll to print the exact words of the advertisement he drew up in 1733. So he writes a letter as P. T., of which only a torn scrap came to be published in the later accounts. That scrap reads:

> Sir, I should not deal thus Cautiously or in the Dark with you, but that 'tis plain from your own Advertisement, that you have been Treating with Mr. *Pope*.
>
> (*Nar.*, p. 21)

Pope was creating for P. T. a plausible response to Curll's advertisement: he had P. T. explain his caution as a result of his fear of double dealing by Curll—a fear P. T. might legitimately have had on the basis of Curll's indirect admission that he had given Pope notice of the letters. It seems likely that this letter also reiterated P. T.'s request to see his advertisement for the book published.

8 April 1735. Either prompted by this letter or merely remembering that P. T.'s letter of 4 April asked to "see my Advertisement of the Book printed first, within these Four or Five days," Curll at last places that advertisement, following the text first sent to him in 1733 (presumably he retained a copy when he sent it to Pope) and adding, at the end, "*E. C.* as before in the like Case, will be faithful."

About 15 April 1735. Pope sees Curll's advertisement as evidence of his willingness to comply with P. T. on P. T.'s terms. As P. T., he sends Curll a letter naming a new price, which is considerably more than costs. He asks for "3 *l*. a Score for 650" (i.e., ninety-seven pounds, ten shillings), and requires a down payment of seventy-five pounds. To show his compliance, Curll is to place another advertisement, which is to read: "*E. C.* will meet *P. T.* at the *Rose Tavern* by the Play-House at Seven in the Evening *April 22d.*" If he places the advertisement, "one will come, and show you the Sheets." Again, only a piece of this letter came to be printed. What it contained, if anything else, remains unknown. Further confusion arises from Curll's later summarizing of the contents of this fragment, the scrap of 6 or 7 April, and the letter of 4 April as if they were all part of one letter.[7] But this seems impossible. The letter of 4 April is a coherent whole, and asks for reimbursement for costs of printing and a fee for the copyright. The scrap of 6 or 7 April is evidently a response to Curll's public advertisement of 5 April. The fragment of 15 April proposes new and much more specific terms, presumably in response to Curll's advertisement of 8 April. Whatever the date, the absence of any promise that Curll would have the original letters was an important and strategic omission.

15-21 April 1735. Curll hesitates—probably realizing that he has committed himself in the public advertisement of 8 April to show authenticating originals, yet is now being asked to pay seventy-five pounds to an unknown agent for printed sheets. He does not place the dictated advertisement.[8]

Noticing Curll's failure to place the advertisement, Pope loses his nerve, or simply has trouble lining up an agent to appear at the proposed meeting; he postpones the assignation. It was difficult for Pope to devise a suitable excuse for P. T. If Curll's later account can be believed, Pope had P. T. send word to Curll that he feared a physical assault from Pope's agents. If true, this message was a serious mistake, for such fears would have been credible only if Curll *had* placed the advertisement about the meeting. Curll's later account of his transaction requires quoting in full:

> But on the Day appointed I received a Countermand, that he thought he had lost his Wits by making such an Appoint-

ment, and seemed in a terrible Panic lest Mr *Pope* should
send some of his *Twickenham-Bravoes*, to assault us; but
how Mr *Pope* was to know of this Meeting is the Cream
of the Jest.   I sent him word that I commiserated his fears,
but as to my own part, I did not at all dread any *Assassina-
tion* whatever from Mr *Pope*, even tho' it were a *Poetical
One*.   To this P. T. rejoined, that a Gentleman should
call at my House precisely at eight in the Evening in a
Week's time.

(*In. Corr.*, p. 13)

28 April 1735.   Pope delays for one more day (perhaps the
actor Worsdale, who has been engaged to play his agent, has a
task at the theatre).   So Curll receives a message, according to
his later account, that a gentleman with "full Commission" to
negotiate will appear at eight the next evening.

29 April 1735.   Curll decides not to meet the gentleman, and
leaves instead a long letter *"For P. T. or the Gentleman who
comes from him."*   His letter complains of P. T.'s manifest in-
consistency in his various proposals.   Curll particularly emphasizes, as well he might, the suspicious circumstance of
P. T.'s groundless fear in postponing the proposed meeting
of 22 April: "You put off this meeting, fearing a Surprize from
Mr. *Pope*.   How should he know of this Appointment, unless
you gave him Notice?" (*Nar.*, pp. 22-3).   Curll asks for open
dealing, at his own house.

30 April 1735.   James Worsdale, a sometime actor and painter,
arrives at Curll's house and introduces himself as the Reverend
Mr. R. Smythe, P. T.'s cousin.   He wears (according to Curll's
account) a clergyman's gown and a lawyer's neckband.   Why
Worsdale chose this bizarre costume is another mystery.   He
shows Curll "a Book in sheets, almost finished, and about a
Dozen original Letters" (*In. Corr.*, p. 14).   Curll, familiar with
Pope's handwriting from the Cromwell correspondence, recognizes the letters as genuine.   Curll's later account placed this
meeting on 7 May; in fact, all of Curll's later remarks about the
timing of events after this date make little sense when compared
with the dates of the letters he printed.   Probably he was con-

fused rather than deceitful when putting together the *Initial Correspondence*—at least about the dates.

1 or 2 May 1735. Curll writes to Smythe with a definite counter-offer, which amounts to a reiteration of the terms P. T. had proposed on 4 April. Curll is now "ready to discharge the Expence of Paper, Print, and Copy-Money, and make the Copy my own, if we agree. But if I am to be your Agent, then I insist to be solely so." Always shrewd, Curll recognized the importance of securing the copyright and of preventing other booksellers from becoming involved.

3 May 1735. Pope (for whom money was never the principal object anyway) decides that this offer is good enough. As P. T., he sends a letter which does not explicitly accept Curll's terms, but implies that financial arrangements "will be left to your Honour" (*In. Corr.*, p. 14). P. T. promises to deliver fifty books "in five or six Days' time," without title pages. Curll may devise his own title page, and he need not pay for the books until the end of the next week; the book is to be published on 12 May. P. T. again encourages Curll to advertise, again unsuccessfully.

4 May 1735. Pope creates, for P. T., another strange flurry of fear of exposure. In another letter to Curll, P. T. reiterates his promise that R. S. will deliver the books, and asks that Curll return his own letters. Then, most strangely, he expresses great concern about Curll's use in an advertisement (presumably that of 30 March 1733, quoted above, pp. 30-31) of information from one of his letters. He stresses his fear of being discovered by Pope:

> The Clergyman you saw will bring you the Books, to whom I insist you will deliver my former Letters concerning Mr *Pope*, whom I must be concealed from, and he [presumably R. S.] tells me you had written an *Advertisement of Mr Pope's Life*, in which if you insert any one Circumstance of what I told you in a private Letter, I shall be discovered and exposed to his Resentment. I insist on your Honour in returning them therefore.
>
> (*In. Corr.*, p. 15)

Knowing that Curll would eventually discover that he had been
cheated in one way or another, Pope naturally wanted to have
the P. T. correspondence in his own hands.   But in using the
old advertisement as a pretext for P. T.'s fear, he perhaps forgot
that the first letter communicating the anecdotes in question
was signed by E. P., not by P. T.

   5 or 6 May 1735.   Curll tries to reassure the suddenly wary
P. T.   He mentions the E. P. letters and points out that since
only initials have appeared in the public prints, P. T. need
not fear exposure:

> But consider, sir, as the Publick, by your Means entirely
> have been led into an Initial Correspondence betwixt *E.C.*
> and *P.T.* and betwixt *A.P.* and *E.C.* the Secret is still as
> recondite as that of the Free-Masons.   *P.T.* are not, I dare
> say, the true Initials of your Name; or if they were, Mr.
> *Pope* has publickly declar'd, *That he Knows no such Person*
> *as* P.T. how then can any thing you have communicated
> to me, discover you, or expose you to his Resentment?
>   I have had Letters from another Correspondent, who
> subscribes himself *E.P.* which I shall print as Vouchers,
> in Mr. *Pope*'s Life, as well as those from *P.T.* which, as
> I take it, were all sent me for that Purpose, or why were
> they sent at all?
>
> *(Nar.*, p. 24)

In a postscript, Curll defends himself again from the implicit
charge of collusion with Pope.

   7 May 1735.   R. S. pays his second visit to Curll, and at last
delivers fifty books, without title pages.   He reiterates P. T.'s
request for the return of his letters.

   8 May 1735.   Pope now decides, having created a wary and
not entirely dependable personality for P. T., that the more
pragmatic and sensible R. S., who has successfully visited Curll
twice, will start to write some of the necessary letters.   Accordingly, R. S. writes to Curll (of course, Pope, not Worsdale,
writes the letter) and asks him to send "by the bearer the Title
and the Preface, and an Estimate, and the Papers you promised

me last Night; I mean the Letters." In a postscript, he reports that "the old Gentleman is vastly pleas'd at our Meeting last Night" (*In. Corr.*, p. 16). Curll immediately replies that he "cannot send the Letters now, because I have them not all by me, but either this Evening or To-morrow, you shall not fail of them" (*Nar.*, pp. 25-6). He requests fifty more books. Although he claimed that the P. T. letters were "in a Scrutore of mine out of Town," Curll was probably seeking a delay in order to have time to take careful copies of the letters.

(?) **9 May 1735.** On or about this date, Curll does return some of the P. T. letters.

10 May 1735. Pope, again as Smythe, writes to Curll:

Dear SIR,
My Cousin desires you will get 600 of the Titles printed with all Expedition, and assures you that no Man whatever shall vend one Book but your self, for you shall have the whole Impression to be sure. He says Tuesday [i.e., 13 May]. I am,

SIR,
Your Friend
and Servant,
R.S.

P.S. Why don't you advertise.

(*In. Corr.*, pp. 16-17)

There had been talk on 3 May of an advertising campaign of five or six days. Pope insisted on having the book advertised for a reason which would quickly become apparent: the advertisement would provide legal grounds for the book's seizure.

12 May 1735 (Monday). The *Daily Post-Boy* carries this advertisement:

This Day are published, and most beautifully printed, Price five Shillings, Mr. Pope's *Literary Correspondence* for thirty Years; from 1704 to 1734. Being a Collection of Letters, regularly digested, written by him to the Right

> Honourable the late Earl of Hallifax, Earl of Burlington,
> Secretary Craggs, Sir William Trumbull, Honourable J.
> C. General ********, Honourable Robert Digby, Esq; Honour-
> able Edward Blount, Esq; Mr. Addison, Mr. Congreve
> Mr. Wycherley, Mr. Walsh, Mr. Steele, Mr. Gay, Mr.
> Jarvas, Dr. Arbuthnot, Dean Berkeley, Dean Parnelle, &c.
> Also Letters from Mr. Pope to Mrs. Arabella Fermor, and
> many other Ladies. With the respective Answers of each
> Correspondent. Printed for E. Curl in Rose-street, Covent-
> Garden, and sold by all Booksellers. N.B. The *Original
> Manuscripts* (of which Affidavit is made) may be seen at
> Mr. Curl's House by all who desire it.

Pope's *Narrative* (p. 27) would suggest that the advertisement
was written by Curll; but Curll's reprint (p. x), no doubt correctly, insisted that "Mr *Curll* . . . copied the Advertisement,
and returned the Original." The advertisement betrays Pope's
authorship in the phrase "With the respective Answers of each
Correspondent." Curll, by placing the advertisement, was
claiming, thanks to that phrase, to be printing letters by Lords.
This, according to law, was an illegal "breach of privilege."
In fact, the book contained no such letters, but the advertisement
would give Pope the ammunition he needed to act publicly
once again.

Curll's failure to notice the danger of the advertisement is
remarkable. He writes to R. S. to explain that he has just
received Smythe's letter of 10 May (Saturday) late on Sunday
night; he promises to finish the title pages, and hopes that
P. T. will let him have more books and the all-important
manuscripts. He mentions the advertisement and expresses
his hope that R. S. and P. T. approve it. R. S. replies immediately, sending a messenger with some printed title pages
and this covering note:

> Sir,
> You see how earnest *P. T.* is to have these Books out, there-
> fore you will receive by the Bearer some Titles. By one
> a-Clock, you shall have more Books; but he must insist
> on some Money to pay the Printer. The Number I shall

bring you will be near 200, be at home at 12, for I may
get them before. I am,

Your Friend
and Servant,

R. S.

(*In. Corr.*, p. 17)

This promise delights Curll.   He need now run no risk of
selling out, having advertised the book with only fifty copies
on hand; R. S. promises "near 200" more.   The only pressing
financial demand is "some Money to pay the Printer."   Perhaps
R. S. will even bring some manuscripts; Curll hopes so.

At 1 p.m., R. S. sends for Curll, who meets him at the Standard
Tavern in Leicester Fields.   Curll pays Smythe (i.e., Worsdale)
ten pounds in cash and two notes, one for fifteen pounds and
one for five.   Five bundles of books, which Smythe is careful
to tell Curll have come by water, arrive in the care of two porters,
loaded onto a horse.   Curll dispatches the horse-load to his
shop, where his wife receives it.   Back at the shop, Curll's assis-
tants have sold out the fifty title-less books he had on hand.   At
2 p.m., officers of the Black Rod, armed with a warrant from
the House of Lords, arrive at the shop and seize the entire ship-
ment.   They order Curll and Wilford (the publisher of the *Post-
Boy*, in which the advertisement appeared) to report for ques-
tioning on 13 May.

This flawlessly-timed seizure is one of the most overwhelming
evidences of Pope's masterminding the entire scenario.   While
R. S. had been dealing with Curll, Pope had presumably seen
to it that his friend Lord Ilay was aware of the suggestive phrase
in the advertisement.   It was at Ilay's insistence that the books
were ordered seized.[9]   They disappeared before Curll could
discover he had been bilked, whether by Pope's intention or
not.   He had received only 190 books, and five signatures from
the middle (containing letters to Jervas, Digby, and Edward
Blount) and two signatures from the end (containing correspondence with Gay, Arbuthnot, and Burlington) were missing
from all these copies.

13 May 1735.   Curll and Wilford are examined by the House
of Lords. Wilford is dismissed, but Curll is ordered to appear
again the next day.   When he returns home, he finds a letter
of instructions, signed by Smythe, coaching him as to his
testimony:

Sir,

As soon as I heard of our Misfortune of the Books being
seiz'd, I posted away to P. T. he said he found his great
Caution was but necessary; but tho' he knew Mr *Pope*'s
Interest with the Great, he apprehended only his personal
Revenge, or a Chancery Suit; (knowing he would spare
no Cost to gratify his Revenge) he said, if you had been
more cautious, than to *name Lords* in your Advertisement,
this could not have happen'd: but since it has happen'd,
you shall not only find him punctual, but *Generous.* He
immediately sent me with Money to pay off the Printer,
and I have the whole Impression in my hands; I then found
that the Rogue had deliver'd your last Parcel imperfect: but
I will bring you both those Sheets, and the whole Impression, the very first day they can be safely deliver'd you.

P. T. says he never intended any more Advantage, but
meerly not to be out of pocket. (Except you had been willing to gratify me a little), but now he will be Just, and act
handsomely to you, tho' ever so much to his own Loss:
provided you keep secret our whole Transaction—As it
is plain that *Pope*'s whole Point is only to *suppress the
Books*, and find out *who gave the Letters.* You will intirely
disappoint him in both, if, whatever Questions the Lords
ask, you will answer no more than thus: *that you had the
Letters* from *different Hands*, some of which you *paid* for,
that *you printed these as you did Mr Cromwell's* before,
without Mr *Pope*'s ever *gainsaying* it; and that as to the
Originals, many you can shew now, and the rest you can
very speedily.

It is well that an Accident hinders you at present from
the Originals, which now, they would seize. P. T. thinks
it was indiscreet to advertise the Originals so very quick
as the first Day, until you actually had them, which by his

own falling ill, he cou'd not come at so soon in the place where they lay.

The Lords cannot stop the Books above two or three Days, if at all.

And P. T.'s wonderful Caution as it happens, will enable you to sell them whatever Orders they may make. For he, apprehending Injunctions in Chancery might suppress the Book, had already printed *another Title and Preface,* which throws the Publication intirely off you, and might be safely vended even in that case.

In short, if you absolutely conceal all that has passed between P. T. Me, and Your self, you win the old Gentleman for ever. For his whole Heart is set upon publishing the Letters, not so much for this Volume as, *in Ordine ad* to much more important Correspondence that will follow, *viz.* with SWIFT, late Lord Ox——D, Bp. ROCHESTER and Lord BOL.

You shall hear soon from me. I hope this will be quickly over. I remain,

Your Faithful Servant,
R. Smythe
(*In. Corr.*, pp. 19-22)

This letter is a minor masterpiece. Pope's imagination, warming to the task, supplies dramatic details: R. S. has "posted away" to P. T., and P. T. has been delayed in getting at the originals by "falling ill." The letter seeks to shift the blame from the fictitious conspirators for each of their failures to deal fairly with Curll: the imperfections in the delivered copies are blamed on the printer ("the Rogue"); Curll should be glad he has no originals, as they would be seized; and the seizure of the books is really Curll's fault for his incautious advertisement (an odd assertion if the advertisement was sent him by P. T.). Smythe promises that it will be to Curll's advantage to tell the lies outlined in his letter. If Curll cooperates in hiding P. T., the financial settlement will be sweet, he will be able to sell the books no matter what, and (most tempting) there will be more and better material for a subsequent volume.

14 May 1735. The House of Lords meets in Committee. Pope himself attends.[10] Lord Ilay advises the Committee that in his copy of the book, bought at Curll's shop, there is an "abuse of the Earl of Burlington" on page 117. The seized books are in sheets, however, so Curll is called in to fold up a copy. There is no page 117 to be found, that being a part of the last sheets left out of the horse-load copies. Questioned about the advertisement, Curll wisely chooses not to follow the coaching in Smythe's letter; instead, he summarizes for the Lords his negotiations with P. T., and claims that P. T. sent him copy for the troublesome advertisement. He is questioned about originals, and admits that the only ones he has now are the old Cromwell letters he purchased from Mrs. Thomas. The Committee seem satisfied with this, but they are still curious about the missing letter to Jervas, in which the suspected abuse of Burlington is supposed to occur, so they order their officers to search for that letter.[11] Curll is to attend the next day, with any original letters he has.

On Curll's return home, he finds another letter, which shows detailed knowledge of his testimony, and reports that P. T. "is charmed with your behavior yesterday."[12] In this letter, Smythe reiterates some of his earlier instructions about Curll's concealing the conspirators, and gives him more information about P. T. than he has ever had:

> If you observe all the old Gentleman's Directions you will soon be fully acquainted both with his Person and Designs; in the mean Time, to shew you he will take off the Mask, and clear the *Mysterium magnum* you complain of, I have this Leave to tell you these things which he would have writ to you himself, but that his Arm is now disabled by the Rheumatism.
>
> He is no Man of Quality, but conversant with many, and happening to be concern'd with a noble Lord (a Friend of Mr *Pope*'s) in handing to the Press his Letters to *Wycherley*, he got some Copies over and above. This Incident put first into his Head the Thought of collecting more, and afterwards finding you did not comply in printing his Advertisement, he went on with it by himself. Found *Crom-*

well's Answers in the same Lord's Possession, with many others, which he printed as near as possible to correspond with the Letter and Paper, &c.

Why did Pope send Curll this information? The logic of the letter is simple enough: R. S. hopes that the promise of a future meeting with P. T. and the revelation of these details about P. T.'s identity and his method of procuring the letters will strike Curll as gestures of good faith and keep him from disclosing what he knows to the Lords. But that logic is fictional. Pope must actually have suspected that Curll would double-cross R. S. and say anything he felt would get him off. Therefore, he provided P. T. with a plausible false identity. If Curll summarized or read this letter to the Lords, the Lords would presumably conclude that P. T. was someone involved with Oxford and thus able to get copies of Pope's letters from the Harleian Library. This planted theory would hide Pope's actual complicity. Still, Pope did seem to be giving a great deal away. By having Smythe mention the forgotten and withdrawn volume including the Wycherley letters, he gave Curll the clue he needed to discover the source of the first section of the new volume. Bibliographers now unanimously assert that the letters to Wycherley in the first printing of the 1735 volume are actually the remainder sheets from the suppressed 1729 *Posthumous Works*. The rest of the volume was printed so as to match closely, though not exactly, and the paper from the Wycherley letters, having sat unbound for six years, is discolored in most extant copies. True, the Lords would hardly know that Pope himself had these remainder sheets of a forgotten book on hand, but Curll might think to ask Gilliver, who would remember.[13] Pope's apparent incaution in including these details is another puzzle.

15 May 1735. Curll dashes off a note to Smythe at 9 a.m. He is "going to the Lords to finish *Pope*" (*Nar.*, p. 31), and he wants the sheets to perfect the horse-load, as well as the other 300 books. He arrives at the Lords, who have determined that they cannot stop the volume, and who are beginning to be impatient with the whole affair. As Pope must have anticipated, Curll shows the Lords the letter he has received the previous evening.

They release him and the books, which sell quite briskly, thanks
to the free publicity accorded them by the dramatic seizure and
subsequent hearings. A note soon arrives from Smythe, con-
gratulating Curll on his release and announcing (again in
dramatic detail) "the Coach waits, and I am going with this
joyful News to the old Gentleman" (*In. Corr.*, p. 25). A subsequent note carries the drama further: R. S. writes that he has
found P. T. "in a very different Humour from what I left him"
(*In. Corr.*, p. 26). Apparently, P. T. has now learned the details
of Curll's testimony, which he calls "blabbing." Terribly
afraid that he and Smythe will now be identified, he demands
more money as a test of Curll's fidelity. Pope imagined this
change of heart for P. T. not to extort more money for himself
(he knew that Curll was unlikely to pay), but to create a situation he could later describe in his *Narrative* as a quarrel over
profits among the conspirators.

16 May 1735. Curll writes Smythe a surly reply, claiming
that he is "falsely accus'd" (*Nar.*, pp. 32-4). But he offers one
final way to close the deal: he will pay twenty pounds in gold
if the necessary sheets are delivered "tomorrow Morning."
Otherwise, he will "instantly *reprint*," which he is perfectly
able to do, needing only one copy of the initial fifty from which
to set up the section of pages missing from the horse-load copies.
He also threatens to add his correspondence with the initialled
agents "as a Supplement." Curll probably began to have type
set at this point.

19 May 1735. Curll's deadline has obviously not been met.
Nonetheless, a short note arrives from Smythe, implying continued cooperation. Smythe says he will "bring you the Remainder of the Impression Thursday evening," i.e., 22 May (*In.
Corr.*, p. 27). Pope was evidently stalling, hoping to delay
Curll's imminent reprint for a few more days while searching
for another bookseller.

20 May 1735. Pope takes public action to cover his tracks,
advertising in three papers in his own name. His advertisement
suggests that the letters have been stolen from his own library
and from "that of a Noble Lord" (i.e., Oxford). He offers a
reward if either P. T. or R. S. will turn the other in or "discover

the Whole of this Affair." His money, needless to say, is safe.

21 May 1735. Curll realizes that he is the victim of the final double-cross. The remaining 360 copies he has been asking for have been delivered, not to him, but to other booksellers, Innys and Mannby. Curll rushes ahead with his reprint.

22 May 1735. Curll retalitates in grand form. He writes a letter to the Lords declaring that he has been cheated, threatens Innys and Mannby with legal action and underselling, and advertises his reprint, to include the *Initial Correspondence* (see *In. Corr.*, Appendix, pp. 28-9).

23 May 1735. Pope strikes back in the newspapers, with advertisements in which P. T. and R. S. allege that Curll's notes have "prov'd *not Negotionable*." They insist that Curll has no copyright, and threaten to publish Curll's letters to them.

About 12 June 1735. *A Narrative of the Method by Which the Private Letters of Mr. Pope have been Procur'd and Published by Edmund Curll, Bookseller* is published by Cooper, who has applied for the copyright to the letters. In the *Narrative*, Pope (surely the author, although the pamphlet is of course anonymous) adduces as evidence those portions of the correspondence returned to him by Curll, and Curll's letters to P. T. and R. S. Not having the letters P. T. and R. S. sent to Curll after 15 April, he is unable to print them, but he summarizes those portions of the story he must omit.

14 July 1735. Curll, despite his advertisements, has not yet published his promised *Initial Correspondence*. Probably he did have it printed before the *Narrative* came out. Now, as front matter for *Mr. Pope's Literary Correspondence. Volume the Second*, he reprints Pope's *Narrative* with adversary footnotes, and adds the already-prepared *Initial Correspondence*, with his own narrative links between the letters. Although this composite account actually gave a much fuller and more accurate picture of the intrigues than did the *Narrative*, Curll was a thoroughly discredited man, thanks to his persistent chicanery. There was no public outcry against Pope, whose version was apparently generally accepted.

15 July 1735. Pope, unhappy about the inclusion of two

spurious letters supposedly written to him by Atterbury in the Curll volume, advertises in the *London Gazette*:

> Whereas several Booksellers have printed several surreptitious and incorrect Editions of *Letters* as mine, some of which are not so, and others interpolated; and whereas there are Daily Advertisements of *Second* and *Third Volumes* of more such *Letters*, particularly my Correspondence with the *late Bishop of Rochester*; I think myself under a Necessity to publish such of the said Letters as are genuine, with the Addition of some others of a Nature less insignificant; especially those which pass'd between the said *Bishop* and my self, or were any way relating to him: Which shall be printed with all convenient Speed.
>
> A. Pope.

This advertisement, despite Pope's later protestations that he merely intended it to forestall Curll and others, was the final goal of his whole plot: to create the impression that he was indeed "under a Necessity to publish."

26 July 1735.   Curll replies angrily but ineffectually.

> I hereby declare, That the *First Volume* of [Pope's] LETTERS which I publish'd on the 12th of May last, was sent me ready printed, by himself . . .
>
> (III, 476)

Having thus (accurately!) "discover[ed] the Whole of this Affair," he claims the reward offered in Pope's advertisement of 20 May. The reward was not paid, nor was Curll generally believed.

15 September 1735.   In his third volume of *Mr. Pope's Literary Correspondence*, Curll reprints Pope's advertisement of 15 July with frequent parentheses correcting Pope's falsehoods (see III, 493-5).   He reiterates the truth about the sheets of the Wycherley correspondence, which he has learned from Gilliver (see above, note 13).

Various piratical reprints of the *Letters* first printed in May continued to be issued by various booksellers. Curll's continuing series by this point contained little or no genuine material. The *Letters*, thanks to the controversy, were the literary event of the year.

To attempt to sort out this insane history is to develop some imaginative sympathy for that historian who will try to explain the Watergate scandal some 150 years from now. The similarities are striking: charges and counter-charges, pseudonymous agents, documents of questionable authenticity, legislative committees. But Pope's chicanery was not at all analogous to Watergate in its effects or motives. No one, after all, was really harmed. James Worsdale, the actor who probably played the Reverend R. Smythe, was no doubt adequately reimbursed.[14] Lawton Gilliver, if Curll's testimony is correct, was paid for the Wycherley remainder sheets. Even Curll, for all his protests, netted a considerable profit. For the 240 books he actually received, he paid thirty pounds *if* his notes were ever cashed (which seems unlikely); he may well have paid only ten pounds in cash. At five shillings a book, his income was sixty pounds, not to mention all he made from reprints and subsequent volumes.

NOTES

Notes to the Preface

1. To date, additional letters have been published as follows: by Sherburn in *RES* n. s. IX (1958), 389-406; by Rawson in *RES* n. s. X (1959), 371-387; by Arlidge in *RES* n. s. XII (1961), 398-402; by Link in *RES* n. s. XV (1964), 398-99; by Rousseau in *PQ* XLV (1966), 409-18; by Eddy in *Cornell Library Journal* III (1967), 56-57; by Rogers in *PQ* L (1971), 306-8; by Erskine-Hill in *N&Q* XX (1973), 207-8; and by Lunn in *RES* n. s. XXIV (1973), 207-9. Heyworth published what he thought was an unpublished letter in *TLS* (3 July 1969), 731; however, while not in Sherburn, this letter had been published by A. S. Turberville in *A History of Welbeck Abbey* (London: Faber and Faber, 1938), I, 342-43.

Notes to Chapter 1

1. "Apparently correspondents were flattered to have their letters used in any way the editors saw fit. For that matter, some of them are more than aware of their own shortcomings and suggest quite frankly that Steele do some revising." William H. Irving, *The Providence of Wit in the English Letter Writers* (Durham: Duke University Press, 1955), 169. See also the Introduction to *New Letters to the Tatler and Spectator*, ed. Richmond P. Bond (Austin: University of Texas Press, 1959).

2. See Ault's thorough introduction to *The Prose Works of Alexander Pope* (Oxford: Shakespeare Head Press, 1936). Some subsequent commentators have suggested that Ault's assignments to Pope are excessively generous.

3. Following the text of *The Spectator*, ed. Donald F. Bond (5 vols., Oxford: Clarendon Press, 1965), III, 517.

4. Introduction to *Prose Works*, xxxiv.

5. Cf. the serious tone of the letters published in Sherburn's "Letters of Alexander Pope, Chiefly to Sir William Trumbull," *RES* n.s. IX (1958), 388-406.

6. In Bond, IV, 397.

7. In Bond, IV, 396.

8. Sherburn labels the letter as a suspected fabrication, but concedes in a footnote, "Evidently Pope must have written Steele in a somewhat similar manner."

9. Introduction to *Prose Works*, lvii.

10. Following the text of *The Guardian* (2 vols., London: J. and R. Tonson, 1751), II, 91.

11. Irving, *Providence of Wit*, 23.

12. For a full account, with a facsimile title-page of Pope's pamphlet, see Ralph Straus, *The Unspeakable Curll* (London: Chapman and Hall, 1927), 49-64.

13. One of Pope's letters to Jacob Tonson, Jr., dated [16 or 23 May 1722?], provides evidence about Pope's methods: "I'm resolvd to pass the next whole week in London, purposely to get together Parties of my acquaintance ev'ry night, to collate the several Editions of Shakespear's single Plays" (II, 118). By "the several Editions," Pope meant the quartos; he was not certain what to do with them, but he was the first editor of Shakespeare to suspect their value and collate them.

14. For a full text of Pope's interesting preface, see Sherburn, I, xxxv.

15. "Pope, Theobald, and Wycherley's *Posthumous Works*," *PMLA* LXVIII (1953), 227.

16. Dearing, 236.

17. Did someone see that Swift got a copy of the Wycherley volume? His chiding of Pope in this letter sounds as if he had actually seen the book and concluded Pope was responsible. But perhaps he was only responding to Pope's hint.

18. Later, in his *Narrative* (p. 10), Pope would allege that a copy of his correspondence with Wycherley was extant, annotated by Curll for a new edition. If this charge was true, Curll's notes were certainly antagonistic to Pope, and made for further animosity.

19. Perhaps it is significant that the phrase "it is at your service," used here by E. P., is the same phrase used to introduce the letter from the sickly young gentleman in *Guardian* 132 (see p. 16 above).

20. I follow the text given in Vinton A. Dearing's unpublished Harvard

dissertation, *A History of the Publication of Alexander Pope's Letters during his Lifetime* (1949), 46-47. Dearing transcribes a photograph of the original.

21. In the *Initial Correspondence* (p. 10), Curll says "Notice was accordingly given, at the time appointed, in *the Daily Advertiser.*" Straus, in *The Unspeakable Curll* (p. 157), accepts Curll's claim and asserts that "Such a notice duly appeared." Where? *Not* in the *Daily Advertiser* for 18 October, or for any other date in October.

22. "*Thursday* the 10th" is a misprint for "18th," as Curll's text shows, and as would only be logical from P. T.s request, in his letter of 11 October, for a reply "this Day-sennight."

23. "Sheet" is a misprint for "Shilling." Again Curll's text is correct.

24. Straus (pp. 158-9) blames the delay on Curll's being particularly busy at this time. It seems simpler, given how busy Curll *always* was, to conclude that he was suspicious, as well he might have been, and unwilling to make the next move.

25. It was Charles W. Dilke who first pointed out the convenience of Caryll's death, in *Papers of a Critic* (London: John Murray, 1874), I, 307-8.

26. On the importance of the Roberts octavo, see Vinton A. Dearing, "The 1737 Editions of Alexander Pope's Letters," in *Essays Critical and Historical dedicated to Lily B. Campbell* (Berkeley: University of California Press, 1950), 185-197.

27. *The Counterfeiters* (Bloomington: Indiana University Press, 1968), 30-31.

Notes to Chapter 2

1. *The Epistles of Erasmus*, tr. Francis Morgan Nichols (3 vols., London: Longmans, Green, and Co., 1901), I, 390.

2. Nichols, III, 178.

3. See Erasmus's letter to Gillis (Nichols, I, xxix), and the resulting prefatory letter from Gillis to Clava (Nichols, I, lxxv).

4. In the *Catalogus Lucubrationum*, following the translation given by J. W. Binns in "The Letters of Erasmus," Chapter III of *Erasmus*, ed. T. A. Dorey (London: Routledge & Kegan Paul, 1970), 56.

5. Nichols, I, lxxxix.

6. Ordinem in Epistolis, vel a natura, vel ab arte licebit petere, sed ab arte infrequentius. Nam si in actionibus forensibus, omnis fere dispositio a consilio sumitur, non praeceptis: quanto magis id faciundum in literis quae leguntur, non audiuntur: & leguntur a docto, non a vulgo. Postremo quae nullum omnino nonnunquam habent ordinem: & si habent maxime, melius dissimulant, quam ostendunt. Quare superstitiose faciunt, qui libertatem illam Epistolarem, certis partibus alligant, atque ejusmodi servituti includunt, cujusmodi ne orationes quidem tenere Fabio placet. In simplicibus argumentis eum sequamur ordinem, quem consilium nobis dictaverit, non praeceptiunculae. In confusaneis Epistolis, in quibus innumerabilium prope rerum acervus congeritur: aut ut quicquid in buccam venerit, ita effundemus: aut ordinem aliquem a tempore, loco, personis, aut rebus imaginabimur, eum crebris transitiunculis breviter significamus.

I follow the text of *Desiderii Erasmi Roterdami Opera Omnia,* ed. John Le Clerc (Leyden, 1703; reprinted in facsimile, Hildesheim: Georg Olms, 1961), col. 376, D-E, translation mine.

7. For a full account of Erasmus's classification, see Binns, 72-76.

8. *Opera Omnia,* col. 973-1026.

9. Hoole, pp. 2-3; the letter is *Ad Familiares,* xiv, 22.

10. See, for example, Atterbury to Pope (28 September 1720; II, 55), Bolingbroke to Swift ([9 April 1730]; III, 102-3, quoted below, pp. 68-9), Swift to Pope (19 July 1725; II, 310). Swift's invention comes in a letter to the Duchess of Queensberry, Gay's protector: "Non te civitas, non Regia domus in exilium miserunt, sed tu utrasque, so says Cicero (as your Grace knows) or so he might have said" (28 August 1731; III, 220).

11. *Ad Familiares,* 4 (in the 1620 translation, 59-60; brackets original).

12. *Ad Familiares* IV, 4 (in the 1620 translation, 158).

13. *Ad Familiares* V, 12 (in the 1620 translation, 218).

14. Mearum epistularum nulla est συναγωγή; sed habet Tiro instar septuaginta; et quidem sunt a te quaedam sumendae. Eas ego oportet perspiciam, corrigam. Tum denique edentur.

Ad Atticum VI, 5, following the text and translation of *The Letters of Cicero to Atticus,* ed. E. O. Winsedt (3 vols., London: William Heinemann, 1925), III, 388-9. Swift's interest in and knowledge of the history of letter writing is indicated by the following entries in the sale catalogue of his library:

108 Senecae Philosophi Opera	—Paris	1587
116 Voiture ses Oeuvres I. & II. partie	Bruss.	1695
123 Lettres choisies de Mons. Guy Patin	—Franc.	1683

152 Plinii Epistolae   —Elzev L. Bat.   1640
174 M. Tulii. Ciceronis Opera in 11 vols.
                                        —apud Gryphium Lugd.   1546
185 Erasmi Obscurorum Virorum Epistolae   —Franc.   1643
204 Costar ses Letters.   —Par.   1658
308 Richelet, Les plus Belles Lettres avec des Notes
                                                  —Amst.   1690
353 Voiture ses Oeuvres   —Paris   1652
402 Ciceronis Opera cum Annot. Lambini, in 8 vols.
                                              Argentor.   1581

See the facsimile of the sale catalogue in Harold Williams, *Dean Swift's Library* (Cambridge: Cambridge University Press, 1932).

15. Following the translation in Hoole's *Century of Epistles*, 56-7.

16. See I, 479, 493. Gay was with Pope on the visit to Stanton Harcourt during which the incident occurred, and may have collaborated in writing this account. Still, the close similarities in all three versions (the "Gay to Mr. F___" version was the only one published) argue for Pope's authorship.

17. Following Tom Brown's translation, in *Familiar and Courtly Letters* . . . (London: for Sam. Briscoe, 1700), 126.

18. *The Providence of Wit*, 22.

19. In Brown's translation, 133-4.

20. For accounts of the rural lovers, see I, 479, 482, 493, 497. For the Stanton Harcourt letters, see I, 505, 508. Manuscript fragments of the letter on the hermaphrodite (see I, 277) at Mapledurham and among the Marriot papers indicate that Pope sent versions to the Blounts and to Betty Marriot.

21. *Opera Omnia*, col. 350 C, translation mine.

22. I quote from Roger L'Estrange's *Seneca's Morals by Way of Abstract*, a remarkably popular selective translation, which first appeared in 1682 and had been reprinted thirteen times by 1739. My quotations follow the ninth edition (1705), 382.

23. In L'Estrange, 474, 427.

24. The phrase and the idea are William Irving's; see *The Providence of Wit*, 47.

25. In "The translator to the Reader," unpaginated.

26. In Tirwhyt, 315 (misprinted as 335).

27. In Tirwhyt, 94.

28. In Tirwhyt, 290-91.

29. Readers of the 1735 *Letters,* in which this letter appeared in a highly edited form, may have noticed an even closer resemblance; Martha is replaced there by "my sovereign Lady *Sylvia.*"

30. Printed as an introductory letter in the unpaginated front matter of *A Collection of Some Modern Epistles of Mounsieur de Balzac* (Oxford: printed by Leonard Lichfield for Francis Bowman, 1639).

31. Curll accuses Pope of having "politely pillaged" Voiture in his letter of 15 September 1735 (III, 495). The Voiture letter in question appears as Epistle xviii of Volume I of Ozell's "translation" of Voiture's *Works* (1715). I cite by Volume and Epistle numbers, as pagination differs in the numerous reprints, many of which combine the two volumes as one.

32. See Pope to Cromwell (24 June 1710; I, 89), Cromwell to Pope (3 August 1710; I, 95), Pope to Cromwell (12 October 1710; I, 98). For a full discussion of this and other borrowings, see Emile Audra, *L'influence Francaise dans L'oeuvre de Pope,* 315-346.

33. In Ozell, I, xxxvi.

34. This letter, dated 28 May 1709, was first printed in Sherburn's "Letters of Alexander Pope, Chiefly to Sir William Trumbull," *RES* n.s. IX (1958), 395.

35. In Ozell, II, xvi.

36. See, for example, the letter of 19 January 1707/8 (I, 37), in which Pope discusses the "innumerable Litle faults" he was discovering while translating sections of Statius. On the Cromwell correspondence and the progress of this translation, see TE I, 346-352.

37. In Ozell, I, lxxix.

38. Michael J. Pretina, Jr., *Vincent Voiture, Creation and Reality: A Study of his Prose* (unpublished Ph.D. dissertation, Yale, 1967), 105.

39. Richelet's "Account of Voiture" was printed as part of the front matter in the Ozell *Works*; in the first edition (1715), this phrase occurs on p. xx.

40. In Ozell, I, lxxvii.

41. In Tom Brown's *Familiar Letters: Written by the Right Honourable John late Earl of Rochester, And several other Persons . . .* (2 vols., usually bound as one, London: for Sam. Briscoe, 1697). My citations follow the fourth edition, 1705. Rochester's letter is at I, 4.

42. *Familar Letters,* I, 73-74.

43. In *Familiar Letters,* I, 189-90. For an admirable account of Brown's vigorous career, see Benjamin Boyce, *Tom Brown of Facetious Memory* (Cambridge, Mass.: Harvard University Press, 1939).

44. In the preface to the "authorized" edition of 1737, Pope describes himself (in the third person) as "recalling as many [letters] as he could from those who he imagin'd had kept any. He was sorry to find the number so great, but immediately lessen'd it by burning three parts in four of them" (I, xxxvii). Needless to say, this is a dubious claim, but it may function as evidence that Pope did manage to collect a good many letters.

Notes to Chapter 3

1. Not insignificantly, this letter, with its dramatic *apologia*, was the one printed by Curll in *New Letters of Mr. Pope* (1736). No one knows how Curll got the letter (see below, Chapter 5, 187-8).

2. This letter, dated 16 February 1715/16, was first printed in Sherburn's "Letters of Alexander Pope, Chiefly to Sir William Trumbull," *RES* n.s. IX (1958), 405.

3. Maynard Mack, *The Garden and the City* (Toronto: University of Toronto Press, 1969), 121.

4. Cf. the similarly execrable puns used by Christopher Smart in *Jubilate Agno*. Smart was a Cambridge man. Was this sort of humor then current in Cambridge?

5. See lines 153-4; TE IV, 87-9.

6. See Joseph Spence, *Observations, Anecdotes and Characters of Books and Men*, ed. James M. Osborn (Oxford: Oxford University Press, 1966), 119-128, for evidence of the respect Pope accorded Bolingbroke. In emphasizing that respect, I do not mean to accept the now thoroughly discredited view that Bolingbroke was in any way the "author" of the *Essay on Man*.

7. Spence, 158.

8. See George Sherburn, *The Early Career of Alexander Pope* (Oxford: Clarendon Press, 1934), 107-112.

9. See III, 354; for an earlier example of the same stratagem, see I, 178-9.

10. See I, 119, 123, 132, 142, and *Early Career*, 99-100.

11. See, among other references, I, 129; II, 58, 434, 449; III, 17-18, 36.

12. "Two different Cornish towns confidently claim him as a native son," explains Benjamin Boyce in The *Benevolent Man* (Cambridge: Harvard University Press, 1967), 1. Boyce's account of Pope's relations with Allen, especially Chapters V and VII, is admirably complete.

13. As Boyce puts it, Allen's "acquaintance with literature and writers was at this point [1735] slight, and throughout his life he never quite acquired the Castilian refinement in grammar of matching a plural verb to a plural subject." "The Poet and the Postmaster: The Friendship of Alexander Pope and Ralph Allen," *PQ* XLV (1966), 115.

14. For the letter to Lyttelton, see IV, 142; for Pope's claims to Allen that he is above party, see IV, 281, 383-4, 386-7, etc.

15. For a reconstruction of the conflicting reports about this fiasco, see The *Benevolent Man*, 146-49. There are two theories. One is that Mrs. Allen was suspicious of Martha Blount's relationship with Pope, because her niece, Gertrude Tucker, who later married Warburton, heard Martha go into Pope's room early in the morning and "talk earnestly" with him. This was the version the Warburtons told to Mason; it was first printed in Duncan C. Tovey's *Gray and his Friends* (Cambridge: Cambridge University Press, 1890), 280-82. The other theory, based on the conversation of Warburton's friend Thomas Newton, but reported by Thomas Birch, is that Allen refused to lend Martha Blount his coach to go to mass. Martha's letter to Pope at the time (IV, 462) and his reply (IV, 463-4) make it clear that she was extremely upset. It is worth pointing out, as some tellers of this story have not, that Martha had lost her mother just a few months before, which may have increased her depression and susceptibility to insult.

16. See *Early Career*, 157. For an example of Pope's claims, see I, 47.

17. Marjorie Nicholson and George S. Rousseau, *"This Long Disease, My Life"* (Princeton: Princeton University Press, 1968), 66.

18. Spence, 111. The "slander" was Cibber's claim that he had rescued Pope from what might have been the dangerous embraces of a prostitute (in his *Letter from Mr. Cibber, to Mr. Pope . . .* , published in 1742). Cibber's letter occasioned a number of satirical prints; for one example, see J. V. Guerinot, *Pamphlet Attacks on Alexander Pope* (London: Methuen, 1969), opposite p. 288. The account of the Pope-Cibber quarrel in Norman Ault's *New Light on Pope* (London: Methuen, 1969), 301-7, is thorough and judicious.

19. Martha Blount told Spence that she was "a very little girl" when she met Pope, but also said that the meeting occurred after the publication of the *Essay on Criticism*, i.e., 1711. Osborn, reckoning backwards from Pope's jocular phrase about "the three hundred eighty-ninth week of the reign of your most serene majesty" (I, 258), dates the meeting in May or June 1707. Pope's sense of time was never very precise, but in this case his numbers lead to a plausible date.

20. *Early Career*, 48.

21. William K. Wimsatt, Jr., *Alexander Pope: Selected Poetry and Prose* (New York: Holt, Rinehart, and Winston, 1951), Introduction, xii.

22. Geoffrey Tillotson, in his introduction to the *Eloisa*, argues plausibly that the letter to Martha, placed in Holy Week of 1716 by Elwin (and by Sherburn), actually belongs in Holy Week of 1717, suggesting that the poem was nearly finished and that "Pope *did* 'find in [his] heart to leave out the conclusion [he] once intended for it' " (TE II, 312). Pretty clearly, the lines in the conclusion about absence (361-2) fit Lady Mary far better than Martha, but Tilloston's postulation of an earlier, cancelled conclusion written specifically for Martha may be considered an attractive conjecture.

23. *New Light*, 359.

24. *Poetical Miscellanies: the sixth part* (London: for Jacob Tonson, 1709), 342-3. This volume, in which Pope's *Pastorals* were first printed, was part of a series originally edited by Dryden, and continued after his death by Tonson.

25. Quoted in *Early Career*, 92.

26. See, for example, the description of Sherborne (II, 236), the two-part description of Bristol (IV, 200, 204), and Pope's wonderful account of his "voyage" with Peterborow, published by G. S. Rousseau in *PQ* XLV (1966), 409-18.

27. As the review articles of the Sherburn edition were quick to point out, this is one of a very few letters there misdated. It belongs in the late summer of 1718.

28. As Sherburn explains (V, 1-2), Lady Mary seems to have misdated this letter.

29. Our source for the hypothesis that Pope refused to join Lady Mary and Lord Hervey in some satirical enterprise is Lady Mary herself; she told Spence that Pope had made that explanation to Arbuthnot, but she denied its veracity (see Spence, p. 306). Her break with Pope cannot be dated with certainty, and may have been more gradual than violent. See Robert Halsband, *The Life of Lady Mary Wortley Montagu* (Oxford: Clarendon, 1956), 129-32.

30. Our source for these lines is a letter from Lady Mary herself to her sister, the Countess of Mar, dated 1720.

31. *Alexander Pope: A Critical Anthology*, ed. F. W. Bateson and N. A. Joukovsky (Middlesex: Penguin Books, 1971), 24. This bald statement represents the hardening into dogma of a position Professor Bateson once expressed more tentatively. In his notes for *Epistles to Several Persons*, which he edited for the Twickenham Edition in 1951, he provided a summary of the gossip upon which such an assertion might be based, and concluded, "It is not improbable that she was Pope's mistress" (TE III ii, 46).

32. The "lady of your acquaintance" is Caryll's wife. A letter from her to Martha, which confirms Pope's assertions here, is printed in *Early Career*, 294. "Those very people," i.e., those who had spread the rumor, may well have included Teresa.

33. See III, 40, 90, 122.

Notes to Chapter 4

1. Good discussions of the problems of authors during the period include A. S. Collins, *Authorship in the Days of Johnson* (London: Holden & Co., 1927); Ian Watt, "The reading public and the rise of the novel," Chapter II of *The Rise of the Novel* (Berkeley: University of California Press, 1957), 60-92; and Watt's later article, "Publishers and Sinners: The Augustan View," *SB* XII (1959), 3-20.

2. The best recent discussion of the political dangers Pope faced as a Roman Catholic comes in Jean Béranger's ambitious study of religious and political issues in the period, *Les Hommes de Lettres et La Politique en Angleterre de la Revolution de 1688 a la Mort de George Ier* (Bordeaux: Biscaye Frères, 1968). Especially relevant to Pope are pp. 25-34, 130-132, 495-500, 571-574.

3. His profits from the *Iliad* translation were over 5,000 pounds. Lintot, despite the generous terms he made with Pope, and despite his losses due to a piracy by Johnson, still netted "un revenu considérable pour ses héritiers." Alexandre Beljame, *Le Public et les Hommes de Lettres en Angleterre au Dix-Huitième Siècle* (Paris: Hachette, 1897), 394n. See also *Early Career*, 188-89.

4. For a fine account of Pope's knowledge of and interest in pamphlet literature, see the introduction to Guerinot's *Pamphlet Attacks on Alexander Pope*. Pat Rogers's *Grub Street: Studies in a Subculture* (London: Methuen, 1972) surpasses all previous studies of the lives and milieu of the Dunces.

5. On Tonson, see Kathleen M. Lynch, *Jacob Tonson: Kit-Cat Publisher* (Knoxville: University of Tennessee Press, 1971), and Harry M. Geduld, *Prince of Publishers* (Bloomington: Indiana University Press, 1969).

6. Boswell's *Life of Johnson*, ed. G. B. Hill, rev. L. F. Powell (6 vols., Oxford: Clarendon Press, 1934), III, 19.

7. See Johnson's *Life of Pope*, par. 239, following the text of *Lives of the English Poets*, ed. G. B. Hill (3 vols., Oxford: Clarendon Press 1905), III, 188.

8. Par. 278; in Hill, III, 209.

9. This weekly paper, which ran from 1730-37, was consistently friendly to Pope. He may occasionally have even written anonymous pieces for it. It seems at least likely that he occasionally was in touch with its editors. For a full account, see James T. Hillhouse, *The Grub-Street Journal* (Durham: Duke University Press, 1928). Hillhouse's assignments of various pieces to Pope have been thought overly speculative by Sherburn and others.

10. Cf. Pope's similar letter to William Trumbull of 10 August 1711 in "Letters of Alexander Pope, Chiefly to Sir William Trumbull," *RES* n.s. IX (1958), 397.

11. Again, there is no evidence that Pope was directly responsible, but he may have been.

12. See Pope's letters to Hill (III, 166, 171).

13. For what seems to me the correct interpretation, see Ault, *New Light on Pope*, 286-97.

14. One possible exception is his last letter to Addison (I, 263). But this is lesss than forthright, and may be a fabrication.

15. Thomas R. Lounsbury, *Shakespeare and Voltaire* (New York: Charles Scribner's Sons, 1902), 87. Professor Lounsbury's account of Hill is marvelous; of Hill's predilection for "the feminine resource of italicized words," Lounsbury remarks: "These are so abundant in some of his writings that one of his pages frequently gives the impression that a contest must have gone on in the printing-house between the two kinds of type, in which the roman got distinctly the worst of it" (p. 84).

16. See William H. Irving, *John Gay: Favorite of the Wits* (Durham: Duke University Press, 1940), 27-29.

17. *Aaron Hill* (New York: Columbia University Press, 1913), 208. Ms. Brewster's account of Hill's relations with Pope is solid and useful.

18. *Shakespeare and Voltaire*, 86.

19. *Early Career*, 248-69, gives full details of the facts here summarized.

20. Spence, 56. For an account of the history and productions of the Club, see the splendid edition of the *Memoirs*, ed. Charles Kerby-Miller (New York: Russell and Russell, 1966).

21. Professor Martin Price has suggested to me that the references to the "mantle" and "water-tabby" echo the clothing imagery in Swift's *Tale*

of a Tub, and that the phrase about the sun "prop'd under the Chin by the Tops of the distant Mountains" echoes Milton's similar lines in the *Nativity Ode:*

> So when the Sun in bed,
> Curtain'd with cloudy red,
> Pillows his chin upon an Orient wave . . .

22. There is no incontrovertible evidence for this story, but Arbuthnot was abused in the same libel, and it would have been fully in character for him to take physical action. See Lester M. Beattie, *John Arbuthnot: Mathematician and Satirist* (Cambridge: Harvard University Press, 1935), 278-9.

23. 26 February 1727/8; II, 475.

Notes to Chapter 5

1. In Book I of Pope's *Iliad*, lines 81, 233, 299, 434, 464, 512, 748. Swift was being his usual pedantic self, as these eye-rhymes were quite normal in the period, e.g., in Dryden's *Aeneid*.

2. Archibald C. Elias, Jr., in his unpublished Ph.D. dissertation, *Jonathan Swift and Letter-Writing: The Natural and the Playful in his Personal Correspondence* (Yale, 1973), argues that Swift and Pope, because of Pope's plans to publish their letters, engaged in "a routine of mutual deference, usually on high-minded topics like friendship, benevolence, or philosophy" (p. 197). But this description arises from a more suspicious attitude toward the correspondents than mine.

3. Swift later compared Bolingbroke to Cincinnatus: "I will come in person to England, if I am provok'd, and send for the Dictator from the plough" (21 March. 1729/30; III, 99). Did he specifically remember Pope's metaphor, or was he merely responding to Bolingbroke's favorite pose?

4. "Verses on the Death of Dr. Swift," ll. 47-52, following the text of *The Poetry of Jonathan Swift*, ed. Harold Williams (3 vols., Oxford: Clarendon Press, 1958), 555. Bolingbroke had similar praise for Pope's compression in prose: "I have taken up more of this paper than belongs to me, since Pope is to write to you; no matter, for upon recolection the rules of proportion are not broken; He will say as much to you in one Page, as I have said in three" (19 November 1729; III, 71).

5. An act Swift had explicitly praised: "You were pretty bold in mentioning Lord Bolingbroke in that Preface" (28 June 1715; I, 301-2).

6. 20 June 1716; I, 341-2.

7. This is but one of many futile invitations issued in both directions. For others, see II, 460; III, 276; III, 378-9; IV, 6.

8. Later Swift became less careful and more defiant. On 10 November 1730, he wrote angrily to Gay that the Court "deserves no better Genius's than those by whom it is celebrated,—so let the Post rascal open this letter, and let Walpole read it" (III, 149).

9. Elias's unpublished dissertation includes a very full account of the jokes and double-talk in the Pope-Swift letters. See especially pp. 201-233.

10. Pope had imitated Virgil's poem in his first Pastoral, *Spring*; see TE I, 59-70.

11. In Williams, 482-3.

12. For a very full account of this phase of the disagreement, see Elias, pp. 201-209. Elias is somewhat more disparaging of Pope than I would be.

13. For detailed commentary on Swift's undercutting techniques in this letter, see Elias, pp. 219-220.

14. In *The Gutenberg Galaxy* (Toronto: University of Toronto Press, 1962), 308.

15. For an account of Swift's decay free of mythology and full of facts, see the chapters on "Madness" and "Old Age" in Irwin Ehrenpreis, *The Personality of Jonathan Swift* (Cambridge: Harvard University Press, 1958), 117-47. Swift did read and enjoy Pope's increasingly political and satirical poems of the 1730's; see for example his praise of the dialogue "1738" (IV, 115).

16. If Pope had kept copies of the letters he wrote (a normal eighteenth-century practice), he would not have needed to secure the return of the originals from Swift. But it is quite clear that neither Pope nor Swift normally bothered to take copies.

17. Elias, 243.

18. Elias makes the ingenious suggestion that Pope used as a scribe for this note "someone whose hand only Swift could recognize. Patty Blount is a possibility" (p. 180, n. 88). But the text of the letter and the fact of the volume would be enough basis for Swift to conclude that Pope was responsible but wanted his anonymity protected.

19. On the question of whether Swift or Pope added this letter, which was put into the book by means of a cancel, see Maynard Mack, "The First Printing of the Letters of Pope and Swift," *The Library* XIX (1939), 465-85.

20. For a full description, see Mack's article. Elias's Appendix B, "Negotiations over the Irish Printing of the Pope-Swift Letters, 1740" (pp. 260-64) explains in detail some matters summarized here.

21. Sherburn's note (IV, 337). Of course, Pope may have arranged the volume in such a way in order to make it seem Swift's doing or at least the doing of the people in Dublin, thus keeping himself free of blame. Given an admirable and a self-serving motive for the same act, both plausible, it seems impossible to choose.

Notes to Epilogue

1. "When he rose he was invested in boddice made of stiff canvass, being scarce able to hold himself erect till they were laced. . . . His legs were so slender that he enlarged their bulk with three pair of stockings." Johnson's *Life of Pope*, par. 257 (in Hill, III, 197).

2. The definitive study is William K. Wimsatt's *The Portraits of Alexander Pope* (New Haven: Yale University Press, 1965).

3. Johnson's *Life of Pope*, par. 258 (in Hill, III, 198).

Notes to Appendix

1. In the letters quoted below, I follow the texts of Pope's *Narrative* for those letters which appear there; Curll's reprints, except for the footnotes, vary little. For those many letters found only in Curll's *Initial Correspondence*, I follow the text of the original printing (part of the front matter of *Mr. Pope's Literary Correspondence. Volume the Second*), silently correcting a few confusing misprints in punctuation. Another part of that front matter is a long letter *To Mr. Pope*, which is also relevant to the controversy. Dilke's reconstruction of the history, though neither correct nor complete, was the basis upon which Elwin wrote his diatribe against Pope's methods (in *The Works of Alexander Pope* (London: John Murray, 1871), I, xxxvi-lxv). Straus attempts to tell the story from Curll's point of view, but falls into confusing errors by accepting Curll's dating. Dearing, in his unpublished thesis (cited above, p. 223, n. 20), gives a very thorough account, easily the most sensible to date. I concur with Dearing's judgments about most of the facts, although I have dated some parts of the sequence of events differently.

2. On the importance of the Harleian transcripts, see Sherburn, "Pope's Letters and the Harleian Library," *ELH* VII (1940), 177-87.

3. Curll's reprint (p. iv) more or less admits this charge.

4. Straus suggests (p. 159) that Curll may have seen an advertisement in the *Grub-Street Journal* (a periodical favorable to Pope) on 20 March, which announces an auction of love letters and jokingly bars Curll from bidding. Straus suggests that Pope planted this advertisement, hoping to remind Curll of the earlier approach. This seems a rather wild guess.

5. Curll's reprint (p. v) notes that Pope also advertised in the *Daily Journal* and the *Grub-Street Journal*. There, the advertisement takes a slightly different form, beginning "Whereas *E. C.* Bookseller, has written to Mr P____ . . . "

6. In his reprint of the *Narrative* (p. vi), Curll insists again that he was "directed" to approach Pope.

7. In this third paragraph of his letter of 29 April, he mentions "your Third Letter of the Fourth Instant," and includes references to all three pieces (see *Nar.*, p. 22).

8. At least, no one, myself included, has ever found the advertisement.

9. Curll's later comment perhaps betrays some chagrin at not having caught the deadly phrase in the advertisement: "Upon your Complaint to *some* Lords (whom *you make* Patrons to the *Abuse* of *others*) it was owing that the Books were *seized*, and not to the Advertisement, which was but the Shoeing-Horn to your groundless Resentment against me" (*To Mr. Pope*, p. x).

10. Pope did not testify, but his attendance would have been logical and even expected under the circumstances, and would have been the fastest way for P. T. and R. S. to learn the details of Curll's testimony. The actions of the House are recorded in the *Journals of the House of Lords*, xxiv, 550-556.

11. How did Pope get Ilay to make this suggestion? In fact, the passage in question (which does occur on p. 117 of complete copies) is fulsome praise of Burlington.

12. *In. Corr.*, 22-4. Pope summarizes this letter in indirect discourse (*Nar.*, pp. 29-30) suggesting that he had a rough copy by him. The *Narrative* says that the letter is from P. T., and Curll's text of the letter is signed P. T., but the letter frequently refers to "the old gentleman." Surely it is meant to be written by R. S., or perhaps by R. S. with a final paragraph and signature by P. T. The fact that Pope continues to have R. S. speak for P. T. here sets up P. T.'s later changes of mood, which R. S. will be unable to explain. Pope has succeeded in establishing the conspirators as distinct characters.

13. By the time he published the *Initial Correspondence*, Curll had consulted Gilliver: *"Lawton Gilliver* has declared that you bought of him the Remainder of the Impression of *Wycherley's* Letters, which he printed, by your Direction, in 1728, and have printed Six Hundred of the additional Letters, with those to Mr. Cromwell, to make up the Volume" (*To Mr. Pope*, p. xiv).

14. He never betrayed Pope, which he might easily have done, and he may have been helpful again during the negotiations about the Swift correspondence. Dilke (I, 326) notes that he was in Dublin on 18 April 1740.

WORKS CITED

Addison, Joseph, and Richard Steele. *The Spectator*, ed. Donald F. Bond. 5 vols., Oxford: Clarendon Press, 1965.

Audra, Émile. *L'influence Francaise dans L'oeuvre de Pope*. Paris: H. Champion, 1931.

Ault, Norman. *New Light on Pope*. London: Methuen, 1969.

Balzac, Jean Louis Guez de. *The Letters of Mounsieur de Balzac Translated into English, according to the last Edition, by W[illiam] T[irwhyt] Esq*. London, 1634.

————. *A Collection of Some Modern Epistles of Mounsieur de Balzac*. Oxford, 1639.

Bateson, F. W., and N. A. Joukovsky, eds. *Alexander Pope: A Critical Anthology*. Middlesex: Penguin Books, 1971.

Beattie, Lester M. *John Arbuthnot: Mathematician and Satirist*. Cambridge, Mass.: Harvard University Press, 1935.

Beljame, Alexandre. *Le Public et les Hommes de Lettres en Angleterre au Dix-Huitième Siècle*. Paris: Hachette, 1897.

Béranger, Jean. *Les Hommes de Lettres et La Politique en Angleterre de la Revolution de 1688 a la Mort de George Ier*. Bordeaux: Biscaye Frères, 1968.

Binns, J. W. "The Letters of Erasmus." In *Erasmus*, ed. T. A. Dorey. London: Routledge & Kegan Paul, 1970.

Bond, Richmond P., ed. *New Letters to the Tatler and Spectator*. Austin: University of Texas Press, 1959.

Boswell, James. *The Life of Samuel Johnson*, ed. G. B. Hill, rev. L. F. Powell. 6 vols., Oxford: Clarendon Press, 1934.

Boyce, Benjamin. *Tom Brown of Facetious Memory*. Cambridge, Mass.: Harvard University Press, 1939.

_____ . *The Benevolent Man.* Cambridge, Mass.: Harvard University Press, 1967.

_____ . "The Poet and the Postmaster: The Friendship of Alexander Pope and Ralph Allen," *PQ,* XLV (1966), 114-122.

Brewster, Dorothy. *Aaron Hill.* New York: Columbia University Press, 1913.

Brown, Tom. *Familiar Letters: Written by the Right Honourable John late Earl of Rochester, And several other Persons . . . .* 2 vols., London, 1697.

_____ . *Familiar and Courtly Letters.* London, 1700.

Cicero, Marcus Tullius. *The Familiar Epistles of Marcus Tullius Cicero Englished and Conferred with the French Italian and other Translations.* London, 1620.

_____ . *The Letters of Cicero to Atticus,* trs. and ed. E. O. Winsedt. 3 vols., London: William Heinemann, 1925.

Collins, A. S. *Authorship in the Days of Johnson.* London: Holden & Co., 1927.

Curll, Edmund. *The Initial Correspondence.* In *Mr. Pope's Literary Correspondence, Volume the Second.* London, 1735.

_____ . *New Letters of Mr. Pope.* London, 1736.

Dearing, Vinton A. *A History of the Publication of Alexander Pope's Letters during his Lifetime.* Unpublished Ph.D. dissertation, Harvard University, 1949.

_____ . "The 1737 Editions of Alexander Pope's Letters." In *Essays Critical and Historical dedicated to Lily B. Campbell.* Berkeley: University of California Press, 1950.

_____ . "Pope, Theobald, and Wycherley's *Posthumous Works,*" *PMLA,* LXVIII (1953), 223-236.

Dilke, Charles W. *Papers of a Critic.* 2 vols., London: John Murray, 1874.

Ehrenpreis, Irvin. *The Personality of Jonathan Swift.* Cambridge, Mass.: Harvard University Press, 1958.

Elias, Archibald C. *Jonathan Swift and Letter-Writing: The Natural and the Playful in his Personal Correspondence.* Unpublished Ph.D. dissertation, Yale University, 1973.

Erasmus, Desiderius. *Desiderii Erasmi Roterdami Opera Omnia,* ed. John Le Clerc. Leyden, 1703; repr. in facsimile Hildesheim: Georg Olms, 1961.

———. *The Epistles of Erasmus,* trs. Francis Morgan Nichols. 3 vols., London: Longman's, Green, & co., 1901.

Geduld, Harry M. *Prince of Publishers.* Bloomington: Indiana University Press, 1969.

Guerinot, J. V. *Pamphlet Attacks on Alexander Pope.* London: Methuen, 1969.

Halsband, Robert. *The Life of Lady Mary Wortley Montagu.* Oxford: Clarendon Press, 1956.

Hillhouse, James T. *The Grub-Street Journal.* Durham: Duke University Press, 1928.

Hoole, Charles. *A Century of Epistles English and Latine . . . By imitating of which, children may readily get a proper style for writing Letters.* London, 1660.

Irving, William H. *John Gay: Favorite of the Wits.* Durham: Duke University Press, 1940.

———. *The Providence of Wit in the English Letter Writers.* Durham: Duke University Press, 1955.

Johnson, Samuel. *Lives of the English Poets,* ed. G. B. Hill. 3 vols., Oxford: Clarendon Press, 1905.

Kenner, Hugh. *The Counterfeiters.* Bloomington: Indiana University Press, 1968.

L'Estrange, Roger. *Seneca's Mortals By Way of Abstract.* London, 1682.

Lounsbury, Thomas R. *Shakespeare and Voltaire.* New York: Charles Scribner's Sons, 1902.

Lynch, Kathleen M. *Jacob Tonson: Kit-Cat Publisher.* Knoxville: University of Tennessee Press, 1971.

Mack, Maynard. "The First Printing of the Letters of Pope and Swift," *The Library,* XIX (1939), 465-85.

———. *The Garden and the City.* Toronto: University of Toronto Press, 1969.

McLuhan, Marshall. *The Gutenberg Galaxy.* Toronto: University of Toronto Press, 1962.

Nicholson, Marjorie, and George S. Rousseau. *"This Long Disease, My Life": Alexander Pope and the Sciences.* Princeton: Princeton University Press, 1968.

[Pope, Alexander.] *A Narrative of the Method by Which the Private Letters of Mr. Pope have been Procu'rd and Publish'd by Edmund Curll, Bookseller.* London, 1735.

Pope, Alexander. *The Prose Works of Alexander Pope,* ed. Norman Ault. Oxford: Shakespeare Head Press, 1936.

——————. *The Correspondence of Alexander Pope,* ed. George Sherburn. 5 vols., Oxford: Clarendon Press, 1956.

——————. *The Twickenham Edition of the Poems of Alexander Pope,* gen. ed. John Butt. 10 vols., London: Methuen, 1950-1967.

Pretina, Michael J. *Vincent Voiture, Creation and Reality: A Study of his Prose.* Unpublished Ph.D. dissertation, Yale University, 1967.

Rogers, Pat. *Grub Street: Studies in a Subculture.* London: Methuen, 1972.

Sherburn, George. *The Early Career of Alexander Pope.* Oxford: Clarendon Press, 1934.

Spence, Joseph. *Observations, Anecdotes and Characters of Books and Men,* ed. James M. Osborn. Oxford: Oxford University Press, 1966.

Steele, Richard. *The Guardian.* 2 vols., London, 1751.

Straus, Ralph. *The Unspeakable Curl.* London: Chapman and Hall, 1927.

Swift, Jonathan. *The Poetry of Jonathan Swift,* ed. Harold Williams. 3 vols., Oxford: Clarendon Press, 1958.

Tonson, Jacob. *Poetical Miscellanies: the sixth part.* London, 1709.

Tovey, Duncan C. *Gray and his Friends.* Cambridge: Cambridge University Press, 1890.

Voiture, Vincent. *The Works of the celebrated Monsieur Voiture . . . Done from the Paris edition, by Mr. Ozell.* London, 1715.

Watt, Ian. *The Rise of the Novel.* Berkeley: University of California Press, 1957.

——————. "Publishers and Sinners: The Augustan View," *SB,* XII (1959), 3-20.

Williams, Harold. *Dean Swift's Library.* Cambridge: Cambridge University Press, 1932.

Wimsatt, William K.   *The Portraits of Alexander Pope.*   New Haven: Yale University Press, 1965.

INDEX

Addison, Joseph, 14, 33, 40, 54, 66, 70-1, 90-1, 212, 232.
Allen, Ralph, 39, 86, 97-100, 193, 199, 228-9.
Anne, Queen, 75-6, 127, 145-6, 151, 155, 167, 177.
Arbuthnot, Dr. John, 30, 118, 127, 139, 145-6, 149-50, 155, 160-64, 170-1, 196, 198, 212-13, 130.
Aristaenetus, 63.
Atterbury, Francis, Bishop of Rochester, 29, 46, 76, 82-83, 201, 215, 220, 225.
Audra, Émile, 227.
Augustine, St., 45.
Ault, Norman, 14, 16, 111, 222-3, 229-30, 232.

Bacon, Francis, 31.
Balzac, Jean Louis Guez de, 14, 43, 49, 55-8, 66, 72, 227.
Barber, John, 150.
Bateson, F. W., 120, 230.
Bathurst, Allen, 76, 79-81, 83, 85, 123-4, 170-1.
Beattie, Lester, 233.
Beljame, Alexandre, 231.
Bentley, Richard, 78, 147.
Béranger, Jean, 231.
Berkeley, George, Bishop of Cloyne, 212.

Bethel, Hugh, 24-5, 86, 91-7, 99-100, 170-1, 199, 201.
Binns, J. W. 224-5
Birch, Thomas, 229.
Blackmore, Sir Richard, 126.
Blount, Edward, 212-13.
Blount, Martha, 47, 57, 84, 86, 88-90, 94-6, 98, 102-11, 113-16, 120-23, 159, 201, 226, 229-30, 234.
Blount, Teresa, 18, 57, 86, 88, 102, 104-5, 106-11, 113-16, 121-2, 226, 230.
Boiardo, Matteo, 62.
Bolingbroke, Henry St. John, Viscount, 46, 49, 76, 80-1, 86, 150, 170-1, 173-5, 177, 182, 187, 215, 225, 228, 233.
Bond, Donald F., 222-3.
Bond, Richmond P., 222.
Boswell, James, 127, 231.
Boyce, Benjamin, 97-8, 227-9.
Brewster, Dorothy, 134, 232.
Bridges, Ralph, 60.
Briscoe, Samuel, 58-9, 226-7.
Broome, William, 22, 38, 69, 120, 139-45.
Brown, Tom, 14, 58, 63, 64-6, 72, 226-7.
Budgell, Eustace, 129.
Burlington, Richard Boyle, 3d Earl of, 69, 83, 85, 177, 212-13,